Effective Business and Professional Writing

from Problem to Proposal

Second Edition

William Magrino

Michael Goeller

RUTGERS, THE STATE UNIVERSITY OF NEW JERSEY

Kendall Hunt
publishing company

Kendall Hunt
publishing company

www.kendallhunt.com
Send all inquiries to:
4050 Westmark Drive
Dubuque, IA 52004-1840

Printed in the United States of America
10 9 8 7 6 5 4 3 2

Contents

The Project Proposal from the Ground Up

Chapter

Someone once said, "those who know *how* will always have a job, but those who know *why* will lead the way." When you write a project proposal, you need to answer two critical "why" questions: "why do this?" and "why *this way* as opposed to some *other* way?" A key premise of this text is that you can only answer those "why" questions through research. Without research, you will not have knowledge (or, at least, you will not be able to persuade other people that you have knowledge), and without knowledge you cannot answer "why" in a way that persuades people to follow you.

We live in a society where knowledge is at the heart of the decision-making process. In this "knowledge society," as Peter Drucker has called it, "knowledge workers" need many complex skills and abilities to get things done. They need to be able to:

- guide their own learning to master new knowledge and skills,

- analyze new situations, assess information needs, and locate that information,

- understand and digest both factual and theoretical material,

- think creatively to combine or improve available ideas,

- harness knowledge to justify a plan,

- develop and explain complex plans of action to others, and

- manage people and resources by putting information into action.

Knowledge workers need to be prepared for the creative challenge of solving problems through research, and they need practice in communicating their research to others. Having the experience of writing a project proposal where they use research to rationalize a plan of action can be a great first step toward professional competence. This book is designed to help you through the process of writing such a proposal.

The Six Parts of the Project Proposal

Though formats differ from organization to organization, there are always six basic parts to any strong project proposal:

- Patron (the person who will fund your proposal)

- Population (the people who will benefit from it)

- Problem (the need or opportunity that your proposal addresses)
- Paradigm (the research rationale for your plan)
- Plan (the way you will address the problem)
- Price (the budget to implement your plan)

A good project proposal will always help a specific *population* to address a *problem* by developing a *paradigm*-based *plan* of action that stays within the *price* that your *patron* is willing to pay. Though formats will differ from place to place, all strong proposals will have these six basic elements. The difficult part of developing a strong proposal is having all of the parts fit together into a coherent whole.

The *Six P Formula* can be used to organize both your written product and your writing process. The ideal process will follow the Six P's in order, more or less, focusing first on identifying a population to assist, a problem to solve, and a patron who would be willing to fund; then developing a paradigm through research that will help you design a well-justified plan of action; and once you have your plan you can develop your budget. Until you have a firm grasp on the first three P's, you will not be able to deal adequately with the last three. The first three help direct you to the right research to justify your plan and the last three present that research and use it to advance a coherent plan of action.

Patron

Who will fund your project? This is the person to whom you will literally address your proposal, and therefore the person whose name will be on your cover letter or memo. He or she will be your chief audience or reader. This is the person you most need to persuade. The patron could be your boss, the people at headquarters, a government group, or any public or private foundation. Like the "patrons" of the arts who paid for public and private projects during the Renaissance, your patron is the person whose hand controls the purse. Recognize that the interests of your patron must ultimately influence the proposal. If you choose a funding source that is most compatible with your approach, you will have fewer problems justifying your plan to them.

Population

Who will benefit from your project? These are the people who will directly or indirectly be affected by your proposal. This must be a significant, measurable number of people. In a business setting, they may be your customers or people in your organization. In the case of a scientific project, the population should be thought of as both the people in your field who want certain questions answered and the people in the world who might benefit from your research. In any case, a persuasive project proposal will have a well-thought-out human dimension. After all, why should a proposal be funded if no one but you will benefit from it?

Sometimes students choose a project proposal (such as any reform at their college) where they themselves are part of the population to be served. If you do that, it is especially important for you to remain objective. No one wants to fund a self-serving project, and until you can imagine other beneficiaries for your work (the larger population of students to be served, for example) you will not be able to make a persuasive case for funding.

Problem

What instigates your project? This could be a theoretical question (in the case of scientific research), or an opportunity not to be missed (in the case of an entrepreneurial endeavor), or a persistent issue that needs remedying (in the narrowest sense of problem). All good proposals begin with a problem. If you find yourself beginning with a plan of action, then you have really jumped to conclusions.

Before anyone should consider acting, after all, they need to be convinced that the problem is objectively real and that it needs to be addressed. You must first define and quantify your problem so that your patron can understand its scale, scope, and significance. In the case of a theoretical question, you will need to show how this question arose in prior research. In a business proposal, you will typically need to quantify the problem so that your patron can weigh the costs and benefits of action and inaction. Why does the problem even need to be addressed? Ultimately, you need to provide evidence to answer that question. You are not advancing a course of action just "because it sounds like a good idea." If there is no problem, then there is no need to write a proposal.

Paradigm

Why is your plan of action the best one available for addressing the problem? To answer "why" you need a research-based rationale that answers these two questions: *How do you know* that your plan will solve the problem? And *why* try to solve the problem *this way* rather than any number of other ways? A good research-based rationale will show that you have a consensus within your field that justifies your approach. It might also show that the plan you want to implement has strong precedents to suggest that it will succeed. This is basically what we mean by a "paradigm."

The way we use the term "paradigm" today has been greatly influenced by the work of Thomas Kuhn. In Kuhn's view, experiments form the basis of scientific knowledge by being what he called "exemplars," or models of how problems can be solved. The larger theory that explains why the models work, which he called the "disciplinary matrix," often comes much later. But the part and the whole are mutually dependent. When there is a consensus within a field of endeavor that this model and this matrix agree with each other, you have a paradigm. In terms of writing a persuasive project proposal, a paradigm can be either a model of success (or benchmark) that you think should be imitated or it can be a theoretical framework for understanding why your plan should succeed. The ideal paradigm will feature both an exemplar and a disciplinary matrix: it will have both a model of success and a theory of why that model succeeds. It will have both the part and the whole.

Paradigms describe the rhetorical and conceptual spaces that practitioners of any discipline generally follow. In the sciences and some areas of social research, paradigms are so commonly shared that a shorthand has developed for describing them, so that many paradigms can be summed up in a phrase that names a theory within a specific discipline: "integrated pest management" in agriculture, or "experiential learning" in education, or "ecological risk assessment" in environmental planning, or "the broken window theory" in sociology or law enforcement. These terms grew out of exemplary practices that became common knowledge within a field of endeavor.

If you want to develop a paradigm for your project, you might ask these questions: How have other people solved this problem or addressed this question in the past? What models of successful practice are available to give me ideas and help justify a plan or experiment? What theories or ideas might help me to develop a logical approach to this problem or to develop experimental procedures? How might language from my discipline help describe and understand the problem?

Once you have a paradigm, you will be able to construct your plan based on research. Without a paradigm you will be inventing your plan out of whole cloth with nothing but your own ethos to justify it, and that is not likely to take you very far with your patron.

Plan

Your plan might be a construction project, a training or education program, an experiment to test a hypothesis, a study to determine what course of action is best, or some other specific initiative. Since a good plan will have to grow organically out of the people, problem, and paradigm, it is generally not the first thing you will work on for the project. It has to be responsive to your research findings.

How you present your plan will depend upon your project, but you should strive to be as explicit as possible about all that will be involved. If you can find a way to visually organize this part of your proposal, it will help your reader to understand it better. If the project will take place in a series of steps, you might be able to set up a calendar showing the sequence of events. If the plan requires construction, you will probably want to draw a diagram of the thing you are going to build. But a good plan needs to look back at its problem and paradigm: it should detail the specific ways you are going to address the problem and suggest how it follows logically from your models and theoretical research.

Price

Once you have your plan in place, you will need to calculate a budget. Often, your budget is restricted before you begin your project, and you should recognize the ways that price can have a strong influence over choices you make in dealing with the other five P's. If you are making a case for overall long-term savings from your project, you may want to include those in your calculations. If the materials for your project can be broken down and detailed, then do so. Find out the price of the materials you need, either by contacting suppliers or looking up prices online. Talk to people who have done this sort of work before if you can. Use your judgment if you are not certain of costs, but try to be as realistic as possible.

Other Considerations

The Six P's are not an exhaustive list, but they should handle the critical issues you need to cover in any good proposal. We could add some other P's here, and I would like to mention two more, since they often come up: Partners and Politics.

By *partners* I mean the people who will help you achieve your goals yet who will not necessarily be benefiting from the project or providing funding for it. They might be other organizations or other people in your company. They can sometimes be very important to discuss in your proposal, since mentioning their support will show that you already have convinced other people that you have a good project idea.

By *politics* I mean the larger cultural, economic, legal, or political situation that may impact your proposal. As we know, projects that might gain support at one time or in one place will not gain support in another time or place. If your project runs counter to prevailing ideology, you may have a problem on your hands. For example, it would be politically difficult to get backing to promote the medical use of illegal drugs in a state with tough anti-drug laws; it would be difficult to organize a deer hunt to address a deer overpopulation issue in a community that is anti-hunting; it might be foolhardy to propose new accounting tricks in the wake of accounting scandals like Enron's; and costly projects will not be well received during times of fiscal difficulty. At the very least, you may need to give special attention to your rhetorical frame (that is, how you argue for your project) or you may need to adjust some of your assumptions to make your proposal more feasible given current realities (or "politics").

The Interdependence of the Six P's

You should imagine the Six P's spatially, as the parts of a coherent project that might come together in any temporal order. Making the Six P's fit together can sometimes feel like building a structure with six interlocking parts. As previously stated, the last three P's rely upon your command of the first three. The Six P's are completely interdependent entities, so choices in one area impact choices in other areas. You need to be open to revising the different parts of your project as it develops. How will decisions about the funding source (the addressee for your proposal) affect the way you approach the problem? How will the population to be served by the project impact the approach you might take?

For example, suppose your lab has expanded beyond its present capacity to give experimental space to all who need it. The people in charge of finding a solution to this problem will begin by asking themselves a number of questions:

- Patron: Where might we get money to solve this problem?

- Population: Who is most affected by the problem?

- Problem: What are some of the causes of the problem? What is its scope? What nonsubjective evidence do we have that there really is a problem?

- Paradigm: How have other labs succeeded in solving this problem? What innovative approaches (such as time sharing) have they used? What areas of knowledge can be brought to bear on the problem?

- Plan: What plans are feasible given current fiscal and political realities?

- Price: How much do you think you might be able to raise to fund your project? How much have similar projects cost?

If you find a patron willing to give you whatever money you need, then that will make it possible to build additional space. However, if your funds are limited and you need to make do with the space available, then that will clearly change your approach. In the case of limited funds, you may need to make decisions about which researchers should have priority over others, and that will create a narrower population that needs extra assistance. At each step of your project you should recognize how your choices can have cascading effects down the line.

The Six P's in Action

Because you are likely to make changes in your proposal at each step of its development, you should be prepared to revise your project as you go in order to make it more coherent. While not every project develops in a coherent step-by-step process following the order of the Six P's, they all need to put the Six P's together in a way that meshes. The order in which they are discussed here, however, is the order in which they will appear in the final proposal. Some projects begin logically but then require extensive revision to resolve conflicts between various areas of the Six P's (as when the patron doesn't like the price).

A Rutgers computer science student taking one of our professional writing courses—let's call her Sandy—wanted to build a web page for a restaurant where she worked, but she didn't see how that web page could be used to improve business. She had begun with the plan ("I want to build a website"), and her dilemma was that she didn't see the problem to be solved or the paradigm to solve it. As a result, she had to go back to the beginning and ask some of the questions that had been skipped over in leaping to the plan of action. This is why you should avoid "working backward" and find the best research before identifying a course of action. You do not want to advocate for a plan for which there is no justification.

Sandy already knew the funding source: the restaurant owners would pay to develop a good website. But she had not yet thought about the people to be served (Who are our customers? Do they even have access to the Internet?), or the problem (How could a website improve business? What opportunities are we missing out on by not having one?), or the paradigm to guide her (What principles or models of success might give us ideas?). Without answers to these questions, the website could very well become a waste of resources. She had to work on the Six P's from the beginning.

A good project always depends on good research. And what Sandy most needed was a paradigm to guide her research. Always remember that the success of a proposal is dependent upon the quality of the paradigm research—not the ambition of the plan.

In her initial writings about the project, Sandy had made the textbook distinction between "target marketing," which seeks to attract new consumers from a specific group, and "relationship marketing," which involves improving loyalty among the base of consumers who already use your product or service. She suggested that the Internet was probably more useful for relationship marketing than for target marketing because of how expensive and difficult it is to reach consumers who haven't already heard of your business. In fact, she recognized it might be easier to attract people to the website by using the restaurant than to attract people to the restaurant by using the website.

What Sandy did not recognize right away was that the term "relationship marketing" describes a researchable concept, literally a marketing paradigm. Sandy had stumbled upon the term in her initial research, but because she was not a marketing major (she was a computer science major, after all) it had not occurred to her that she could explore that concept further through more focused research and reading. To do that, she needed to look at resources in the marketing field and examples of relationship marketing in action. A brief stop at the library index *Business Source Premier* (which indexes business sources and even offers full-text versions online) showed her that there was a wealth of source material within easy reach. A single search turned up almost 500 potential sources on "relationship marketing" alone. Though she found no examples of restaurants using the concept, she did discover quite a few service-sector models for using a website to build relationships with loyal customers. One of the best examples she found, described at length in one article, was of a dry cleaner that used a sophisticated website not only to communicate with customers but also to offer other services that helped to develop a sense of community around the establishment. The site even had a singles meeting page that allowed people going to this dry cleaner to connect with local singles, many of whom would post their pictures both online and in the lobby of the establishment.

You might say that Sandy's paradigm was supported by both the exemplar (or example) of the dry cleaner and the disciplinary matrix (or theory) of "relationship marketing," two things she knew nothing about when she began her research. There were other approaches she could have explored (for example, there is a large body of research on building a "virtual community," a term coined by Howard Rheingold). But the approach she found gave her what she needed to begin developing a paradigm for a workable plan. The idea Sandy ended up developing was quite creative and went beyond the things she had learned as a computer science major. In many ways, the project helped her to understand the human dimensions of her field.

After looking at how a number of other companies used their websites to develop relationships with customers, Sandy was able to synthesize an original yet proven plan for her workplace. She decided to work on developing a sense of community around the restaurant, so that even when customers were not there they could participate in the social life of the institution, developing a relationship with it like the patrons of the television bar "Cheers." To entice current customers of the restaurant to visit the website, she would offer them online coupons, based upon the models offered by a number of other establishments. Customers visiting the site could find out more about the staff, e-mail suggestions directly to the chef, check out the calendar of upcoming events, join the restaurant "listserv" to receive announcements and advertisements, or check out what was going on at one of the live chat rooms. In a business built on loyal customers, a website that helped build loyalty was a concept worth implementing.

It took research to lead the way.

Works Cited

Drucker, Peter F. "The Age of Social Transformation." *The Atlantic Monthly* 274.5 (November 1994): 53–80. Print.

Kuhn, Thomas. *The Structure of Scientific Revolutions*. Chicago: University of Chicago Press, 1970. Print.

Newspaper Exercise

Preparation

To participate in this exercise, you should read several newspapers and choose **one** article that could be the basis for a project proposal. The best articles will suggest a problem that you can imagine trying to address. The purpose of this exercise is *not* to get you to choose the topic that you will actually work on for this class (though it is possible that some of you might stumble upon your topic this way). Rather, this exercise is intended to get you to practice the process of project development. After reading Chapter One, take notes on the Six P's that you could imagine developing from the article you have chosen. This may be collected and used in class discussions.

In Class

Get into small groups, and do the following:

1. Each of you, in turn, should present your article to the other group members. Describe the article and explain how this might make a good project idea. (About 10 minutes)

2. After the individual presentations, decide, as a group, which of them would make the most interesting basis for a project. (About 5 minutes)

3. Elect a group leader. This person does not have to be the one whose article was chosen, but he or she should present your ideas to the class. (About 5 minutes)

4. Once you have elected a group leader, begin developing a project idea based upon the article and on your own general knowledge. Obviously, to develop a strong project you would have to do a significant amount of research, but do the best you can with the information provided in the article. Use the following questions as a guide to discussion: (About 20 minutes)

   • Patron. Who might fund your idea? Why would they fund it?

   • Population. Who is affected by this problem? What specific population will your project serve?

   • Problem. What is the basic problem or need your project will address? Why is it a problem? How could you illustrate the extent of this problem? What are the tangible effects of this issue upon the population?

   • Paradigm. What disciplines (e.g., marketing, education, nutrition, medicine, etc.) might be useful in addressing this problem? What specific types of research would help?

   • Plan. How might you address the problem you have identified? What is your plan of action? Who will carry out this plan?

   • Price. What resources or assistance will you need? How much do you think your project might cost?

5. Present your ideas to the class and answer any questions. (5 minutes for each group)

Chapter 1 ■ The Project Proposal from the Ground Up

Six P's Exercise

Use the following form in a class exercise as directed by your instructor to analyze your project idea or the idea of someone else in your class.

Patron

Who would be willing to fund this project? Why would they want to fund it?

Population

Who does the problem affect? That is, who has a stake in seeing that there is a solution to the problem? Does your population have the same interests as the patron?

Problem

What are the main problems that need to be addressed? How could research shed light on these problems to emphasize their scale, scope, and significance? What sources of information about the problem would the patron find most persuasive?

Paradigm

What disciplines (e.g., computer science, marketing, education, psychology, etc.) might be useful in developing a disciplinary matrix for providing a rationale for action? Where might models of success be found to help shape the plan? What specific types of research would help?

Plan

What possible plans of action can you already imagine at this point? What plans are politically feasible? What would you need to know in order to develop a logical plan?

Price

How might your budget be limited? How much do you think the project might cost? How can that spending be justified?

Chapter 1 ■ The Project Proposal from the Ground Up

Six P's Exercise

Use the following form in a class exercise as directed by your instructor to analyze your project idea or the idea of someone else in your class.

Patron

Who would be willing to fund this project? Why would they want to fund it?

Population

Who does the problem affect? That is, who has a stake in seeing that there is a solution to the problem? Does your population have the same interests as the patron?

Problem

What are the main problems that need to be addressed? How could research shed light on these problems to emphasize their scale, scope, and significance? What sources of information about the problem would the patron find most persuasive?

Paradigm

What disciplines (e.g., computer science, marketing, education, psychology, etc.) might be useful in developing a disciplinary matrix for providing a rationale for action? Where might models of success be found to help shape the plan? What specific types of research would help?

Plan

What possible plans of action can you already imagine at this point? What plans are politically feasible? What would you need to know in order to develop a logical plan?

Price

How might your budget be limited? How much do you think the project might cost? How can that spending be justified?

Chapter 1 ■ The Project Proposal from the Ground Up

Six P's Exercise

Use the following form in a class exercise as directed by your instructor to analyze your project idea or the idea of someone else in your class.

Patron

Who would be willing to fund this project? Why would they want to fund it?

Population

Who does the problem affect? That is, who has a stake in seeing that there is a solution to the problem? Does your population have the same interests as the patron?

Problem

What are the main problems that need to be addressed? How could research shed light on these problems to emphasize their scale, scope, and significance? What sources of information about the problem would the patron find most persuasive?

Paradigm

What disciplines (e.g., computer science, marketing, education, psychology, etc.) might be useful in developing a disciplinary matrix for providing a rationale for action? Where might models of success be found to help shape the plan? What specific types of research would help?

Plan

What possible plans of action can you already imagine at this point? What plans are politically feasible? What would you need to know in order to develop a logical plan?

Price

How might your budget be limited? How much do you think the project might cost? How can that spending be justified?

Readings in Business and Professional Writing

Chapter **2**

A large part of your success in this course depends upon understanding some important concepts, including culture, paradigm, and leadership. These concepts are best grasped in the context of discussing readings that offer commentary on the social situation of writing, descriptions of the paradigm concept, and examples of paradigms and paradigm shifts in action.

Each reading is chosen to help reinforce a major lesson of the course. Joel Arthur Barker's discussion of paradigms, for example, offers an accessible representation of Thomas Kuhn's ideas. Without understanding the paradigm concept, you may have trouble conducting your research and successfully supporting your argument. You will also have difficulty envisioning ways of making change within an organization, which often depends less on what Kuhn calls "normal science" than on what he calls a "paradigm shift." John T. Bowen and Stowe Shoemaker's discussion of loyalty helps us see how a paradigm—in this case relationship marketing—can shape business strategy and improve practices. Importing paradigms is one way to bring about change within an organization. Malcolm Gladwell's essay on designs for working demonstrates that the paradigms that guide our plans can come from theoretical sources we might not expect to find useful. Who would have thought, after all, that the ideas of sociologist and urban planner Jane Jacobs would be so useful in designing office space? Ronald Heifetz and Donald Laurie's essay on leadership helps us understand the larger social implications of making change within an organization and responding to them appropriately. Ian Parker's essay on PowerPoint helps us to recognize some of the limitations of relying on standardized forms of business writing to shape our presentations of ideas.

We hope that you find these essays worthwhile both in the course and in your professional lives.

Works Cited

Barker, Joel Arthur. "Defining a Paradigm." Chapter 3 from *Paradigms: The Business of Discovering the Future* (New York: Harper Business, 1993), 30–41. Print.

Bowen, John T. and Stowe Shoemaker. "Loyalty: A Strategic Commitment." *Cornell Hotel and Restaurant Administration Quarterly* 39.1 (February 1998): 12–25. Print.

Carroll, Brigid, Lester Levy, and David Richmond. "Leadership as Practice: Challenging the Competency Paradigm." *Leadership* 4.4 (2008): 363–379. Print.

Gladwell, Malcolm. "Designs for Working." *The New Yorker* (December 11, 2000): 60–70. Print.

Parker, Ian. "Absolute PowerPoint: Can a Software Package Edit Our Thoughts?" *The New Yorker* (May 28, 2001): 78ff. Print.

Defining a Paradigm

"It's Twenty Cents, Isn't It?"

Joel Arthur Barker

■ ■ ─ ■

When I began talking about paradigms in 1974 to corporate audiences, a lot of people asked me why I was wasting my time with such a strange idea. Most people didn't even know how to pronounce the word, much less define it.

Most of the changes [in the business environment] were driven by a special phenomenon—a switch in paradigms (pronounced pair-a-dimes). And, in the jargon of futurists, they would be called "paradigm shifts."

The concept of paradigms and paradigm shifts can help you better understand the nature of those unexpected changes [in the business environment]. Being able to understand what caused them will give you a better chance to anticipate other paradigm shifts.

Today, "paradigm" is a buzzword and people use it loosely. But it is not a loose idea.

What is a paradigm? If you look up the word in the dictionary, you discover that it comes from the Greek *paradeigma,* which means "model, pattern, example."

Let me give you some definitions that have appeared in various books since 1962. Thomas S. Kuhn, a scientific historian, and author of *The Structure of Scientific Revolutions,* brought the concept of the paradigm to the scientific world. Kuhn wrote that scientific paradigms are "excepted examples of actual scientific practice, examples which include law, theory, application, and instrumentation together—[that] provide models from which spring particular coherent traditions of scientific research." He adds: "Men whose research is based on shared paradigms are committed to the same rules and standards for scientific practice" (page 10).

Adam Smith's definition, in his *Powers of the Mind,* is: "A shared set of assumptions. The paradigm is the way we perceive the world; water to the fish. The paradigm explains the world to us and helps us to predict its behavior." Smith's point about prediction is important. We will see that most of the time we do not predict things with our paradigms. But paradigms do give us the added advantage of being able to create a valid set of expectations about what will probably occur in the world based on our shared set of assumptions. "When we are in the middle of the paradigm," Smith concludes, "it is hard to imagine any other paradigm" (page 19).

In *An Incomplete Guide to the Future,* Willis Harmon, who was one of the key leaders of the Stanford Research Institute, writes that a paradigm is "the basic way of perceiving, thinking, valuing, and doing associated with a particular vision of reality. A dominant paradigm is seldom if ever stated explicitly; it exists as unquestioned, tacit understanding that is transmitted through culture and to succeeding generations through direct experience rather than being taught."

In *The Aquarian Conspiracy,* Marilyn Ferguson, who first made her name as editor and publisher of the *New Sense Bulletin,* writes: "A paradigm is a framework of thought . . . a scheme for understanding and explaining certain aspects of reality" (page 26).

Let me offer my definition:

A paradigm is a set of rules and regulations (written or unwritten) that does two things: (1) it establishes or defines boundaries; and (2) it tells you how to behave inside the boundaries in order to be successful.

And how do you measure success?

For most situations success is really measured by your ability to solve problems, problems from trivial to profound. If you think about that definition, you should immediately get a sense of how widely it could be applied. For example: Based on my definition, is the game of tennis a paradigm? If you think about it for a minute, you'll discover that it is. Does the game of tennis have boundaries? Of course, that's the easy part. The tricky part has to do with success and problem solving. What is the problem in tennis? It's the ball coming over the net. And you must solve that problem according to the rules of tennis.

You must hit the problem with the tennis racket; not a baseball bat or your hand or your foot. And if you hit it back over the net so that it drops inside the boundaries on the other side, you have solved the problem. And your successful solution becomes your opponent's problem. In a very real sense, you and your opponent exchange problems until one of you offers the other a problem that he or she cannot solve. Tennis is a paradigm. All games are paradigms. The beauty of games is that the boundaries are so clearly defined and the requirements for winning—problem solving—are so specific. Games allow for clear winners and losers. It is that aspect that generates much of any game's attraction. It is also that aspect that greatly disconnects them from reality.

Let us look at more important paradigms. Like your field of expertise. Almost everyone has one, either at work or at home. You may be an engineer, or a salesperson, or a chef or a carpenter or a nurse or an economist. Are these paradigms?

Again, let us apply the test. What does the word "field" suggest? Boundaries. How do you feel when you are outside your field? Not competent, right? Not competent to do what? Solve problems. Why do people come to you? To receive help from you in solving problems in your field. That sounds like paradigms, doesn't it?

Do artists have paradigms? I used to tease and say artists were just wild and crazy folks. Then I got straightened out by an artist. She came up after one of my speeches and said, "I'm a sculptor. What do you think the piece of marble I work with is?" I saw that it was her "field" and then realized she was going to work "inside the field" by chiseling into that block of marble.

"Okay," I said to her, "but you can do anything you want with that piece of marble."

"Not if I want to be judged successful," she retorted. And then she told me of the rules of "texture" and "form" and "balance' and "content" that she had to follow in order to be considered successful.

Since that encounter, I have begun to listen to artist's talk, especially about the "problems" they have solved in their work, whether it is a problem of perspective, or of color, or of tonality, or of character development. Artists have paradigms.

In a sense, I am constructing a hierarchy. At the top sits science and technology. That's where Thomas Kuhn focused. Science and technology deserve top billing because they are so careful with their paradigms, in terms of writing them down, and of developing measurement devices of increasing precision to tell whether they have solved a particular problem.

And, once a scientist has performed a successful experiment, it is expected that he or she should be able to hand the notes and the apparatus to another scientist who should then be able to replicate that experiment, getting the same results.

We would never expect a tennis player to be able to "replicate" Boris Becker's serve by just reading his notes and using the same tennis racket. Or someone to replicate an artist's work by being given the same pigments, paintbrushes, and canvas. The requirement of reproducibility constitutes a very important difference between science and all other fields. It results in science and its technologies having much more power to manipulate reality. But, even though they are more powerful, if you apply the definition I offered to science and technology, you will see that it holds true.

Over the years, I have collected words that represent subsets of the paradigm concept. Below they are ordered on a spectrum ranging from challengeable to unchallengeable. You may disagree with my arrangement, but take a look at the words and think about the boundaries and rules and regulations for success that is implicit in them.

1. Theory	10. Patterns	19. Prejudices
2. Model	11. Habits	20. Ideology
3. Methodology	12. Common Sense	21. Inhibitions
4. Principles	13. Conventional Wisdom	22. Superstitions
5. Standards	14. Mind-set	23. Rituals
6. Protocol	15. Values	24. Compulsions
7. Routines	16. Frames of Reference	25. Addictions
8. Assumptions	17. Traditions	26. Doctrine
9. Conventions	18. Customs	27. Dogma

Please note that nowhere in the list do the words "culture," "worldview," "organization," or "business" appear. That is because cultures, worldviews, organizations, and businesses are **forests of paradigms.** IBM is not one paradigm; it is a collection of many. That is true for any business. Large or small, they have management paradigms, sales paradigms, recruitment paradigms, marketing paradigms, research and development paradigms, human resource development paradigms. It goes on but I am sure you get the point. And there are even more paradigms in our cultural life: how we raise our children; how we deal with sex; how we define honesty; the food we eat; the music we listen to.

And the interrelationship of all these paradigms is crucial to the success and longevity of any culture or organization. That is captured in the word "forest"—a highly interdependent structure. As we know from the environmental paradigm, when one thing in the forest is altered, it affects everything else there. So when someone within your organization starts messing with their paradigm and says, "Don't worry, it's got nothing to do with you," start worrying. It is never just one paradigm that is changed.

A paradigm, in a sense, tells you that there is a game, what the game is, and how to play it successfully. The idea of a game is a very appropriate metaphor for paradigms because it reflects the need for borders and directions on how to perform correctly. A paradigm tells you how to play the game according to the rules.

A paradigm shift, then, is a change to a new game, a new set of rules.

It is my belief that changes in paradigms are behind much of society's turbulence during the last thirty years. We had sets of rules we knew well, then someone changed the rules. We understood the old boundaries, then we had to learn new boundaries. And those changes dramatically upset our world.

In *Megatrends,* the best-seller of 1982, John Naisbitt reflects in an indirect way how important paradigm shifts are. Naisbitt suggested that there were ten important new trends that would generate profound changes in our society in the next fifteen to thirty years.

I believe that if you look for what initiated those trends, you will find a paradigm shift. What Naisbitt identifies for us in Megatrends is important, because he shows us a pathway of change that we can follow through time to measure how we are getting more of something or less of something.

But even more important than the pathway is our understanding of what instigated that change in the first place. We almost always find that at the beginning of the trend, someone created a new set of rules. The trend toward decentralization is an excellent example of a paradigm shift. The old rules, the old game, required that we "centralize the organization and make the hierarchy complex." But the game ultimately created big problems. Then somebody discovered that there was a different way to deal with the problems, which was to decentralize the organization and simplify the structure; in other words, to change the rules. The result was a paradigm shift.

So if you want to improve your ability to anticipate the future, don't wait for the trends to develop. Instead, **watch for people messing with the rules, because that is the earliest sign of significant change.**

Four Questions

One of the difficulties I have with Thomas Kuhn's *Structure of Scientific Revolutions* is his insistence that paradigms exist only in science. In his afterword, Kuhn takes great pains to talk about all the other disciplines as being "preparadigmatic" because they do not have the exactness of science. And yet, again and again I saw the phenomena he writes about in nonscientific settings and situations. Then I realized that a key element in one of his most powerful examples was not scientific but cultural—a simple deck of cards. The cards were used in a scientific experiment to prove that people have great difficulty perceiving "red" spades and "black" hearts when they are intermixed with standard cards and flashed very quickly to an observer. But even though the experiment was scientific, the objects of the experiment, the cards, are cultural artifacts. And the expectations about the correct colors are cultural expectations, not scientific expectations.

So the experiment was actually a measure of the power of a simple cultural paradigm—the card-deck paradigm—to set up boundaries that dramatically influenced the way the subjects of the experiment saw the anomalous cards.

I am convinced that what Thomas Kuhn discovered about paradigms is a description not just of science but of the human condition.

When we look back to the 1960's, we see nonscientific paradigm shifts: Parents responded so violently to drugs and long hair on their children because these things represented a cultural paradigm shift; we missed the OPEC revolution because of an economic paradigm shift. Our country's inability to understand the Iranian revolution had to do with religious paradigms. Much of the confusion we have about the future is because of changes in paradigms.

These paradigm changes are especially important for all of us because, whether it is in business or education or politics or our personal lives, a paradigm change, by definition, alters the basic rules of the game.

And, when the rules change, the whole world can change.

The points that Kuhn makes about scientific paradigm shifts are true for any situation where strongly held rules and regulations exist.

I should also add the following disclaimer: I doubt very much if Kuhn appreciates the extent to which I, and others, have generalized his concepts. In his book he states that only in science, where the rules and examples and measures are precise, can paradigms exist. He also contends that only with the subtlety and accuracy possessed by science can changes in paradigms be measured so as to trigger the search for a new paradigm. I accept the obligation imposed by Kuhn's own careful qualification. In spite of his argument to the contrary, I still believe that his observations can be applied in a broader sense with great utility. I hope you will find this true as well.

To frame this broader discussion, we will ask four questions about paradigms:

1. **When do new paradigms appear?** This question is all about timing. If we can know when the new rules are going to show up, then we can anticipate our future with much greater accuracy. Timing may not be everything, but it's a great place to start.

2. **What kind of person is a paradigm shifter?** It is as important to understand who are the paradigm shifters, the people who change the rules, as it is to know when they show up. Of the four kinds of paradigm shifters that will be described, three are already inside your organization. But typically, we do not understand how to use them to our advantage. In fact, we usually are very hard on these people.

3. **Who are the early followers of the paradigm shifters and why do they follow them?** I call these people paradigm pioneers. Without them, paradigm shifts take much longer. Paradigm pioneers bring the critical mass of brainpower and effort and key resources necessary to drive the new rules into reality. Very few of us can be paradigm shifters; many more of us, if we understand our roles, can be paradigm pioneers.

4. **How does a paradigm shift affect those who go through it?** It is crucial to answer this last question if we are going to understand why there is so much resistance to new paradigms. It also explains the great gulf between old and new paradigm practitioners.

When we have answered these four questions, we will have identified the Paradigm Principles.

Name: _____ **Date:** _____

Chapter 2 ■ Defining a Paradigm

Questions for Discussion

1. Barker says of the term "paradigm" that "people use it loosely. . . but it is not a loose idea." Yet he goes on later to list 27 loosely equivalent terms, suggesting that the definition is not so set in stone. Does Barker finally settle on a definition? What is it? Based on your reading of Barker, how would you define a paradigm in your own words?

2. As part of the process of developing a definition, get into groups of three and try, as a group, to draw a picture of a paradigm. Of course, the word describes an abstract concept and so there can be no actual picture of a paradigm. But in drawing a picture you will be able to objectify it and thus make it easier to describe in your own words. Give it a try. What does a paradigm look like? How might you describe it metaphorically?

3a. Students often say that they are prevented from being original by the requirement that they use research to provide a rationale for their plan. After all, they ask, where is the room for pure invention if everything needs to be supported by research into what other people have done? How can new ideas come out of old ones?

3b. How might Barker respond to these questions? Can tradition actually *support* original work? Can the fact that fields outside of science do not have the same reproducibility introduce an element of creativity? Or does creativity get introduced through the concept of paradigm shifts?

4. How do you research a paradigm? For example, if you wanted to solve the common problem of parking on campus, how would you find a paradigm? How would you research it? What would you look for?

Loyalty: A Strategic Commitment

John T. Bowen and Stowe Shoemaker

Building a group of loyal customers is money in the bank for a hotel, but loyalty requires a long-term relationship in which a hotel earns its guests' trust.

The hotel industry has in recent years become interested in developing loyal guests through relationship marketing, but that initiative has progressed only by fits and starts. The industry's approaches to relationship marketing have so far focused largely on transactional tactics, such as frequent-user programs, gifts for repeat customers, and familiarization trips for meeting planners. As the weaknesses of the transactional approach become apparent (primarily, anyone can copy those tactics), new concepts of relationship marketing are employing a strategic perspective intended to develop guests' loyalty in a way that cannot easily be duplicated by competitors. This study of relationship marketing focuses on loyalty—a relationship built on trust and commitment between the buyer and the seller. Based on the information we garnered from our research, hotels that seek to employ the relationship marketing strategies discussed here may have to undergo fundamental changes in the way they conduct business. This article explains our investigation of how luxury hotels might take a strategic approach to relationship marketing based on loyalty.

Aiming for the Bottom Line

The benefits of relationship marketing come from the continuing patronage of loyal customers who display decreased price sensitivity over time, a concomitant reduction of marketing costs, and "partnership" actions on the part of those customers. The reduction in marketing costs is a result of the facts that it takes fewer marketing dollars to maintain a customer than to create one and that loyal customers help create new customers through positive word of mouth. Loyal customers are less likely to switch to a competitor solely because of price, and loyal customers also make more purchases than comparable non-loyal customers.[1] Partnership-like activities of loyal hotel customers include offering strong word of mouth, making business referrals, providing references and publicity, and serving on advisory boards. The combination of these attributes of loyal customers means that a small increase in loyal customers can result in a substantial increase in profitability. Reichheld and Sasser found that a 5-percent increase in customer retention resulted in a 25- to 125-percent increase in profits in nine service-industry groups they studied.[2] These researchers concluded that building a relationship with customers should be a strategic focus of most service firms.

Customer loyalty is particularly important to the hotel industry, because most hotel-industry segments are mature and competition is strong. Often there is little differentiation among products in the same segment. For example, general managers from ITT Sheraton in Asia were shown pictures of hotel rooms from their own chain and three competitors. Most managers could not identify the

[1] Frederick E. Reichheld and W. Earl Sasser, Jr., "Zero Defections: Quality Comes to Services," *Harvard Business Review* 68 (September–October 1990): 105–111.

[2] *Ibid.*

brand of one room—not even their own—although they were given a list of eight brands from which to choose.[3] The difficulty faced by hotel brands of differentiating themselves on physical attributes is one of the factors that drew the industry's attention in the 1990s to relationship marketing. The goal of relationship marketing is to build customers' loyalty based on factors other than pure economics or product attributes.[4] In essence, relationship marketing means developing customers as partners, a process much different than traditional transaction-based marketing.

Building Relationships

Our study examined the antecedents and consequences of building relationships with customers in the luxury-hotel segment. To test a proposed model of service relationships, the study needed to meet the following sub-objectives.

- Identify the type of benefits (e.g., upgrades, frequency points) luxury hotels must offer so that guests want to develop a relationship with (and consequently a feeling of loyalty for) the hotel;

- Identify the behavioral outcomes of this relationship (e.g., increased product use, willingness to promote the hotel);

- Evaluate the current practices of luxury-hotel operators (e.g., revenue management, last-room availability) and the impact of such practices on developing relationships with customers;

- Identify actions undertaken by luxury hotels that affect consumers' feelings of trust in the hotel (whether positive or negative); and

- Determine whether relationship issues vary according to purpose of stay (i.e., business or pleasure), demographic characteristics, and frequency of use.

Satisfaction Isn't Loyalty

Customer satisfaction measures how well a customer's expectations are met by a given transaction, in this case a hotel stay. Customer loyalty, on the other hand, measures how likely a customer is to return and also gauges how willing that person is to perform partner-like activities for the hotel—starting with recommendations to friends.

Satisfaction

A customer who receives what she or he expected in a hotel stay is most likely to be satisfied. If the guest's expectations were exceeded, she or he may be extremely satisfied. Customer satisfaction of this kind is a requisite for loyalty, but satisfied customers may not become loyal customers. Some of the reasons for the failure of satisfaction to translate into loyalty are unrelated to either satisfaction or loyalty. Travelers who do not regularly visit a particular area, for instance, cannot be loyal to an individual property simply because they never return to the area. Additionally, some luxury-hotel guests seek variety and sample a different property each time they return to an area. These customers may be satisfied with a hotel, but their drive for novelty inhibits their loyalty to a given hotel. Some guests remain price sensitive, even at the luxury level, and shop for the best deal. Even though they were satisfied with a particular hotel, they will try another one that makes a better offer. As a final consideration, customers at this level simply expect that they will be satisfied with their

---

[3] Philip Kotler, John T. Bowen, and James C. Makens, *Marketing for Hospitality and Tourism* (Englewood Cliffs, NJ: Prentice Hall, 1996): 355.

[4] David Cravens, "Introduction to Special Issue," *Journal of the Academy of Marketing Science* 23.4 (Fall 1995): 235.

Exhibit 1
Relationship Marketing Compared with Traditional Marketing

Relationship marketing	Traditional marketing*
Orientation to customer retention	Orientation to single sales
Continual customer contact	Episodic customer contact
Focus on customer value	Focus on product features
Long-term horizon	Short-term horizon
High customer-service emphasis	Little emphasis on customer service
High commitment to meeting customer expectations	Limited commitment to meeting customer expectations
Quality concerns all staff members	Quality concerns only production staff

*Traditional marketing can also be considered transactional marketing, in which each sale is considered to be a discrete event. This table is based on an idea from: F. Robert Dwyer, Paul Schurr, and Sejo Oh, " Developing Buyer-Seller Relationships," *Journal of Marketing*, Vol. 51, April 1987, pp. 11–27.

purchase and that the hotel will perform as advertised. If there were any likelihood of failure, the guest would not have made the purchase in the first place. As a consequence, hotels generally garner solid satisfaction ratings, but not necessarily loyal customers.

Loyalty extends beyond simple satisfaction. As an example of the weak effect satisfaction has on repeat purchases, researchers Reichheld and Aspinwall found in 1993 that 90 percent of customers who changed from one supplier to another—in this case their bank—were satisfied with their original supplier.[5] A study by Heskett, Sasser, and Schlesinger found that the link between customer satisfaction and customer loyalty was the weakest relationship in their service-profit-chain model, which attempts to capture the influence on profit of operating strategy, service-delivery system, service concept, and target market.[6] In the Heskett group's study, fewer than 40 percent of those giving a particular service a rating of satisfactory (score of 4 on a five-point scale) intended to return, while 90 percent of those who rated the service very satisfactory (score = 5) intended to return.

Although keeping customers satisfied is important, loyal customers are more valuable than satisfied customers. A satisfied customer who does not return and spreads no positive word of mouth has no net present value to the company. On the other hand, Kotler, Bowen, and Makens calculated that a loyal customer of a luxury hotel who both returns and spreads positive word of mouth has a net present value of more than $100,000.[7]

Model for Relationship Marketing. The extent of customer loyalty indicates the likelihood of a customer's returning to a hotel and that person's willingness to behave as a partner to the organization. Morgan and Hunt developed a model of relationships that proposed trust and commitment as central to the development of long-term relationships. We developed the model of service relationships (MSR) shown in Exhibit 2 based on the work of Morgan and Hunt.[8] The MSR also builds on the research

---

[5] Frederick F. Reichheld and Keith Aspinwall, "Building High-Loyalty Business Systems," *Journal of Retail Banking* (Winter 1993–94): 21–29.

[6] James L. Heskett, Earl W. Sasser, Jr., and Leonard A. Schlesinger, *The Service Profit Chain* (New York: Free Press, 1997): 22.

[7] Kotler, Bowen, and Makens, 346.

[8] Robert Morgan and Shelby D. Hunt, "The Commitment-Trust Theory of Relationship Marketing," *Journal of Marketing* 58 (July 1994): pp. 20–38.

undertaken by Gundlach, Achrol, and Mentzer, who investigated the structure of commitment.[9] The difference between the MSR and previous models is that our model focuses on services in which one of the partners is the end user, whereas previous models have examined relationships between firms.

Two concepts at the heart of a relationship are trust and commitment. Cravens and Piercy, for instance, state that trust is important to the success of a partnership. With trust as a precursor, a customer becomes loyal to a firm and forms a commitment to that firm. Morgan and Hunt found a significant connection between trust and relationship based on commitment. Our model also proposes that a positive connection exists between commitment and trust in a relationship.

Commitment

Relationship marketers generally believe that the future of buyer-seller relationships depends on the commitment made by the partners to the relationship.[10] Gundlach et al. defined commitment as "an implicit or explicit pledge of relational continuity between exchange partners."[11] Based on our reading of the literature, we define commitment as the belief that an ongoing relationship is so important that the partners are willing to work at maintaining the relationship and are willing to make short-term sacrifices to realize long-term benefits. As an example, a hotel would make the short-term sacrifice of holding a block of rooms at a reduced corporate rate for the long-term benefit of working with a regular customer, even though those rooms might be sold at a higher rate if the block were released. With an individual customer, the hotel would, for instance, make good on a service failure by forgoing revenues on a particular item to secure the customer's future business (and positive word of mouth).

Trust

Trust has been defined by one set of authors as the "willingness to rely on an exchange partner in whom one has confidence."[12] A second author defines trust as "a generalized expectancy held by an individual that the word, promise, or statement of another individual can be relied upon."[13] Trust is considered so important to commitment and to long-term relationships that Sullivan and Peterson stated: [W]here the parties have trust in one another, then there will be ways by which the two parties can work out difficulties such as power conflict, low profitability, and so forth.[14] Central to all of these definitions of trust are reliability and working for the interests of the partner.[15]

Natural Opportunistic Behavior

Within the daily operation of a partnership, one partner often has the opportunity to take advantage of the other. For trust to develop, we hypothesize that partners in a relationship must suppress this natural opportunistic behavior, resist the desire for an advantage, and instead work toward a

---

[9] Gregory T. Gundlach, S. Ravi Achrol, and John T. Mentzer, "The Structure of Commitment in Exchange," *Journal of Marketing* 59 (January 1995): pp. 78–92.

[10–11] For example, see: Margaret Beaton and Caron Beaton,"Marrying Service Providers and Their Clients: A Relationship Approach to Services Management," *Journal of Marketing Management* 11.1–3 (1995): 55–70; and Inge Geyskins, Jan-Benedict Steenkamp, E. M. Steenkamp, Lisa K. Scheer, and Nirmalya Kumar, "The Effects of Trust and Interdependence on Relationship Commitment: A TransAtlantic Study," *International Journal of Research in Marketing* 13 (1996): 303–317.

[12] Christine Moorman, Rohit Deshpande, and Gerald Zaltman,"Factors Affecting Trust in Market Research Relationships," *Journal of Marketing* 57 (January 1992): 81–101.

[13] J. B. Rotter,"Interpersonal Trust, Trustworthiness, and Gullibility," *American Psychologist* 35 (1980): 1–7.

[14] Jeremiah Sullivan and Richard B. Peterson, "Factors Associated with Trust in Japanese-American Joint Ventures," *Management International Review* 22 (1982): 30–40.

[15] Scott W. Kelly and Mark A. Davis,"Antecedents to Customer Expectations for Service Recovery," *Journal of the Academy of Marketing Science* 22 (1994): 52–61.

Exhibit 2
Antecedents and Consequences of Commitment and Trust in Service Relationships—Model of Service Relationships (MSR)

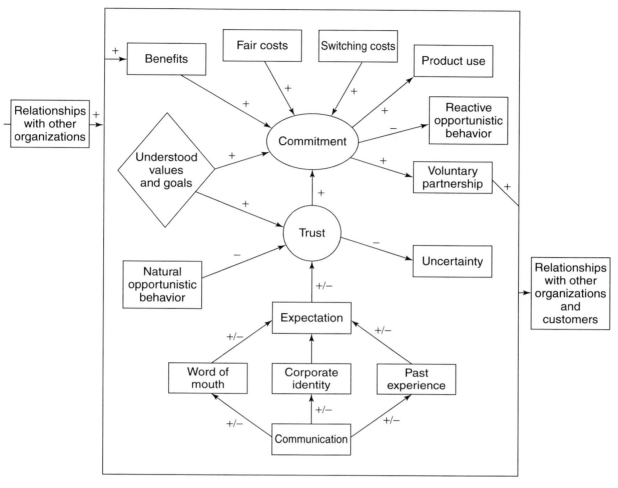

The model of service relationships is based in part on: Robert Morgan and Shelby D. Hunt, "The Commitment–Trust Theory of Relationship Marketing," *Journal of Marketing*, Vol. 58, July 1994, pp. 20–38, supported by concepts from: Gregory T. Gundlach, S. Ravi Achrol, and John T. Mentzer, "The Structure of Commitment Exchange," *Journal of Marketing*, Vol. 59, January 1995, pp. 78–92.

mutually beneficial situation. An example of natural opportunistic behavior is a revenue management system that enables a hotel to change its rates according to demand. We propose that there is a negative relationship between natural opportunistic behavior and trust.

Benefits

The benefits component of our model captures the benefits a customer will need to receive from the service provider to make a commitment to that provider. Benefits are related to commitment.

For a customer to enter into a relationship, the relationship must provide value for that customer. Hotel chains recognize this fact. For example, Sheraton reworked its housekeeping system to allow its Sheraton Club International members to check out as late as 4:00 PM. Kelly and Davis found that health club customers receiving higher levels of service quality are more committed to the health club than those whose service experience was average. We propose a positive relationship between benefits and commitment.

Fair Costs

Fair costs can be categorized as day-to-day costs and switching costs.[16] In our study the day-to-day cost was operationalized as the perceived value of the room rate and the fairness of the costs. In this study costs were measured as being fair, or having a positive sign. Switching costs (i.e., the costs associated with changing from one product or provider to another) were measured by asking respondents directly about those costs.[17] We propose there is a positive relationship between switching costs and relationship commitment and between switching costs and value.

Understood Values

Values have been defined as follows:

- "generalized, enduring beliefs about the personal and social desirability of modes of conduct or end-states of existence";[18]
- "the extent to which partners have beliefs in common about what behaviors, goals, and policies are important or unimportant, appropriate or inappropriate, and right or wrong";[19] and
- "beliefs held by an individual or group that speak to the actions and goals (ends) organizations ought to or should identify in the running of an enterprise."[20]

Myers states the impact of shared values on commitment depends on the degree to which a value is conflicting or shared, the intensity of the value to each of the relationship partners, and the value of the relationship. Values are affected by international cultural differences, organizational culture, and the values held by key individuals involved in the relationship.[21] Although values are an important component of relationships, we did not measure values in this study because of their complexity.

Reactive Opportunistic Behavior

Reactive opportunistic behavior apparently stems from lack of commitment. This tit-for-tat behavior occurs when one party attempts to take advantage of another party because the first party concludes that the other party has failed to look after the first party's best interest. Because our sample included only loyal customers, we did not measure reactive opportunistic behavior as a component of the model.

Product Use

Product use in this instance measures the incremental business a guest is likely to bring to a hotel with which the guest has developed a relationship. Reichheld and Sasser found that loyal customers purchase more from a firm than similar non-loyal customers.[22] Kelly and Davis stated that

---

[16] Hakan Hakansson and Ivan Snehota, *Developing Relationships in Business Networks* (New York: Routledge, 1995).

[17] Dwayne D. Gremler, "The Effects of Satisfaction, Switching Costs, and Interpersonal Bonds on Service Loyalty" (Tucson, AZ: Arizona State University dissertation, 1995).

[18] Boris Kabanoff, Robert Waldersee, and Marcus Cohen,"Espoused Values and Organizational Change Themes," *Academy of Management Journal* 38 (August 1995): 10–75.

[19] Morgan and Hunt, 20–38.

[20] Cathy Enz, *Power and Shared Values in the Corporate Culture* (Ann Arbor: UMI Research Press, 1986): 27.

[21] C. S. Myers, "Trust, Commitment, and Shared Values in Long-term Relationships in Services Marketing" (Las Vegas: University of Nevada, Las Vegas working paper, 1996).

[22] Reichheld and Sasser, 105–111.

a customer's commitment to the organization results not only in repeat purchases but also a greater willingness to become an advocate for the organization.[23]

A committed hotel guest, for example, would be more likely to use the food and beverage facilities at the hotel with which he or she has developed a relationship rather than go someplace else to eat. In contrast, the guest who does not have a relationship with the hotel will more likely go out of the hotel for meals. The attributes used to measure this construct were related to the luxury-hotel market. We propose a positive relationship between relationship commitment and product usage.

Voluntary Partnership

Voluntary partnership comprises the variety of activities that one member of the relationship is likely to undertake on behalf of the other member. We discuss the hotel's possible partnership activities throughout this article. Guests in voluntary partnership may give favorable word of mouth, make business referrals, provide references and publicity, and serve on advisory boards.

Another element of voluntary partnership is that when disputes occur the partners make a determined effort to work things out. Instead of dissolving the partnership when a dispute arises, committed partners use the dispute as the basis for new understandings.

This functional conflict can prevent stagnation, stimulate interest and curiosity, and provide a medium through which problems can be aired and solutions achieved.[24] For customers to become involved in functional conflict, however, they must be committed to the relationship or they will simply switch vendors. We propose a positive relationship between commitment and voluntary partnership.

Expectation

We derived the expectation component of our model from past research on service quality.[25] Since this area has already been tested in previous research, we did not specifically test it.

Questionnaire Development

After our review of relevant literature, we conducted a series of in-depth interviews with 22 luxury hotel guests of the New York Palace and the Waldorf Towers who had paid a minimum of $350 per night for their hotel stay. From the interviews and our literature review we began developing a model of guest loyalty and a questionnaire to test that model. We subsequently presented the proposed model to other researchers at two academic conferences on relationship marketing. We received helpful comments on the model as a result of these presentations.

Next, we pre-tested the survey instrument as follows. Based on comments received during the interviews and from the conference presentations, we developed an initial questionnaire that we mailed to approximately 100 people from a list supplied by a luxury hotel in New York.[26] We also conducted personal interviews with six guests at the Rancho Bernardo Inn in California, showed the survey to guests, and asked for their comments, particularly on survey length, format, and readability.

---

[23] Kelly and Davis, 52–61.

[24] Morgan and Hunt, 26.

[25] See: A. Parasuraman, Leonard L. Berry, and Valerie A. Zeithaml, "Understanding Customer Expectations of Service," *Sloan Management Review* (Spring 1991): 39–48.

[26] The name of the hotel is intentionally omitted.

Exhibit 3
Structural Model and Statistical Relationships

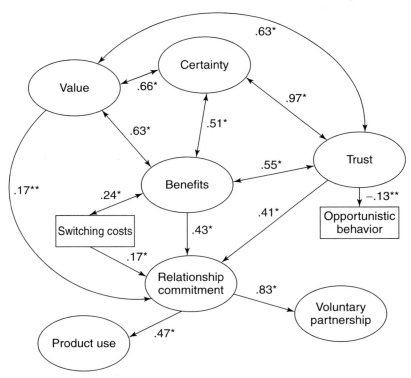

Note: * = significant at *p* < .01; ** = significant at *p* < .05.

With the pre-test completed, we mailed the survey to 5,000 American Express-card holders who had stayed at least three times in one of a pre-selected list of specific luxury hotels.[27]

Results

We received 892 usable questionnaires. Allowing for undelivered (returned) surveys, the response rate was 18 percent, a level common to surveys of this kind. The sample predominantly comprises men (85.4 percent). The participants' median age is 48 and their median income is $260,000. The most frequently mentioned occupations included attorney (13.5 percent), executive (9.3 percent), consultant (7.3 percent), investment banker (7.3 percent), and marketing or sales representative (6.6 percent).

Within the last year, 60.5 percent of the respondents stayed in a luxury hotel when traveling on a combination of business and leisure. Slightly more than one-third stayed in luxury hotels when traveling primarily for business and a small percentage used the hotels primarily for leisure. More than four out of ten participants (44.1 percent) stayed in luxury hotels more than 12 times in the year preceding the survey. More than two out of ten participants stayed either 2 to 6 times (26.9 percent) or 7 to 12 times (28.9 percent) in the last year. Less than 1 percent of the respondents stayed in a luxury hotel only once in the last year.

To determine whether the respondents were representative of the total sample, we interviewed 196 non-respondents via telephone. We could find no significant difference between respondents and

[27] We selected the hotels jointly with representatives of the travel-research division of American Express. We screened the hotels according to the hotel's Mobil rating and by checking room rates in Reed/Elsevier's Hotel and Travel Index. We limited our sample to business-oriented properties because we wanted a substantial sample of business travelers. Hotel chains that we reviewed included Ritz-Carlton, Four Seasons, Leading Hotels of the World members, and Preferred Hotels members.

non-respondents on such characteristics as gender, age, and use of luxury hotels. Looking at the subset of business travelers, our analysis suggests that, compared to those who responded, non-respondents were older, stayed in the luxury hotel to which they are loyal more frequently, and were more loyal. We concluded, therefore, that the results presented in this report are conservative, and that the findings may understate the relationships that exist.

When traveling to their favorite luxury hotel, 48.3 percent of the participants were traveling primarily on business, 13 percent were traveling primarily for leisure, and 38.7 percent were on business combined with leisure. Although we found noteworthy differences between those whose reason for stay was primarily business and those who stayed primarily for leisure, we restrict our discussion to the business travelers. As examples of the differences, however, leisure travelers were more interested than business travelers in the following features: hotel helps you with other reservations (e.g., meals, shows, tee times); hotel provides you with occasional gifts (such as fruit baskets); hotel sends out newsletters; and you can request a specific room. Moreover, leisure travelers were less interested in rooms with business equipment than were business travelers.

Statistical Tests

To develop a path diagram for testing the model of service relationships, we applied Amos, a structural modeling program distributed by SPSS. By adjusting the model according to procedures suggested by Arbuckle, by Bentler and Chou, and in a conversation with Werner Wothke, we were able to produce a model with a good fit.[28] We compared the final model to a baseline model using the normed-fit index (NFI) developed by Bentler and Bonett.[29] The final model had a NFI of .98 which, according to Bentler and Bonett, indicates a good fit.

Building Commitment

The results support the proposition that benefits, trust, switching costs, and perceptions of value (the day-today-cost measure) lead to relationship commitment, the behavioral outcome of loyalty. These results are shown by examining the regression weights relating to commitment.[30] As indicated by the regression weights, benefits and trust are the most important antecedents to commitment. The constructs of value (day-to-day cost) and switching costs have less impact on relationship commitment (each having a Beta of .17) than do benefits and trust, but there is still a positive relationship.

As expected, natural opportunistic behavior is negatively related to trust, albeit weakly, as evidenced by a Beta of −.13. This result suggests that if a hotel practices opportunistic behavior, the customer will be less likely to have trust in the hotel, and, in turn, the less likely there will be relationship commitment.

The results also support the proposition that commitment to a relationship results in increased product use and voluntary partnership activities by the customer. The relationship between relationship commitment and voluntary partnership is quite strong, as evidenced by a degree of .83. The findings that product use and voluntary partnership are outcomes of relationship commitment suggest that it is worthwhile for luxury-hotel firms to develop relationships with their guests.

Customers will give back to the hotel to which they feel loyalty. For instance, data from the study indicate that a guest who feels loyal to a specific property will relay positive comments about the hotel to a median of 10 people and will also spend more money at the hotel.

[28] See: J. L. Arbuckle, *Amos Users Guide,* Version 3.6 (Chicago: SmallWaters Corporation, 1997); and P. Bentler and C. Chou, "Practical Issues in Structural Modeling," *Sociological Methods and Research* 16.1, pp. 78–117.

[29] P. Bentler and D. Bonett, "Significance Tests and Goodness of Fit in the Analysis of Covariance Structures," *Psychological Bulletin* 88 (November 1980): 588–606.

[30] Note that one can compare regression weights in this model because all variables are measured on the same scale.

The reader should realize that the model was tested using responses to questions regarding practices at the hotel to which the respondent was most loyal. We thought it would be useful to examine what a hotel might do to increase feelings of loyalty, as discussed in the next section.

Factors That Build Loyalty

To identify features that build loyalty, we tested the loyalty-creating effects of 18 possible benefits, which were identified in the in-depth interviews. We asked respondents to rate each benefit on a Likert-type scale, where 1 meant the factor would have no impact on loyalty and 7 meant the factor would have a great impact on loyalty. Guests staying in a luxury hotel primarily for business

Exhibit 4
Ratings of Factors Intended to Engender Loyalty

Feature	n	Top rating (7)	Top two ratings (6 or 7)	Overall mean
The hotel provides upgrades when available.	418	69.4%	94.5%	6.6
You can check in and check out at a time that suits you.	417	59.2%	85.8%	6.4
The hotel uses information from your prior stays to customize services for you.	416	57.7%	87.5%	6.4
You can request a specific room.	418	44.7%	71.3%	5.9
Employees communicate the attitude that your problems are important to them.	418	42.6%	79.9%	6.1
When you return to this hotel your registration process is expedited.	416	41.1%	76.9%	6.1
The staff recognizes you by name.	421	39.4%	60.8%	5.6
The staff recognizes you when you arrive.	418	38.3%	63.2%	5.6
If the hotel is likely to be sold out at a time you normally visit, someone from the hotel will call you to ask whether you would like to make a reservation.	379	37.7%	63.6%	5.4
The hotel offers technologically equipped guest rooms so the room can become an office.	415	37.6%	67.0%	5.7
The hotel has a 24-hour business center.	411	34.1%	60.6%	5.4
The hotel has a frequent-guest program that allows you to earn points toward free accommodation.	406	27.8%	49.2%	4.9
The hotel provides you with occasional gifts.	417	23.7%	48.4%	5.2
When you make your room reservation, the hotel helps you with all other reservations.	403	20.1%	42.4%	5.0
The hotel has a credit card that allows you to accumulate points toward the hotel's frequent-guest program each time you use it.	397	19.6%	24.0%	4.1
The hotel has connections with individuals or organizations that help you enjoy your stay or be more productive.	389	13.4%	28.1%	4.3
The hotel provides programs for children.	363	8.3%	16.3%	3.0
The hotel sends out newsletters.	406	4.4%	12.3%	3.3

purposes said the following features would have the greatest effect in fostering their loyalty; the features are presented here in descending order for their effect on loyalty. The figure in parenthesis following each feature is the percentage of respondents rating that feature a 7, indicating that they believe it has a great impact on loyalty.

- The hotel provides upgrades (69.4 percent rated this feature a 7);
- You can check in and check out at a time that suits you (59.2 percent);
- The hotel uses information from your prior stays to customize services for you (57.7 percent);
- You can request a specific room (44.7 percent);
- Employees communicate the attitude that your problems are important to them (42.6 percent); and
- When you return to this hotel, your registration process is expedited (41.1 percent).

Such common approaches as frequent-guest programs (in the absence of the above features) and affinity credit cards (reward cards) appeal strongly only to a small percentage of business-oriented travelers in luxury hotels. The presence of a frequent-guest program was rated a 7 by just 27.8 percent of the respondents and affinity cards earned a 7 from only 19.6 percent of respondents. This result shows that some guests greatly appreciate those programs, although other efforts would cement relationships with an even larger group of guests.

The Loyalty Gap

To understand what hotels are actually doing to build loyalty with their guests, it is useful to undertake a gap analysis. The gap model has been used extensively in the services and marketing arena.[31] Specifically we looked at GAP #5 of the Parasuraman, Berry, and Zeithaml model. This gap is defined as the difference between what the customer wants and what the hotel actually provides. We judged that we might uncover a gap between expectations and action by comparing the percentage of the sample that gave their hotels an excellent performance rating on a given attribute with the percentage that said this attribute was important.

Gap analysis. We have identified what we believe is a tremendous opportunity for hotels to further increase their guests' loyalty. Only one of the 11 features we tested showed a positive gap—that is, performance exceeding expectations. This particular attribute, involving the hotel's external connections that can make the guest's stay more productive, was not among the most important factors for building loyalty. In contrast, the two most important features—providing upgrades when available and allowing the guest to reserve a specific room—showed the largest gaps but are at the same time relatively easy and inexpensive to implement.

The Downside

Although we were not able to measure reactive natural opportunistic behavior (because our sample comprised guests who were loyal to a specific hotel), we attempted to get at this matter by presenting a hypothetical situation in which a hotel increased its rates temporarily because of anticipated demand. The scenario we offered was meant to simulate a situation where the hotel exhibited opportunistic behavior by taking advantage of high occupancy. Respondents were asked a series of questions relating to this situation to see whether they would exhibit any reactive natural opportunistic

---

[31] For example, by: Valerie A. Zeithaml and Mary Jo Bitner, *Services Marketing* (New York: McGraw-Hill, 1996).

Exhibit 5
Performance Versus Importance of Loyalty Factors

Feature	Top performance rating	Top importance rating	Gap
The hotel provides upgrades when available.	18.7%	69.4%	−50.7
You can request a specific room.	4.9%	44.7%	−39.8
If the hotel is likely to be sold out at a time you normally visit, someone from the hotel will call you to ask whether you would like to make a reservation.	3.0%	37.7%	−34.7
The hotel uses information from your prior stays to customize services for you.	24.3%	57.7%	−33.4
The staff recognizes you when you arrive.	15.7 %	38.3%	−23.2
Employees communicate the attitude that your problems are important to them.	24.0%	42.6%	−18.6
The hotel has a frequent-guest program that allows you to earn points toward free accommodation.	9.6%	27.8%	−18.2
The hotel has a credit card that allows you to accumulate points toward the hotel's frequent-guest program each time you use it.	5.1%	19.6%	−14.5
When you return to this hotel your registration process is expedited.	31.2%	41.1%	−9.9
The hotel provides you with occasional gifts.	18.7%	23.7%	−5.0
The hotel has connections with individuals or organizations that help you enjoy your stay or be more productive.	19.5%	13.4%	6.1

Exhibit 6
Reaction to Room-rate Manipulation

Reaction to rate increase	n	Top rating (7)	Bottom rating (1)	Overall mean
The next time I made a reservation at this hotel, I would be more likely to ask about rate.	413	60.3%	2.7%	6.2
The next time I came to this city, I would check hotel rates at other properties.	412	35.7%	3.6%	5.5
My business-travel policies would not allow me to stay at this hotel for the higher rate.	381	19.7%	28.1%	3.7
My feelings toward the hotel would not change as a result of the rate change.	415	4.8%	49.9%	2.2
What I told others about the hotel would still continue to be positive.	409	2.4%	31.8%	2.8
It is all right for the hotel to increase its rates in this situation.	417	1.4%	65.7%	1.7

Responses are given to the following scenario: "Assume that you go to make a reservation at your favorite luxury hotel and you find out that it is charging you $100 per night more than it usually does because it has only a few rooms left." Responses are on a seven-point Likert-type scale with 7 equal to "strongly agree" and 1 equal to "strongly disagree."

behavior. You might recognize the following scenario as simulating a badly designed effort at revenue management:

> *Assume that you go to make a reservation at your favorite luxury hotel and you find out that it is charging you $100 per night more than it usually does because it has only a few rooms left.*

As shown by the responses to this scenario, the respondents' behavior would change if confronted with the above situation. Such an overt approach to manipulating rates appears to damage the fragile structure of guests' loyalty. These findings suggest that luxury hotels need to be careful when practicing yield management, because inappropriate approaches may drive their loyal customers to consider other hotels. Even if the hotel doesn't lose the guest's business, it seems likely to lose the guest's favorable recommendation.

Implications: Why Loyalty Is Important

Our model uses commitment, or the behavioral outcome of loyalty, as a measure of the strength of customer loyalty, because the behavior of loyal customers makes them valuable. Loyal customers return to make repeat purchases, purchase more of the hotel's products and services (e.g., meals), and perform partnership activities (e.g., serve on advisory panels). Each of the activities performed by loyal customers have substantial financial implications for hotels.

Simply patronizing the hotel is an important function of loyal customers. They like the hotel and will use it. Moreover, our study found a positive relationship between commitment and food and beverage purchases. This means loyal guests are more likely to have breakfast meetings or dinner meetings at the hotel than to use an outside restaurant. The finding supports the work of Reichheld, who identified revenue growth as the most important financial benefit of loyal customers.[32] To illustrate the effect of loyal guests' use of restaurants, say that a 300-room luxury hotel has a 70-percent occupancy with 40 percent of its guests as repeat visitors and average stay of 2.5 days. This hotel will sell 76,650 room-nights a year (300 × .7 × 365). Loyal customers will account for 30,660 (76,650 × .4) of these room-nights during 12,264 visits (30,664 room-nights divided by the average stay of 2.5). Now assume a modest increase in restaurant visits on the part of a loyal customer. Say that, compared to a non-loyal guest, the loyal guest will purchase dinner in the hotel just one more time per every four visits to the hotel. Thus, the hotel would sell 3,066 more dining occasions to loyal customers (12,264/4) than to non-loyal customers. If an average table is two covers, the hotel would serve 6,132 more dinners. Finally, if the average check per person is $75, the hotel would see additional revenue of $459,900 (6,132 × $75). One could carry out a similar exercise with breakfast, meetings, concierge services, and other products.

Loyal customers do more than patronize a hotel; they also encourage other people to try the property. Positive experiences shared by colleagues reduce a person's risk in picking an unknown hotel. Loyal customers create positive word of mouth by being strong advocates for a hotel. Almost one out of five respondents (19.3 percent) strongly agreed (a rating of 7) that they would go out of their way to mention a hotel to which they were loyal when the topic of hotels came up (a total of 41.5 percent gave a 6 or 7 rating). In addition, respondents stated that they told a mean of 12 people (median 10) positive things about the hotel to which they claimed loyalty. Several years ago Ritz-Carlton placed the value of a loyal customer at more than $100,000.[33] The value of positive word of mouth from loyal customers is shown by calculating the value if every loyal customer tells 10 or 12 other customers about your property and just one of those becomes a loyal customer.

---

[32] Frederick F. Reichheld, *The Loyalty Effect* (Boston: Harvard Business School Press, 1996): 33–62.

[33] Koder, Bowen, and Makens, 346.

Beyond their patronage, loyal customers provide information to hotels. Some 19 percent of our respondents said they would be willing to serve on an advisory board. Companies in many industries are creating advisory boards from their target customer markets to help guide the business. Talking directly to customers in this manner can save thousands of dollars of marketing research.

Loyal customers are less price sensitive. Reichheld claims that price premiums are a benefit of loyalty.[34] Two questions on our study confirmed that loyal customers seem less sensitive to price offers from competing hotels. Nearly half of our respondents agreed with the proposition, I feel the room rate that I receive will always be fair (47.8 percent of those responding gave this statement a rating of 5, 6, or 7, while only 16 percent assigned a 1, 2, or 3). Even more telling, 34 percent of those responding disagreed with the following statement: In the future, I will stay at this hotel only if its room rates are the same or lower than those of other luxury hotels.

The responses to these questions indicate that loyal customers feel they are getting a fair value. Moreover, almost a third say they would pay a rate premium to stay at a hotel that has earned these travelers' loyalty.

How to Develop Loyalty

So far we have focused on the portion of the loyalty equation that involves offering benefits to guests to encourage their loyalty. Indeed, our survey respondents gave high marks to such features as providing upgrades, allowing flexible check-in and check-out, customizing services, and allowing guests to request a specific room, as well as expediting registration.

Even though some of these features are easy and inexpensive to implement, the majority of the hotels mentioned in this study do not offer their guests such services. Our respondents have already proclaimed their loyalty to these hotels, even though they do not offer the services customers claim they would like. Rather than count on blind loyalty as competition becomes stronger in the luxury segment, hotels should consider providing such benefits to cement guest loyalty.

Building Trust

While benefits may be the first major element of loyalty, the second major element of loyalty is trust. That is, the hotel must behave in a reliable fashion. The reliability dimension of trust is important because it cannot be easily copied by competitors, unlike many of the benefits. Robert Shaw, author of the book *Trust In Balance,* defines trust as the belief that those on whom we depend will meet our expectations of them.[35]

This definition of trust parallels the reliability dimension of trust put forth by Johnson, Swap, and Swap.[36] Trust and reliability undergird the hypothetical question we posed regarding rate manipulation. One can quickly see the result of a hotel's acting in an unreliable fashion.

The results from our initial focus-group discussions support the definitions of trust advanced by Shaw and the Johnson group. When we asked focus-group participants about the elements of trust in a luxury hotel, they responded:

- The hotel does things as promised;
- I feel that my personal property is safe in my room;

[34] Reichheld, 355.

[35] Robert Shaw, *Trust In Balance: Building Successful Organizations on Results, Integrity, and Concern* (San Francisco: Jossey-Bass, 1997): 22.

[36] George Johnson, Cynthia Swap, and Walter C. Swap, "Measurement of Specific Interpersonal Trust: Construction and Validation of a Scale to Assess Trust in a Specific Other," *Journal of Personality and Social Psychology* 43.6 (1982): 1306–1317.

- If I receive a fax, I know it will be delivered to my room;

- Employees provide quick (and correct) answers; and

- I trust a hotel that trusts its employees.

Of all the comments regarding trust, we found the last comment to be the most trenchant. The participant who made this comment explained that he witnessed another guest at the hotel become enraged with the front-desk clerk because the clerk could not remove a $30 charge from a folio without a manager's approval despite the fact the guest was a frequent visitor to the hotel. Our respondent remarked that if management could not trust an employee with a $30 decision, how could he feel comfortable leaving a $4,000 computer and other valuables in the guest room?

Shaw suggests three building blocks of a high-trust organization. Those are achieving results, which means following through on business commitments; demonstrating concern, which is respecting the well-being of others; and acting with integrity, which means behaving in a consistent manner. Without these building blocks, an organization cannot build trust.

Results

Hotels fall short of the mark in following through, in our respondents' estimation. Less than half of the respondents (44.5 percent) gave a firm rating of 7 to the proposition, If I ask the front desk to arrange for an airport limousine at 3:00 PM, I know the limousine will be waiting for me at 3:00 PM.

The respondents were even less sanguine about their hotels' reliably delivering other services. For instance, just 31.9 percent gave a 7 rating to this statement: If I make a request at this hotel, no matter how trivial that request, it gets taken care of; 28.8 percent rated the following a 7: When an employee at this hotel says that they will do something, I am sure it will get done; and only 27.3 percent scored a 7 for this statement: I feel that any communication, including reservations, with this hotel will always be accurately received and recorded or filed.

Demonstrating Concern

As is the case with following through, hotels have much room to improve the way they demonstrate concern for their guests. This is shown, for instance, by the fact that only 24 percent of the respondents in our study gave a 7 to the statement, Employees (of the luxury hotel to which I am loyal) communicate the attitude that my problems are important to them.

Acting with Integrity

Likewise, the respondents believe their favorite hotels could act with more integrity. Many guests, for instance, apparently do not feel comfortable leaving valuables in the room of a hotel that they have patronized frequently. Just 37.8 percent gave a rating of 7 to the statement, I feel comfortable leaving business papers and valuables in my room at this hotel. A smaller percentage, 34.1 percent, strongly agreed with the proposition, If I ask management or an employee a question, I feel they will be truthful with me.

The relatively low scores given by respondents for hotels' performance on each of the three building blocks of trust suggest that a substantial proportion of guests, despite their loyalty to a given hotel, may not completely trust the hotel. Given the importance of trust in building loyalty, hotels should do more to foster feelings of trust in their guests.

Another dimension of trust is the relationship between employees and management. In fact, without employer-employee trust, hotel management will be hard pressed to convince the guest that the hotel is trustworthy, as noted by the participant in our focus group who witnessed the front-desk scene. Although we did not study the dimensions of trust within an organization, readers need to understand that trust starts within the organization first. For instance, an employee is unlikely to go the extra mile for the guest if she feels she will not be supported by management of the hotel.

Employee Behavior

Guests are sensitive to the hotel's treatment of its employees, because guests respond to the way the employees behave toward them. This came out both in our focus group discussions and in our survey. Focus-group participants said they would be loyal to hotels where employees recognize them and call them by name. While this factor didn't score as highly as others in the main study, those respondents gave a high rating to having a hotel where employees communicate the attitude that the guest's problems are important to the employees. Thus, management should strive to create a culture where employees will do what it takes to foster guests' loyalty.

Opportunistic Behavior

Yield management appears to be the type of opportunistic behavior that can inhibit guests' trust and loyalty. We are not advocating abandoning these programs, but our results indicate that yield management programs should contain carefully designed fences that will demonstrate to guests that different rates are justified under different circumstances (as the airlines often do by offering better prices for advance bookings, midweek departures, and Saturday night stay-overs). Perhaps yield management should be practiced only on customers with whom the hotel does not seek a relationship based on loyalty.

Inconveniences

Annoyances created by petty hotel policies and procedures can be a barrier to loyalty. Just under half of our respondents stated that their hotel offers a hassle-free stay. This factor also came out in the initial focus-group discussions. Examples of hassles from the focus groups include having to wait for the bell staff to bring ice when the guest could just as easily get it herself (if there were an ice machine nearby) and having to wait in line to check in.

A Complex Matter

In considering the results of this study, one should note that the customer preferences examined in this study are those of luxury-hotel customers whose purpose of stay is primarily business. The factors that foster loyalty among these guests may be different from those of guests who frequent other hotel tiers or those who are traveling chiefly for leisure. While we believe that the antecedents and consequences of loyalty are essentially the same for all customers and all product segments, the specific attributes that develop trust may be different in various product segments or for different guests. We believe that this study should be repeated for other tiers and market segments. We note, for example, that respondents staying in their favorite luxury hotel primarily for pleasure did, indeed, have different wants and needs than those staying primarily for business, as we mentioned above.

The study provided empirical support for the model of service relationships. We believe this study offers clarity regarding the antecedents and consequences of building relationships with business-travel customers in the luxury-hotel segment by establishing standardized regression weights for the proposed relationships in the model.

The study also provided a gap analysis showing which types of benefit and action luxury hotels can provide to build their customers' loyalty. We identified behavioral outcomes of loyalty and demonstrated the potential profitability to hotels of loyal customers. Finally, the study found but did not explore differences between the responses of business travelers and pleasure travelers. In conclusion, the study demonstrates that relationship marketing—and building loyalty—is far more than an episodic or tactical effort. Instead, hotels should take an integrated, strategic approach to fostering customer loyalty.

Chapter 2 ■ Loyalty: A Strategic Commitment

Questions for Discussion

1. Many of you have probably experienced "loyalty" programs yourself, from your credit cards, the airline industry, or even your local coffeehouse (which might offer you points toward a free cup for each one you purchase). Judging from your own experience only, how effective are these programs at achieving the goal of repeat business? What are some of the pluses and minuses, in your view, of typical loyalty programs? How does your experience compare with these authors' findings?

2. We chose this article in part because it offers a good model of the type of reading you might find valuable as you write your own proposals. How is this source different from more popular sources, such as newspaper articles and websites? Do you think the article is persuasive? What factors add to its credibility? How might you use a source like this to develop your paradigm in your paper?

3. In developing their material, the authors of this article use both survey data and theory. How does one support the other? Which is more persuasive to you and why?

4. One useful aspect of this article is that it offers a model for conducting a business survey. What issues did the authors consider in putting together their surveys? What did they try to do in analyzing them? If you intend to conduct your own survey as part of your project, are there any things they did that you think you should do in yours?

Designs for Working

Why Your Bosses Want to Turn Your New Office into Greenwich Village

Malcolm Gladwell

■ ■ ■

In the early nineteen-sixties, Jane Jacobs lived on Hudson Street, in Greenwich Village, near the intersection of Eighth Avenue and Bleecker Street. It was then, as now, a charming district of nineteenth-century tenements and town houses, bars and shops, laid out over an irregular grid, and Jacobs loved the neighborhood. In her 1961 masterpiece, "The Death and Life of Great American Cities," she rhapsodized about the White Horse Tavern down the block, home to Irish longshoremen and writers and intellectuals—a place where, on a winter's night, as "the doors open, a solid wave of conversation and animation surges out and hits you." Her Hudson Street had Mr. Slube, at the cigar store, and Mr. Lacey, the locksmith, and Bernie, the candy-store owner, who, in the course of a typical day, supervised the children crossing the street, lent an umbrella or a dollar to a customer, held on to some keys or packages for people in the neighborhood, and "lectured two youngsters who asked for cigarettes." The street had "bundles and packages, zigzagging from the drug store to the fruit stand and back over to the butcher's," and "teenagers, all dressed up, are pausing to ask if their slips show or their collars look right." It was, she said, an urban ballet. The miracle of Hudson Street, according to Jacobs, was created by the particular configuration of the streets and buildings of the neighborhood. Jacobs argued that when a neighborhood is oriented toward the street, when sidewalks are used for socializing and play and commerce, the users of that street are transformed by the resulting stimulation: they form relationships and casual contacts they would never have otherwise. The West Village, she pointed out, was blessed with a mixture of houses and apartments and shops and offices and industry, which meant that there were always people "outdoors on different schedules and . . . in the place for different purposes." It had short blocks, and short blocks create the greatest variety in foot traffic. It had lots of old buildings, and old buildings have the low rents that permit individualized and creative uses. And, most of all, it had people, cheek by jowl, from every conceivable walk of life. Sparely populated suburbs may look appealing, she said, but without an active sidewalk life, without the frequent, serendipitous interactions of many different people, "there is no public acquaintanceship, no foundation of public trust, no cross-connections with the necessary people—and no practice or ease in applying the most ordinary techniques of city public life at lowly levels."

Jane Jacobs did not win the battle she set out to fight. The West Village remains an anomaly. Most developers did not want to build the kind of community Jacobs talked about, and most Americans didn't want to live in one. To reread "Death and Life" today, however, is to be struck by how the intervening years have given her arguments a new and unexpected relevance. Who, after all, has a direct interest in creating diverse, vital spaces that foster creativity and serendipity? Employers do. On the fortieth anniversary of its publication, "Death and Life" has been reborn as a primer on workplace design.

The parallels between neighborhoods and offices are striking. There was a time, for instance, when companies put their most valued employees in palatial offices, with potted plants in the corner, and secretaries out front, guarding access. Those offices were suburbs—gated communities, in fact—and many companies came to realize that if their best employees were isolated in suburbs they would be deprived of public acquaintanceship, the foundations of public trust, and cross-connections with the necessary people. In the eighties and early nineties, the fashion in corporate America was to follow what designers called "universal planning"—rows of identical cubicles, which resembled nothing so much as a Levittown. Today, universal planning has fallen out of favor, for the same reason that the postwar suburbs like Levittown did: to thrive, an office space must have a diversity of uses—it must have the workplace equivalent of houses and apartments and shops and industry.

If you visit the technology companies of Silicon Valley, or the media companies of Manhattan, or any of the firms that self-consciously identify themselves with the New Economy, you'll find that secluded private offices have been replaced by busy public spaces, open-plan areas without walls, executives next to the newest hires. The hush of the traditional office has been supplanted by something much closer to the noisy, bustling ballet of Hudson Street. Forty years ago, people lived in neighborhoods like the West Village and went to work in the equivalent of suburbs. Now, in one of the odd reversals that mark the current economy, they live in suburbs and, increasingly, go to work in the equivalent of the West Village.

The office used to be imagined as a place where employees punch clocks and bosses roam the halls like high-school principals, looking for miscreants. But when employees sit chained to their desks, quietly and industriously going about their business, an office is not functioning as it should. That's because innovation—the heart of the knowledge economy—is fundamentally social. Ideas arise as much out of casual conversations as they do out of formal meetings. More precisely, as one study after another has demonstrated, the best ideas in any workplace arise out of casual contacts among different groups within the same company. If you are designing widgets for Acme.com, for instance, it is unlikely that a breakthrough idea is going to come from someone else on the widget team: after all, the other team members are as blinkered by the day-to-day demands of dealing with the existing product as you are. Someone from outside Acme.com—your old engineering professor, or a guy you used to work with at Apex.com—isn't going to be that helpful, either. A person like that doesn't know enough about Acme's widgets to have a truly useful idea. The most useful insights are likely to come from someone in customer service, who hears firsthand what widget customers have to say, or from someone in marketing, who has wrestled with the problem of how to explain widgets to new users, or from someone who used to work on widgets a few years back and whose work on another Acme product has given him a fresh perspective. Innovation comes from the interactions of people at a comfortable distance from one another, neither too close nor too far. This is why—quite apart from the matter of logistics and efficiency—companies have offices to begin with. They go to the trouble of gathering their employees under one roof because they want the widget designers to bump into the people in marketing and the people in customer service and the guy who moved to another department a few years back.

The catch is that getting people in an office to bump into people from another department is not so easy as it looks. In the sixties and seventies, a researcher at M.I.T. named Thomas Allen conducted a decade-long study of the way in which engineers communicated in research-and-development laboratories. Allen found that the likelihood that any two people will communicate drops off dramatically as the distance between their desks increases: we are four times as likely to communicate with someone who sits six feet away from us as we are with someone who sits sixty feet away. And people seated more than seventy-five feet apart hardly talk at all.

Allen's second finding was even more disturbing. When the engineers weren't talking to those in their immediate vicinity, many of them spent their time talking to people *outside* their company—to their old computer-science professor or the guy they used to work with at Apple. He concluded that it was actually easier to make the outside call than to walk across the room. If you constantly ask for advice or guidance from people inside your organization, after all, you risk losing prestige. Your colleagues might think you are incompetent. The people you keep asking for advice might get annoyed at you. Calling an outsider avoids these problems. "The engineer can easily excuse his lack of knowl-edge by pretending to be an 'expert in something else' who needs some help in 'broadening into this new area," Allen wrote. He did his study in the days before E-mail and the Internet, but the advent of digital communication has made these problems worse. Allen's engineers were far too willing to go outside the company for advice and new ideas. E-mail makes it even easier to talk to people out-side the company.

The task of the office, then, is to invite a particular kind of social interaction—the casual, nonthreat-ening encounter that makes it easy for relative strangers to talk to each other. Offices need the sort of social milieu that Jane Jacobs found on the sidewalks of the West Village. "It is possible in a city street neighborhood to know all kinds of people without unwelcome entanglements, without bore-dom, necessity for excuses, explanations, fears of giving offense, embarrassments respecting imposi-tions or commitments, and all such paraphernalia of obligations which can accompany less limited relationships," Jacobs wrote. If you substitute" office" for "city street neighborhood," that sentence becomes the perfect statement of what the modern employer wants from the workplace.

Imagine a classic big-city office tower, with a floor plate of a hundred and eighty feet by a hundred and eighty feet. The center part of every floor is given over to the guts of the building: elevators, bathrooms, electrical, and plumbing systems. Around the core are cubicles and interior offices, for support staff and lower management. And around the edges of the floor, against the windows, are rows of offices for senior staff, each room perhaps two hundred or two hundred and fifty square feet. The best research about office communication tells us that there is almost no worse way to lay out an office. The executive in one corner office will seldom bump into any other executive in a cor-ner office. Indeed, stringing the exterior offices out along the windows guarantees that there will be very few people within the critical sixty-foot radius of those offices. To maximize the amount of contact among employees, you really ought to put the most valuable staff members in the center of the room, where the highest number of people can be within their orbit. Or, even better, put all places where people tend to congregate—the public areas—in the center, so they can draw from as many disparate parts of the company as possible. Is it any wonder that creative firms often prefer loft-style buildings, which have usable centers?

Another way to increase communication is to have as few private offices as possible. The idea is to exchange private space for public space, just as in the West Village, where residents agree to live in tiny apartments in exchange for a wealth of nearby cafés and stores and bars and parks. The West Village forces its residents outdoors. Few people, for example, have a washer and dryer in their apartment, and so even laundry is necessarily a social event: you have to take your clothes to the Laundromat down the street. In the office equivalent, designers force employees to move around, too. They build in "functional inefficiencies"; they put kitchens and copiers and printers and libraries in places that can be reached only by a circuitous journey.

A more direct approach is to create an office so flexible that the kinds of people who need to sponta-neously interact can actually be brought together. For example, the Ford Motor Company, along with a group of researchers from the University of Michigan, recently conducted a pilot project on the effectiveness of "war rooms" in software development. Previously, someone inside the company who needed a new piece of software written would have a series of meetings with the company's programmers, and the client and the programmers would send messages back and forth. In the war-room study, the company moved the client, the programmers, and a manager into a dedicated con-ference room, and made them stay there until the project was done. Using the war room cut the software-development time by two-thirds, in part because there was far less time wasted on formal meetings or calls outside the building: the people who ought to have been bumping into each other were now sitting next to each other.

Two years ago, the advertising agency TBWA\Chiat\Day moved into new offices in Los Angeles, out near the airport. In the preceding years, the firm had been engaged in a radical, and in some ways disastrous, experiment with a "nonterritorial" office: no one had a desk or any office equipment of his own. It was a scheme that courted failure by neglecting all the ways in which an office is a sort of neighborhood. By contrast, the new office is an almost perfect embodiment of Jacobsian principles of community. The agency is in a huge old warehouse, three stories high and the size of three football fields. It is informally known as Advertising City, and that's what it is: a kind of artfully constructed urban neighborhood. The floor is bisected by a central corridor called Main Street, and in the center of the room is an open space, with café tables and a stand of ficus trees, called Central Park. There's a basketball court, a game room, and a bar. Most of the employees are in snug workstations known as nests, and the nests are grouped together in neighborhoods that radiate from Main Street like Paris arrondissements. The top executives are situated in the middle of the room. The desk belonging to the chairman and creative director of the company looks out on Central Park. The offices of the chief financial officer and the media director abut the basketball court. Sprinkled throughout the building are meeting rooms and project areas and plenty of nooks where employees can closet themselves when they need to. A small part of the building is elevated above the main floor on a mezzanine, and if you stand there and watch the people wander about with their portable phones, and sit and chat in Central Park, and play basketball in the gym, and you feel on your shoulders the sun from the skylights and listen to the gentle buzz of human activity, it is quite possible to forget that you are looking at an office.

In "The Death and Life of Great American Cities," Jacobs wrote of the importance of what she called "public characters"—people who have the social position and skills to orchestrate the movement of information and the creation of bonds of trust:

> *A public character is anyone who is in frequent contact with a wide circle of people and who is sufficiently interested to make himself a public character. . . . The director of a settlement on New York's Lower East Side, as an example, makes a regular round of stores. He learns from the cleaner who does his suits about the presence of dope pushers in the neighborhood. He learns from the grocer that the Dragons are working up to something and need attention. He learns from the candy store that two girls are agitating the Sportsmen toward a rumble. One of his most important information spots is an unused breadbox on Rivington Street. . . . A message spoken there for any teen-ager within many blocks will reach his ears unerringly and surprisingly quickly, and the opposite flow along the grapevine similarly brings news quickly in to the breadbox.*

A vital community, in Jacobs's view, required more than the appropriate physical environment. It also required a certain kind of person, who could bind together the varied elements of street life. Offices are no different. In fact, as office designers have attempted to create more vital workplaces, they have become increasingly interested in identifying and encouraging public characters.

One of the pioneers in this way of analyzing offices is Karen Stephenson, a business-school professor and anthropologist who runs a New York-based consulting company called Netform. Stephenson studies social networks. She goes into a company—her clients include J. P. Morgan, the Los Angeles Police Department, T.R.W., and I.B.M.—and distributes a questionnaire to its employees, asking about which people they have contact with. Whom do you like to spend time with? Whom do you talk to about new ideas? Where do you go to get expert advice? Every name in the company becomes a dot on a graph, and Stephenson draws lines between all those who have regular contact with each other. Stephenson likens her graphs to X-rays, and her role to that of a radiologist. What she's depicting is the firm's invisible inner mechanisms, the relationships and networks and patterns of trust that arise as people work together over time, and that are hidden beneath the organization chart. Once, for example, Stephenson was doing an "X-ray" of a Head Start organization. The agency was mostly female, and when Stephenson analyzed her networks she found that new hires and male staffers were profoundly isolated, communicating with the rest of the organization through only a handful of women. "I looked at tenure in the organization, office ties, demographic data. I couldn't see what tied the women together, and why the men were talking only to these women," Stephenson recalls. "Nor could the president of the organization. She gave me a couple of ideas. She said, 'Sorry I can't figure it out.' Finally, she asked me to read the names again, and I could hear her stop, and she said, 'My God, I know what it is. All those women are smokers.'" The X-ray revealed that the men—locked out of the formal power structure of the organization—were trying to gain access and influence by hanging out in the smoking area with some of the more senior women.

What Stephenson's X-rays do best, though, is tell you who the public characters are. In every network, there are always one or two people who have connections to many more people than anyone else. Stephenson calls them "hubs," and on her charts lines radiate out from them like spokes on a wheel. (Bernie the candy-store owner, on Jacobs's Hudson Street, was a hub.) A few people are also what Stephenson calls "gatekeepers": they control access to critical people, and link together a strategic few disparate groups. Finally, if you analyze the graphs there are always people who seem to have lots of indirect links to other people—who are part of all sorts of networks without necessarily being in the center of them. Stephenson calls those people "pulsetakers." (In Silicon Valleyspeak, the person in a sea of cubicles who pops his or her head up over the partition every time something interesting is going on is called a prairie dog: prairie dogs are pulsetakers.)

In the past year, Stephenson has embarked on a partnership with Steelcase, the world's largest manufacturer of office furniture, in order to use her techniques in the design of offices. Traditionally, office designers would tell a company what furniture should go where. Stephenson and her partners at Steelcase propose to tell a company what people should go where, too. At Steelcase, they call this "floor-casting."

One of the first projects for the group is the executive level at Steelcase's headquarters, a five-story building in Grand Rapids, Michigan. The executive level, on the fourth floor, is a large, open room filled with small workstations. (Jim Hackett, the head of the company, occupies what Steelcase calls a Personal Harbor, a black, freestanding metal module that may be—at seven feet by eight—the smallest office of a Fortune 500 C.E.O.) One afternoon recently, Stephenson pulled out a laptop and demonstrated how she had mapped the communication networks of the leadership group onto a seating chart of the fourth floor. The dots and swirls are strangely compelling—abstract representations of something real and immediate. One executive, close to Hackett, was inundated with lines from every direction. "He's a hub, a gatekeeper, and a pulsetaker across all sorts of different dimensions," Stephenson said. "What that tells you is that he is very strategic. If there is no succession planning around that person, you have got a huge risk to the knowledge base of this company. If he's in a plane accident, there goes your knowledge." She pointed to another part of the floor plan, with its own thick overlay of lines. "That's sales and marketing. They have a pocket of real innovation here. The guy who runs it is very good, very smart." But then she pointed to the lines connecting that department with other departments. "They're all coming into this one place," she said, and she showed how all the lines coming out of marketing converged on one senior executive. "There's very little path redundancy. In human systems, you need redundancy, you need communication across multiple paths."

What concerned Stephenson wasn't just the lack of redundancy but the fact that, in her lingo, many of the paths were "unconfirmed": they went only one way. People in marketing were saying that they communicated with the senior management, but there weren't as many lines going in the other direction. The sales-and-marketing team, she explained, had somehow become isolated from senior management. They couldn't get their voices heard when it came to innovation—and that fact, she said, ought to be a big consideration when it comes time to redo the office. "If you ask the guy who heads sales and marketing who he wants to sit next to, he'll pick out all the people he trusts," she said. "But do you sit him with those people? No. What you want to do is put people who don't trust each other near each other. Not necessarily next to each other, because they get too close. But close enough so that when you pop your head up, you get to see people, they are in your path, and all of a sudden you build an inviting space where they can hang out, kitchens and things like that. Maybe they need to take a hub in an innovation network and place the person with a pulsetaker in an expert network—to get that knowledge indirectly communicated to a lot of people."

The work of translating Stephenson's insights onto a new floor plan is being done in a small conference room—a war room—on the second floor of Steelcase headquarters. The group consists of a few key people from different parts of the firm, such as human resources, design, technology, and space-planning research. The walls of the room are cluttered with diagrams and pictures and calculations and huge, blownup versions of Stephenson's X-rays. Team members stress that what they are doing is experimental. They don't know yet how directly they want to translate findings from the communications networks to office plans. After all, you don't want to have to redo the entire office every time someone leaves or joins the company. But it's clear that there are some very simple principles from the study of public characters that ought to drive the design process. "You want to place hubs at the center," Joyce Bromberg, the director of space planning, says. "These are the ones other people go to in order to get information. Give them an environment that allows access. But there are also going to be times that they need to have control—so give them a place where they can get away. Gatekeepers represent the fit between groups. They transmit ideas. They are brokers, so you might want to put them at the perimeter, and give them front porches"—areas adjoining the workspace where you might put little tables and chairs. "Maybe they could have swinging doors with white boards, to better transmit information. As for pulsetakers, they are the roamers. Rather than give them one fixed work location, you might give them a series of touchdown spots—where you want them to stop and talk. You want to enable their meandering."

One of the other team members was a tall, thoughtful man named Frank Graziano. He had a series of pencil drawings—with circles representing workstations of all the people whose minds, as he put it, he wanted to make "explicit." He said that he had done the plan the night before. "I think we can thread innovation through the floor," he went on, and with a pen drew a red line that wound its way through the maze of desks. It was his Hudson Street.

"The Death and Life of Great American Cities" was a controversial book, largely because there was always a whiff of paternalism in Jacobs's vision of what city life ought to be. Chelsea—the neighborhood directly to the north of her beloved West Village—had "mixtures and types of buildings and densities of dwelling units per acre . . . almost identical with those of Greenwich Village," she noted. But its long-predicted renaissance would never happen, she maintained, because of the "barriers of long, self-isolating blocks." She hated Chatham Village, a planned "garden city" development in Pittsburgh. It was a picturesque green enclave, but it suffered, in Jacobs's analysis, from a lack of sidewalk life. She wasn't concerned that some people might not want an active street life in their neighborhood; that what she saw as the "self-isolating blocks" of Chelsea others would see as a welcome respite from the bustle of the city, or that Chatham Village would appeal to some people precisely because one did not encounter on its sidewalks a "solid wave of conversation and animation." Jacobs felt that city dwellers belonged in environments like the West Village, whether they realized it or not.

The new workplace designers are making the same calculation, of course. The point of the new offices is to compel us to behave and socialize in ways that we otherwise would not—to overcome our initial inclination to be office suburbanites. But, in all the studies of the new workplaces, the reservations that employees have about a more social environment tend to diminish once they try it. Human behavior, after all, is shaped by context, but how it is shaped—and whether we'll be happy with the result—we can understand only with experience. Jane Jacobs knew the virtues of the West Village because she lived there. What she couldn't know was that her ideas about community would ultimately make more sense in the workplace. From time to time, social critics have bemoaned the falling rates of community participation in American life, but they have made the same mistake. The reason Americans are content to bowl alone (or, for that matter, not bowl at all) is that, increasingly, they receive all the social support they need—all the serendipitous interactions that serve to make them happy and productive—from nine to five.

Chapter 2 ■ Designs for Working

Questions for Discussion

1. One of the interesting things about Gladwell's essay is the way it gets you to look again at the spaces that surround you every day: from the city you live in to the school rooms you inhabit. How well are the spaces you live in designed for building trust, engagement, community, and productivity? What could be done to improve those spaces, along the lines that Gladwell discusses?

2. In adapting Jane Jacobs's theories about urban environments to the office place, managers have taken a paradigm from one field and applied it to another. How well does it guide the practice of office design? What parallels between the two does Gladwell draw?

3. Karen Stephenson's study (discussed near the end of the essay) is suggestive of the sort of work you might do yourself to test a hypothesis in the workplace. What other productivity-related issues can you record and measure in order to better understand your workplace or university?

4. If you have been taking this class for at least a week or two, it is likely that relationships and connections have developed in the classroom. And studies have shown that students tend to gravitate to specific areas of the classroom or even specific chairs, unless the teacher requires a special seating arrangement or takes some action to change students' chosen spots. Do you think there is a relationship between where you are sitting and with whom you have a connection—from mere acquaintances, to people you have spoken to outside of class, to people you would consider a friend? How much is the strength of that connection perhaps simply a factor of the physical distance between your chairs?

5. Try to replicate Stephenson's study. Distribute a copy of the class roster to everyone in the classroom and have them rate from 0 (no contact) to 5 (friendship) the level of connection they feel with others in the room. Then draw a seating chart on the board and compare some of the numbers that people put down with the physical space between them.

6. How well does Stephenson's study hold up for your class? What limited conclusions might you draw from your findings? How might those conclusions help to shape some action to change the dynamic of the classroom for the better, perhaps in order to promote more classroom participation?

Leadership as Practice
Challenging the Competency Paradigm

Brigid Carroll, Lester Levy and David Richmond

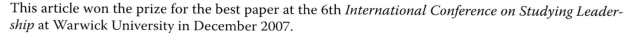

This article won the prize for the best paper at the 6th *International Conference on Studying Leadership* at Warwick University in December 2007.

Abstract Competency frameworks, models, instruments and thinking have long been ingrained and utilized in management and organizational life. Not surprisingly they have been transplanted both swiftly and seemingly easily into the leadership domain. While there certainly have been discomfort and critique from academic and practitioner sources, nothing has emerged strongly enough to date that would provide an alternative mode of framing and translating both leadership and leadership development in the different contexts that seek to make it visible. In this article, consequently, we submit leadership and its development to the 'practice turn' to enable a radically different perspective from a competency orientated one. The ontology, epistemology and methodologies of practice are examined and translated to the leadership field. We argue that a focus on praxis, practitioner and practice offers both challenge and transformation to the ways that leadership is bounded and constrained by current organizational and managerial conventions.

Keywords leadership; micro-emancipatory practices; rationality and rationalization; theory of practice

Introduction

Competencies have been labelled 'ubiquitous' (Bolden & Gosling, 2006: 147) in both management thinking and implementation, thus their transfer into the relatively newer leadership domain is unsurprising. While competencies can and have been critiqued within the management sphere (Cullen, 1992; Grugulis, 1998; Lester, 1994), their dominance and influence in both leadership and leadership development should give new pause for concern and reflection. Consequently, the facility with which competencies have entered the leadership terrain marks the initial point of inquiry of this article.

While it is not too difficult to call attention to the colonization of leadership by such a distinctly managerial concept and framework as competencies, it certainly is more problematic to depose it. For an alternative ontology, epistemology and methodology, we then look to the practice turn and this marks the primary contribution of this article. Practice theory is derived from social theory (Bourdieu, 1990; de Certeau, 1984; Heidegger, 1926/1962), and has undoubtedly made its strongest impact in the organization-related discipline of strategy and strategy-as-practice, a coherent and influential stream of thinking (see, amongst others, Jarzabkowski, 2003; Samra-Fredericks, 2003; Whittington, 1996, 2003).

We argue that the time is ripe for a leadership-as-practice body of work that, for virtually identical reasons as strategy, aims at the demystification, deepening and appreciation of the 'nitty-gritty details' (Chia, 2004: 29) of routine and practice that Chia (2004: 33) calls 'a practical logic'.

In approaching leadership from a practice perspective, it is not our intention, in this specific article, to discuss issues of methodology, outline how the practice approach can be applied directly to leadership theory and development, or offer specific recommendations for leadership practice. However, we are interested in not just calling new theory into the leadership domain, but paying attention to dimensions of leadership thought and practice that in our view are currently neglected, if not actually invalidated, by the competency paradigm. Bolden and Gosling (2006: 158) position neglect as being around the 'subtle, moral, emotional and relational aspects of leadership'. Any dilution or avoidance of such terrain risks rendering leadership an impoverished and largely mechanistic imperative. Equally, a practice orientation has the capacity to put something of the lived experience of such a landscape into words so that researchers engage with what Whittington (2004: 62) terms 'managers' real problems' and Chia (2004: 30) typifies as 'the scene of everyday action'.

Ultimately, the impact of exploring leadership through a practice orientation aims to penetrate how actors 'get on' (Chia and Holt, 2006: 647) with the work of leadership, something which both traditional and mainstream leadership research has shed surprisingly little light on.

The Ubiquity of Competency

It is not difficult at all to understand the appeal of competency models to management and, by extension, leadership. Both, albeit leadership to a much stronger degree, have a quality of vagueness and complexity that invite discomfort and unease in an organizational world which has long privileged rationality, control, clarity and simplicity (Grey, 1999; Townley, 2002). A rather benign interpretation would view competencies as an attempt to usefully describe and thus operationalize what can appear a bewildering and contradictory array of expectations, while a more critical viewpoint would identify them as conscious instruments of managerial manipulation, inculcation and regulation.

A more detailed examination of the definition of competency as 'an underlying characteristic of an individual that is causally related to effective or superior performance in a job' (Boyatzis, 1982: 21) appears to be a useful starting place to explore the meaning of competencies. From the earlier definition, at least four words stand out as critical to any exploration of competency; namely, 'individual', 'causally', 'superior' and 'performance'. Those four words aggregated together constitute the premises of what Chia and Holt (2006: 638) term 'methodological individualism' whereby the individual agent is credited with primacy, a linear relationship is constructed from intention to intervention, and performance is governed by purpose, principles and co-option into an overarching strategic plan.

On the surface of it, those would appear so normative as to not be particularly worthy of comment, but the competency approach has surprisingly little empirical robustness behind it (Bolden & Gosling, 2006: 152). Many of its assumptions do not hold true when subject to active scrutiny.

Competency thinking, due to the difficulty of transposing context, tends to represent individual actors as acting and performing in isolation to others and context; that one achieves or exceeds requisite performance by adopting the same generic prescribed behaviours and roles; and that success comes from being strong across a wide range of behaviours rather than being cognisant and compensatory with where one is stronger and weaker (Grugulis, 2000; Loan-Clarke, 1996).

There are more complex and latent problems with the competency ethos, such as the reliance on processes of reduction and fragmentation. In this process, numerous parts are distilled on the assumption that if they are to be reassembled then a credible, impressive and integrated 'whole' can be attained (Ecclestone, 1997; Grugulis, 1998). Of equal concern is the derivation of competencies from past or present organization scenarios with the assumption that they will be relevant and appropriate for whatever constitutes the future (Lester, 1994)—notably, the reality of competency frameworks as disciplinary mechanisms (Townley, 2002) which seek to define and enshrine an 'ideal' in terms of management and leadership by which others can be measured, evaluated, legitimated and disciplined. Consequently, they become constitutive of identity and a mechanism of domination.

To an extent, competencies by their very nature can only articulate that which is objective, measurable, technical and tangible. It is perfectly legitimate to argue that management is predominantly technocratic, functional, disembodied, objective and instrumental (Townley, 2002). Processes such as budgeting, operational planning, project management and compliance do meet the competency criteria, but little of the leadership realm could be coherently interpreted as pertinent to competency criteria. Consequently, the acceptance of competencies as a basis for leadership seems particularly problematic, inappropriate and misplaced.

Bolden and Gosling (2006: 147) equate the use of competencies for leadership to the notion of a 'repeating, recurring refrain' in music which imposes structure, predictability and constraint to further develop the melody or voice. Competencies do not address or facilitate what gives music (or leadership) its vitality, life, originality and distinctiveness. Bolden and Gosling (2006: 158) conclude that competencies do not provide 'a sufficiently rich vocabulary' for the subtle, textured, complex, embodied and highly situated mindset that is required for leadership. Rather, they breed conformity to a standardized and unfocused leadership model, as opposed to diversity and connectedness which could foster personal and organizational capacity.

We believe it is timely and necessary to both contest and supplant the growing reliance on competency models in the realm of leadership.

The Promise of Practice

A practice approach could be positioned as directly opposite to competency logic. Ontology, epistemology and methodologies as they relate to competency and practice are quite distinctive, as Table 1 illustrates.

We propose that a practice ontology, epistemology and methodology offers different and multiple units of analysis (Jarzabkowski et al., 2007), considerably broader definitional scope, a new vocabulary and a re-theorization of both agency and action (Chia & Holt, 2006). The intent of this section is to explore and consider what is meant by practice theory.

Whittington (2006) proposes three strands of practice theory as characterized by Reckwitz (2002). These are praxis (the interconnection and embeddedness of action, actor and institution), practice (consistent or routine types of behaviour or what Chia and Holt, 2006: 637, term 'a patterned consistency of action'), and practitioner (those actors active in the domain). Each of the three constitutes a different unit of analysis and site of research. Taken together they unite the micro ('the situated

Table 1   *The Competency/Practice Distinction*

Competency	*Practice*
Rooted in objectivism	Explicitly constructionist
Individual level of analysis	Inherently relational and collective
Quantifiable and measurable	Discourse, narrative and rhetoric
Unanchored in relationship and context	Situated and socially defined
Privileges reason Assumes intellect predominantly	Privileges lived or day-to-day experience
	Incorporates embodiment and emotion

doings of individual human beings') and the macro ('different socially defined practices') (Jarzabkowski et al., 2007: 7). This interrelationship between the micro and macro is exceedingly complex. The bulk of the research focus is concerned with micro-action, micro-phenomena and micro-activity with an explicitly relational or non-individualistic stance (Chia & Holt, 2006; Schatzki, 2005). At this point, the ontolological and theoretical nature of practice theory requires elaboration.

Core to practice theory are assumptions of relationality (Chia & Holt, 2006; Cooper, 2005) and a 'logic of practice' (Chia, 2004). Relationality represents the commitment to understanding individuals or collectives not as separate, isolated or discreet entities but as a 'field of re-lat-ionships' (Cooper, 2005: 1693) or 'bundles of practices' (Schatzki, 2005: 12). This means that it is practice that is 'the source of meaning and normativity' (Schatzki, 2001: 12) more than practice constituting the identities (leadership and otherwise) of individual or collective actors. Relationality epitomizes an understanding of practices as 'non-individualistic phenomena' and 'social sites in which events, entities, and meaning help compose one another' (Schatzki, 2005: 480). Wittgenstein (in Dreyfus, 1991b: 7) and Chia and Holt (2006: 639) perhaps best represent relationality in both radical but pragmatic terms in the following rhetorical statement:

> *How could human behaviour be described? Surely only by showing the actions of a variety of humans, as they are all mixed up together. Not what one man is doing now, but the whole hurly-burly, is the background against which we see an action.*

This 'logic of practice' (Bourdieu, 1977/2002: 19) privileges practice over actor and is critical of what Chia (2004: 30) terms 'a means-ends analytical logic'. Bourdieu (1990: 29) refers to this as an 'intellectualocentrism' whereby causal logic, intentionality, deliberateness, instrumental reason or a 'vocabulary of intentions, rules, plans and laws' (Chia, 2004: 30) are imposed by academics on more practical reason and activity. Thus action, behaviour and life are shaped by an academic view of the world which disregards that which isn't linear, progressive, conscious, planned and organized.

A practice perspective in contrast reminds us that the overwhelming majority of action takes place 'on the hoof' (Chia & Holt, 2006: 643), involves 'skilled, improvised in-situ coping' (Chia, 2004: 33) and 'takes place unreflectively, on-the-spot and in the twinkle-of-an-eye' (Chia & MacKay, 2007: 238). The radical nature of a practice perspective invites us into what de Certeau (1984) terms 'the everyday' and Whittington (1996: 734) terms 'the unheroic work of ordinary [strategic] practitioners in their day-to-day routines'.

Heidegger's distinction between building and dwelling (as discussed in Chia, 2004; Chia & Holt, 2006; Chia & MacKay, 2007) speaks very tangibly, if symbolically, to the vast gulf between competency and practice. The building mode is the one that characterizes competency logic. This mode relies on the agency of a motivated and intentional actor to act on a world they stand separate from to achieve preconceived ends and objectives. In a dwelling mode, action is 'immanent' (Chia & Holt, 2006: 637) in that it unfolds along with identity through feeling, responding, coping and negotiating with the day-to-day. Dwelling, for Heidegger, is mindless—not because it lacks sense and efficacy, but because it must 'follow an internalised predisposition: a modus operandi rather than any deliberate conscious intent' (Chia & MacKay, 2007: 236). This is what Bourdieu (1990) calls habitus or a repertoire of background dispositions, improvizations, embodied skills, internalized habits or know-how that shape 'what it is to be a person, an object, an institution' (Dreyfus, 1991a: 17).

While the building mode is purposeful in that it involves a predefined outcome, the dwelling mode is purposive in that it 'gives consistency, stability and ultimately, identity to the agent, be it individual or organization, as a locus of action' (Chia & Holt, 2006: 650). We propose that practice, relationality, a logic of practice and a mode of dwelling provide an equally appropriate paradigm and place within which to explore leadership and its development.

Practice: An Empirical Perspective

The discourse of those engaged in leadership development revealed both explicit and implicit reference to practice as it relates to the construct of leadership. For an article intent on avoiding the trap of 'intellectualocentrism', it is vital to capture the way practice is evoked 'everyday' and 'in the moment' by practitioners.

The qualitative statements presented in Table 3 (Leadership development participants talk of practice) are sourced from interviews with participants from a number of leadership development programmes run by an Australasian provider. Participants were drawn from long-term, intensive leadership programmes orientated at the corporate, community and professional sectors (65 participants in total). These statements were drawn from post-programme interviews where interviewees were invited to reflect on the meaning and value of their development experience. To that end, they were semi-structured and self-directed with the intent that interviewees could express leadership development in ways that made meaning and sense for them.

All participants represented here were on concurrent leadership development programmes designed and delivered by the same university affiliated provider. In each case they undertook a joint selection process whereby they were assessed by the leadership provider (for capacity to learn and readiness for long-term development) and the 'host' organization (for their potential to make a contribution in leadership). The participants were mainly in the 35 to 50 age band with males having proportionately greater representation. The following table (Table 2: Programme demographics) provides a more specific breakdown of this sample group.

The leadership development provider did have an understanding of practice as central to their development pedagogy, philosophy and interactions with participants. While this was not fully or directly evoked and articulated in their communication with these participants, a practice orientation did underpin their development framework which moved from a self to relational to collective orientation (what Day, 2000, and Iles & Preece, 2006, refer to as the shift from human to social capital) and focused on leadership that needs to be reflective, creative and strategic. Activities and processes that would be highly sensitive and conducive to a deeper understanding of practice were a conscious part of all programmes. Thus, participants were supported in peer mentoring groups that ran the duration of the 18 months, engaged consciously in dialogue and conflict processes, participated regularly in critically orientated reflective and collective sense-making opportunities, and took part in experiential activities and forums that enabled tacit knowledge to be accessed and explored. In this, the leadership development programmes relied strongly on concepts of 'reflection-in-action' (Schon, 1983), wisdom (Grint, 2007), 'observable practice' (Kelly et al., 2006), deep learning (Agyris & Schon, 1978) and situated learning (Lave and Wenger, 1991). We would make the

Table 2 *Programme Demographics*

Programme type	Organizations represented	Typical roles, level, positions held by participants	No. of participants	No. of males	No. of females
Corporate	Financial services	General manager or head of division	27	24	3
Community	Mixed	Self-employed SME manager, Public sector manager	16	8	8
Professional	Research science	Senior manager or science division leaders	22	15	7

point that while such leadership development is highly congruent with the practice approach we are exploring in this article, talk of practice cannot be attributed in a more direct way to the prevailing programme discourse.

The specific statements collected in Table 3 were derived from post-programme interviews conducted with all participants immediately after their 18-month programmes had finished. Those interviews were conducted between a programme facilitator and a participant. Since both parties were complicit in the development experience, we assume that these participants were being 'politically conscious actors' (Alvesson & Deetz, 2000: 195) who would have exercised intentionality, reflexivity and even caution in the interview context. Consider too that these interviews were part of a wider analysis project attempting to explore assumptions around multiple dimensions of their leadership development.

The different categories illustrated here were a 'problematic' series of empirical clusterings offered by participants in terms of the value, difference and growth experienced by participants as an outcome of the programme. We use the word 'problematic' in the same sense as Alvesson and Karreman (2007), who interpret it as something that produces puzzlement on the part of the researcher. Our puzzlement was in the process/practice nature of these particular categories as opposed to more tangible outcomes of leadership development such as increased confidence, courage and self-knowledge. What was 'interesting' (Weick, 1989: 525) and 'surprising' (Alvesson & Karreman, 2007: 1270) to us was that a significant amount of the impact and value of their development experience was not the attainment of something new, or the ongoing development of something existing, but instead the movement of an idea or insight between different states of awareness, consciousness and identification. Furthermore, such leadership development 'outcomes' appeared to be recognized, appreciated and valued, judging from the positive language used to represent them.

The data table presented here is really an illustration of the different ways in which participants articulated a sense of practice. The seven headings (habits, process, consciousness, awareness, control, everydayness, identity) reflect seven discourses of dwelling or modes of depicting a shift or change in how knowledge or understanding is held by a participant. The quotes assembled under each heading were primarily chosen for their capacity to convey each practice-related concept but we have by no means represented all references to each topic here. Quotes do come, however, from participants across all these different programmes. It is certainly not claimed that a practice philosophy dominated the sense-making of participants to the exclusion of other forms of meaning-making, but the point is made that an intuitive understanding and articulation of practice was present in a surprisingly large number of them. A range of their statements is shown in Table 3 in order to ground this discussion in the 'mundane' and 'unheroic'.

Talk of habits, consciousness and awareness was apparent and was indicative of the dwelling mode discussed earlier. Central to these statements were the evocation of tacit (as opposed to the technical knowledge of a building mode) knowledge, the linking of leadership to disposition rather than a series of traits or behaviours, and the bringing to consciousness of elements that have been partially or fully hidden and disguised in terms of one's past and existing 'modus operandi'. The leadership that emerges from such a discourse is one of intentionality, depth, authenticity and enquiry.

Sensitivity to practice would appear to surface distinctive questions in terms of both leadership and development. Talk of 'habits' suggests a recognition by participants that change is not achieved or secured until there has been some kind of (in the language of one of the participants) 'undoing' of existing and normative ways of doing things before what is new can be fostered and established. This marks a refreshing difference to the kind of 'instant fix' discourse of much training and development, which appears to presume that a new technique, tool or resource can in itself effect change.

Table 3 *Leadership development participants talk of practice*

Habits

'I am still in the process of actively unlearning. Habits are hard to break.' 'It's a habit now; I actually look through papers for leadership articles.' 'Really it's about changing habits. How do I change my habits?' 'It's the extent to which I undo myself.'

Process

'I've implemented process, more process, instead of just doing things on the spur of the moment. So I've more back-up and follow-through.'

'It wasn't until I started the course or even half-way through that I realised there were processes. I really understand my processes a lot better and I looked at them instead of just reacting to them for a change.'

Consciousness

'This was a real opening up for me as it made something unconscious conscious.'

'I can't say I go back and refer continually to the content that we've covered. But there are just, I don't know, elements in my subconscious.'

Awareness

'So I suppose I am just so much more aware of what people notice. I'd never taken time to actually think about it. Some of those questions in those interviews, I never actually thought about. Questions like, what makes a good leader or what is leadership or how would you describe your leadership styles are something that I have a real awareness of now.'

'Because it's not something I've ever done, which is actually saying why are you acting the way you do and why are you like you are? And what's happened in the past that's consistent with how you're acting now. So I suppose it was that real self awareness.'

Control

'And I think where previously I felt as though leadership was something that I'd just fallen into, rather than something that I had control over being in, or out of.'

'I think I'm a lot more in control of where I'm going, even though I don't know where I'm going. But I'm in a lot more control.'

'Previously I felt I was a bit like a raft. The current was controlling. And now I feel I'm more like a yacht.'

Everydayness

'I look at things more clearly, more carefully and think about it more. And in an everyday sense, if there's something cropping up, I think how am I going to go about this instead of just going out and doing it.'

Identity

'So I thought that leadership was like a coat that one could slip into for in a specific setting. And I realised that leadership is more like a skin that we wear and it can't be taken off.'

'In the end it asks that very existential question about who is the person we are creating through our actions and work. I have reflected on all the half-hearted moments and unrealised moments and the shadow that these live in, compared to the luminescence of the fully lived and engaged moments. The inevitable question is why not more of the one and the less of the other—from where springs the timidity or the fear.'

'For me it's how I articulate me to myself.'

There also appears to be a link between practice and process where participants become aware of the multitude of actions, reactions and interactions that make up 'the everyday' of leadership. Even a moment or situation has processes, which allows the possibility of shaping and intervention, and participants seem to reflect a greater optimism in being able to '*back up*' and avoid '*just reacting to them*'.

The connection between practice and control would appear a critical one for leadership. Such talk of control was not reminiscent of power and authority as one might possibly expect from those engaged in leadership development, but one where participants explored their subjectivity, inner voice and autonomy. While centred on the issue of '*where I'm going*', participants depicted this not as a question of outcome or destination but as one of confidence, composure and self-belief. Thus, being a '*yacht*' and not a '*raft*' is about the journey (dwelling mode) rather than its endpoint (building mode).

Participants used imagery and reference to identity to depict the nature and extent of their development and learning. Most evocatively, the image of leadership as no longer being '*like a coat that one could slip into for in a specific setting*' but '*a skin that we wear and it can't be taken off*'. Such an image speaks to the embedding of the new, whereby fresh practices become fully embedded or integrated in the new system and cannot be simply switched off or on. These participants talk of leadership, then, as a shaping and discovery of self rather than a set of traits or techniques (or competencies) that can be translated into the organizational environment for specific outcomes.

It would be appropriate to also read these quotes as indicative of a more generic growth in the maturity and agency of this particular set of people. Indeed, we often do understand growth as an unfolding of what is latent; a refocusing on what is core or essential, or an unveiling of what has been hidden or obscured. Likewise, these quotes all seem to have what Heifetz (1994, 1999) would call an adaptive quality or 'the achievement of a different consciousness' (1999: 11) which Heifetz sees as the essential work of leadership. In adaptive work, such awareness or consciousness is evolutionary, revelatory, experimental and interdependent. What drives a shift in consciousness is what Heifetz terms 'small "t" transformational change' (1999: 11) which is a combination of reflection (what he terms 'internalizing') and mobilization (engaging relationally and socially). In the context of this discussion, then, what we call a practice logic or mindset would appear to fit closely with adaptive leadership work.

This section suggests that practitioner talk of practice intuitively draws attention to leadership in 'ordinariness' or an ability to comprehend the subtleties of sophisticated dynamics like unlearning, transition and transformation. It desires leadership to be an embodied, embedded way of being and approaching organizations, contexts and the world. If so, then the translation of much of leadership into competencies does not do them or leadership sufficient justice. We argue that a practice perspective and agenda presents as both an alternative research paradigm and set of organizational principles with which to understand and depict leadership and its development.

A leadership-as-practice agenda

Much of what has fuelled the strategy-as-practice research momentum and energy would appear equally valid to the discipline of leadership. Many leadership researchers and scholars would identify strongly with Whittington's (2003) admission that, after decades of successful teaching *about* strategy (or leadership), he was impoverished at enabling practitioners with *how* to strategize (or do leadership). Like strategy, leadership is ripe to throw off 'the epistemological straightjacket' of modernism that has valued 'scientific detachment over practical engagement, the general over the contextual, and the quantitative over the qualitative' (Whittington, 2004: 62). Equally, like strategy, leadership needs to make the journey to 'the internal life of process, the practices by which work is actually done' (Brown & Duguid, 2000: 95).

Whittington (2003: 117) proposed a series of six questions to consider for the strategy-as-practice agenda. We use them verbatim here except for the substitution of 'leadership' for 'strategizing' in non-italics:

Where and how is the work of leadership *actually done; how does this* leadership *work; what are the common tools and techniques of* leadership; *how is the work of* leadership *organized, communicated and consumed?*

As he later clarifies, 'this is the world in boardrooms and away days, on phones and in front of computer screens' (Whittington, 2003: 119). With the amount of ink and paper dedicated to the discipline of leadership, it may seem extraordinary to claim that we do not know enough about these questions, but the challenge of focusing on 'situated activity rather than abstract processes' (Whittington, 2003: 118) should appear, on reflection, as a real one.

We would not be the first to note that the leadership literature has invested significant time and attention on the qualities that leaders are assumed to have (confidence, optimism, charisma and so on), the behaviours that they should be demonstrating (inspiring others, role modelling and so on), the intelligences they need to develop (cognitive, emotional and even spiritual), the orientation required (to task or people), or the nature of their work (interpersonal, adaptive or strategic and so on). There are many leadership typologies and descriptors that highlight or emphasize a certain style, brand or effect (transformational, servant, authentic and ethical leadership and so on) and there are copious lists of leadership skills, tools and competencies that delineate expectations of what needs to be mastered. Yet these shed more light on the 'what' and 'why' rather than the 'how' of leadership (Chia, 2004).

Recent critical and interpretive work on leadership highlights the lack of meaning, conceptual depth and real know-how that leadership practitioners have around the work of leadership. A stream of work by Alvesson and Sveningsson (2003a, b and c) reveals that many managers engaged in leadership work are able to articulate the abstract ideals (vision, inspiration, commitment and so on) of leadership readily, clearly and easily, but are at a loss when challenged to say what they actually do in the pursuit and exercise of such ideals. This has led them to conclude that leadership has more power as a discourse and identity, giving practitioners enhanced self-esteem, significance and 'positive cultural valence' (Alvesson & Willmott, 2002: 620), rather than a specific or distinctive set of practices or interventions in organizational life. The one practice that those engaged in leadership could talk about in detail was listening, which Alvesson and Sveningsson (2003b: 1435) categorized as 'the extra-ordinarization of the mundane' on the rationale that leadership conferred significance on listening, rather than the proposition that listening attests necessarily to the presence of leadership.

In fact, Chia (2004: 30), discussing Bourdieu (1977/2002: 19), reminds us that the academic discourse is so pervasive that even when 'practitioners willingly provide quasi-theoretical accounts of their own practices, they are likely to 'conceal' even from their own eyes the true nature of their practical mastery'. Practice research must seek '"richer versions" of *leadership*' coming from more intimate and sustained interactions with actors and 'a more theoretically incisive understanding of the importance of language use or talk for constituting actions (shaping *leadership*) and more generally for socially constructing "organization/social order"' (Samra-Fredericks, 2003: 142; we again substituted *leadership* for strategy).

Samra-Fredericks' (2003) empirical work offers an interesting exemplar of practice-orientated empirical work. She takes a strong ethnographic approach combined with conversation analysis in investigating the routines and interactions (what she calls 'the ebb and flow of everyday human exchange', 2003: 144) of six strategists. She isolates six practices:

The ability to speak forms of knowledge; mitigate and observe the protocols of human interaction (the moral order); question and query; display appropriate emotion; deploy metaphors and finally; put history 'to work'. (Samra-Fredericks, 2003: 144)

These six, combined with timeliness and the relational domain, can be seen to constitute the practical wisdom that enables the work of strategy. She assessed these as being 'intricate, dynamic, fragile and skilled . . . attempts at improvisation' and 'realtime efforts to assemble a plausible narrative' constituting 'embodied, emotional and moral human beings' (Samra-Fredericks, 2003: 168).

This particular piece of practice empirical work is particularly relevant for leadership, as it would appear completely seamless to read the six practices isolated in this research as leadership practice. Indeed, we could expect that a greater practice focus would radically challenge the ways we have carved up organizational life into 'ideologically loaded labels' (Alvesson & Sveningsson, 2003a: 985) such as 'leadership', 'management', 'strategy' and so on. One could expect that practices do not fall into such neat and discrete packages, and that, through making them more visible, we have the chance of moving closer to 'the contours of [their] lived experience over time/space dimensions' (Samra-Fredericks, 2003: 169).

Implications of a Practice Perspective for Leadership and Its Development

Whittington (2004: 62) claims that a practice perspective 'has a radically decentring effect on traditional conceptions of the discipline's purpose'. We would propose a number of sites where that 'decentring' would be particularly significant. In an earlier article, Whittington (1996: 734) has commented that neither scholars nor practitioners know enough about 'unheroic work' and, while he is referring to strategy practitioners, we know notions of heroism have long permeated leadership studies. We are supposedly entering a post-heroic leadership age (Gronn, 2002), yet much of our data and theory is based on those with profile, status, position and power. One of the impacts of the practice turn in strategy has been the recognition that the work of strategy is distributed far and wide in an organization and that middle and lower level employees engage in strategy practice (Balogun, 2003; Balogun and Johnson, 2004, 2005; Rouleau, 2005). We would argue that both a broadening and redefinition of who is engaged in leadership work is well overdue and promises the potential for research to be more focused and specific on the constitution of leadership in different sites and from different organizational positions (or 'non-positions').

Likewise, hearing the challenge of exploring 'non-deliberate practical coping' as opposed to 'planned, intentional action' (Chia & Holt, 2006: 643) would be truly unsettling to much leadership research. Chia and Holt (2006: 641) quote Heidegger's illustration of the door in support of this distinction. Given that we go through myriads of doors in our day-to-day existence, we in effect stop noticing, or confine to the periphery of our attention, the action of turning the door handle. This reflects what Heidegger calls 'availableness' or a 'non-thematic circumspective absorption' (Chia & Holt, 2006: 640) which is indicative of being fully immersed in the world. However, if the doorknob becomes broken, absent or problematic, we become conscious and attentive to what normally is quite non-reflective, and then begin a conscious analysis and planning of action in response. Thus, failure, dysfunction, obstruction, surprise and dissonance are what can spark conscious, intentional action in the first place, but it is important to note that the bulk of lived reality is of the former not the latter type.

Much of leadership research focuses on this narrower point of action where the actor is in a self-conscious and decisive mode with a crisis, problem, issue, problematic encounter, choice or challenge presenting. Practice theory suggests two options: first, it can reorient us to think about and explore the vast bulk of leadership action or coping that is as non-reflective and non-conscious as the simple opening of doors; second, it could invite us to bring more of the non-conscious and unreflective into the conscious and intentional domain. This would indicate that 'building' and 'dwelling' modes could complement each other in a development context. If we move beyond Heidegger's door example, then we can see that a dynamic process can link building and dwelling modes, whereby knowledge is moved from a state of unconsciousness or unawareness into a more active, intentional state before re-embedding it as a new set of habits. Just giving individuals or groups new 'tools' in themselves without paying attention to 'non-thematic circumspective absorption' (Chia & Holt, 2006: 640) would appeal to focus on the narrowest point of leadership practice. Potentially, as a result of a more dynamic approach, we then learn to extend what it is we pay attention to and actually have leadership choices about.

Furthermore, Whittington's (2004: 62) assertion that 'studying practice can be practical', emphasizes that attention must be paid to how a practice turn can have tangible leadership effects. This is especially pertinent to leadership development. Given that leadership-as-practice orients us to what is internalized, improvised and unselfconscious, then development must be prepared to work with what is 'unspoken', 'inarticulate' and 'oftentimes unconscious' (Chia & MacKay, 2007: 237). Chia and MacKay (2007) speak to a radically different development process than a skill- or tools-based programme:

> *Becoming skilled in a practice therefore, is not simply a question of deliberately acquiring a set of generalized capabilities that can be transmitted from one individual to another. Rather, skills are 'regrown' . . . incorporated into the modus operandi of the developing organism through training and experience in the performance of particular tasks. (p. 233)*

Raelin (2007) proposes the construction of 'reflective communities' (p. 502) and a contemporary form of 'apprenticeship' (p. 503) focusing on meta-competence as two learning or development practices by which habits, awareness and identity are constructed, revised and indeed 'regrown'.

In a similar vein, Dreyfus (2001: 41) reminds us that while academic knowledge and processes seek to produce competence, they do not produce what he terms 'practical proficiency or mastery of the art'. For that to occur 'a particular style of engagement' (Chia, 2004: 33) is required which he typifies as 'discipleship, apprenticeship or extensive periods of understudy' (Dreyfus, 2001: 41). The development of leadership practice would appear acutely experiential, interactive, situated, embodied, sustained and relational which creates a new kind of engagement with self, others and world. Such a new kind of engagement is predicated on learning to operate from a dwelling mode, removing any distinction between subject, object and reliance on mental models and cognitive frameworks (Dreyfus, 1991a: 27). Shotter (2005: 2) calls this 'withness' not 'aboutness' thinking and Dreyfus (1991b: 232) reminds us that 'we are the practices' which are socially embedded and embodied ways of understanding 'what it is to be a person, an object, an institution' and we would add, to be in leadership.

Understanding more effectively 'what it is to be a person, an object, an institution' could (and should) be extended to ask what it means to be a researcher. We note a timely, lively and engaging special issue of *Academy of Management Journal* (2007, 32:4) on just this topic. A number of articles in this special issue propose the need for theory that 'comes from engagement with problems in the world' (Van Maanen et al., 2007: 1149), a 'closer connection with professional practice' (Pfeffer, 2007: 1342), and 'a scholarship of integration' (Bartunek, 2007: 1323) between scholars and practitioners. Most strongly articulated by Raelin (2007) is the capacity of a practice perspective to offer such relationships and energy through its attention to tacit knowledge, its wariness of an overreliance on rationality and its support of third-order learning. Equally pertinent to this specific article is his warning that 'practice epistemology will likely resist our Western inclination, our near obsession, with measuring items so as to believe we know them' (Raelin, 2007: 506), thus confirming that while practice indeed has an oppositional logic to competency, it won't in all likelihood offer a straightforward or practical alternative to it.

Indeed, we are conscious that practice-orientated perspectives, while solving or making progress on many 'mysteries' (Alvesson & Karreman, 2007), have their challenges. We have talked about the focus on micro-action in a practice perspective and have seen this empirically explored in the

Samra-Fredericks (2003) article, yet we still struggle to find methods that capture the complexity of interaction and interrelation rather than an individualistic perspective. While approaching individuals as 'field of re-lat-ionships' (Cooper, 2005: 1693) or 'bundles of practices' might provide an appealing and provocative starting place for researchers, it certainly will challenge our understanding of the identity, agency and boundaries of our research participants. Practice in a leadership sphere, unless it is to replicate leader-centric behaviour, is going to have to be very methodologically sophisticated in order to gain access to leadership interactions without the distortion of pre-fixed categories such as leader, follower, subordinate and boss.

Methodological issues take us to the level of the discipline, where we have the challenge of bringing markedly different research paradigms into conversation. Where this fails to happen, certainly evident in the lack of dialogue between the strategy as practice literature and the mainstream strategy literature, there is limited capacity to influence the wider field and in effect a separate sub-field is created. Leadership perhaps could be characterized as already rift, with division on a number of fronts ranging between often tightly contested philosophical, geographical, contextual, discipline and paradigmatic boundaries. We note and applaud those who are beginning to explore and pay attention to talking across such boundaries; for example, Fairclough's (2007) recent work focusing on bringing together psychological and discursive leadership approaches.

Conclusion

This article can be read in the light of Bryman's (1986) call to interpret leadership in the light of new and alternative paradigmatic thought. That call is decades old now and, while we have seen momentum in critical leadership research (Gemmill and Oakley, 1992; Grint, 2005), interpretative leadership research (Alvesson & Sveningsson, 2003a, 2003b, 2003c) and process leadership theory (Wood, 2005), undoubtedly the leadership field has some way to go before it becomes as dynamic and methodologically rich as it could be. An exploration of a practice perspective presents as intuitively appealing because, like strategy, leadership begs for 'a complementary dialogue' (Wilson & Jarzabkowski, 2004: 15) between the agendas, discourses and audiences of both academics and practitioners. The ubiquity of competency in the current mainstream dialogue, we argue, acts more as a restraint to leadership thinking and development than a facilitator of further leadership richness, texture and possibility. Consequently, we offer the notion of practice in its attentiveness to leadership as discourse, identity and modus operandi, as far more aligned and attuned to what researchers, developers and practitioners will require.

References

Agyris, C., & Schon, D. (1978) *Organizational Learning: A Theory of Action Perspective.* New York: McGraw Hill.

Alvesson, M., & Karreman, D. (2007) 'Constructing Mystery: Empirical Matters in Theory Development', *Academy of Management Review* 32(4): 1265–81.

Alvesson, M., & Sveningsson, S. (2003a) 'Good Visions, Bad Micro-management and Ugly Ambiguity: Contradictions of (Non-) Leadership in a Knowledge-Intensive Organization, *Organization Studies* 24(6): 961–88.

Alvesson, M., & Sveningsson, S. (2003b) 'Managers Doing Leadership: The Extra-ordinarization of the Mundane', *Human Relations* 56(12): 1435–59.

Alvesson, M., & Sveningsson, S. (2003c) 'The Great Disappearing Act: Difficulties in doing Leadership', *The Leadership Quarterly* 14: 359–81.

Alvesson, M., & Willmott, H. (2002) 'Producing the Appropriate Individual: Identity Regulation as Organizational Control', *Journal of Management Studies* 39(5): 619–44.

Alvesson, M., & Deetz, S. (2000) *Doing Critical Management Research.* London: SAGE.

Balogun, J. (2003) 'From Blaming the Middle to Harnessing its Potential: Creating Change Intermediaries', *British Journal of Management* 14(1): 69–84.

Balogun, J., & Johnson, G. (2004) 'Organizational Restructuring and Middle Manager Sensemaking', *Academy of Management Journal* 47(4): 523–49.

Balogun, J., & Johnson, G. (2005) 'From Intended Strategies to Unintended Outcomes: The Impact of Change Recipient Sensemaking', *Organization Studies* 26(11): 1573–601.

Bartunek, J. (2007) 'Academic–Practitioner Collaboration Need Not Require Joint or Relevant Research: Toward a Relational Scholarship of Integration', *Academy of Management Journal* 50(6): 1323–33.

Bolden, R., & Gosling, J. (2006) 'Leadership Competencies: Time to Change the Tune?', *Leadership* 2(2): 147–63.

Bourdieu, P. (1977/2002) *Outline of a Theory of Practice*. Cambridge: Cambridge University Press.

Bourdieu, P. (1990) *The Logic of Practice*. Cambridge: Polity.

Boyatzis, R. E. (1982) *The Competent Manager: A Mode for Effective Performance*. New York: John Wiley and Sons.

Brown, J. S., & Duguid, P. (2000) *The Social Life of Information*. Boston, MA: Harvard Business School Press.

Bryman, A. (1986) *Leadership and Organizations*. London: Routledge and Kegan Paul.

Chia, R. (2004) 'Strategy-as-practice: Reflections on the Research Agenda', *European Management Review* 1: 29–34.

Chia, R., & Holt, R. (2006) 'Strategy as Practical Coping: A Heideggerian Perspective', *Organization Studies* 27(5): 635–55.

Chia, R., & MacKay, B. (2007) 'Post-processual Challenges for the Emerging Strategy-as-practice Perspective: Discovering Strategy in the Logic of Practice', *Human Relations* 60(1): 217–42.

Cooper, R. (2005) 'Relationality', *Organization Studies* 26(11): 1689–710.

Cullen, E. (1992) 'A Vital Way to Manage Change', *Education* 13: 3–17.

Day, D. V. (2000) 'Leadership Development: A Review in Context', *Leadership Quarterly* 11(4): 581–613.

de Certeau, M. (1984) *The Practice of Everyday Life*. Berkeley, CA: University of California Press.

Dreyfus, H. L. (1991a) 'Reflections on the Workshop on the Self', *Anthropology and Humanism Quarterly* 16(1): 1–28.

Dreyfus, H. L. (1991b) *Being-in-the-real-world*. Cambridge, MA: MIT Press.

Dreyfus, H. L. (2001) *On the Internet*. London, New York: Routledge.

Ecclestone, K. (1997) 'Energizing or Enervating: Implications of National Vocational Qualifications in Professional Development', *Journal of Vocational Education and Training* 49: 65–79.

Fairclough, N. (ed.) (2007) *Discourse and Contemporary Social Change*. Bern: Peter Lang.

Gemmill, G., & Oakley, J. (1992) 'Leadership: An Alienating Social Myth', *Human Relations* 45(2): 113–29.

Grey, C. (1999) "We Are All Managers Now"; "We Always Were": On the Development and Demise of Management', *Journal of Management Studies* 36(5): 561–85.

Grint, K. (2005) *Leadership: Limits and Possibilities*. New York: Palgrave Macmillan.

Grint, K. (2007) 'Learning to Lead: Can Aristotle Help us Find the Road to Wisdom?', *Leadership* 3: 231–46.

Gronn, P. (2002) 'Distributed Leadership as a Unit of Analysis', *Leadership Quarterly* 13(4): 423–51.

Grugulis, I. (1998) '"Real" Managers Don't Do NVQs: A Review of the New Management "Standards"', *Employee Relations* 20: 383–403.

Grugulis, I. (2000) 'The Management NVQ: A Critique of the Myth of Relevance', *Journal of Vocational Education and Training* 52: 79–99.

Heidegger, M. (1926/1962) *Being and Time*: Oxford: Blackwell.

Heifetz, R. (1994) *Leadership Without Easy Answers*. Cambridge, MA: Harvard Kennedy School of Government.

Heifetz, R. (1999) *Adaptive Change: What's essential and what's expendable?* Cambridge, MA: Harvard Kennedy School of Government.

Iles, P., & Preece, D. (2006) 'Developing Leaders or Developing Leadership? The Academy of Chief Executives' Programmes in the North East of England', *Leadership* 2(3): 317–40.

Jarzabkowski, P. (2003) 'Strategic Practices: An Activity Theory Perspective on Continuity and Change', *Journal of Management Studies* 40(1): 22–55.

Jarzabkowski, P., Balogun, J., & Seidl, D. (2007) 'Strategizing: The Challenges of a Practice Perspective', *Human Relations* 60(1): 5–27.

Kelly, S., White, M. I., Martin, D., & Rouncefield, M. (2006) 'Leadership Refrains: Patterns of Leadership', *Leadership* 2(2): 181–201.

Lave, J., & Wenger, E. (1991) *Situated Learning. Legitimate Peripheral Participation*. Cambridge, MA: Cambridge University Press.

Lester, S. (1994) 'Management Standards: A Critical Approach', *Competency* 2(1): 28–31.

Loan-Clarke, J. (1996) 'The Management Charter Initiative: A Critique of Management Standards/NVQs', *Journal of Management Development* 15: 4–17.

Pfeffer, J. (2007) 'A Modest Proposal: How Might We Change the Process and Product of Managerial Research', *Academy of Management Journal* 50(6): 1334–45.

Raelin, J. (2007) 'Toward an Epistemology of Practice', *Academy of Management Learning* 6(4): 495–519.

Reckwitz, A. (2002) 'Toward a Theory of Social Practices: A Development in Cultural Theorizing', *European Journal of Social Theory* 5(2): 243–63.

Rouleau, L. (2005) 'Micro-practices of Strategic Sensemaking and Sensegiving: How Middle Managers Interpret and Sell Change Every Day', *Journal of Management Studies* 42(7): 1413.

Samra-Fredericks, D. (2003) 'Strategizing as Lived Experience and Strategists' Everyday Efforts to Shape Strategic Direction', *Journal of Management Studies* 40(1): 141–74.

Schatzki, T. R. (2001) 'Introduction: Practice Theory', in T. R. Schatzki, K. Knorr Cetina, & E. von Savigny (eds) *The Practice Turn in Contemporary Theory*, pp. 1–14. London: Routledge.

Schatzki, T. R. (2005) 'The Sites of Organizations', *Organization Studies* 26(3): 465–84.

Schon, D. A. (1983) *The Reflective Practitioner: How Professionals Think in Practice*. New York: Basic Books.

Shotter, J. (2005) *The Role of 'Withness' Thinking in 'Going On' Inside Charismatically-structured Processes*. Keynote paper presented at the First Organization Studies Santorini Workshop on Theorizing Process in Organizational Research, Santorini, 12–13 June.

Townley, B. (2002) 'Managing with Modernity', *Organization* 9(4): 549–73. Van Maanen, J., Sorenson, J., & Mitchell, T. (2007) 'The Interplay Between Theory and Method', *Academy of Management Review* 32(4): 1145–54.

Weick, K. (1989) 'Theory Construction as Disciplined Imagination', *Academy of Management Review* 14: 516–31. Whittington, R. (1996) 'Strategy as Practice', *Long Range Planning* 29(5): 731–5.

Whittington, R. (2003) 'The Work of Strategizing and Organizing: For a Practice Perspective', *Strategic Organization* 1(1): 117–25.

Whittington, R. (2004) 'Strategy after Modernism: Recovering Practice', *European Management Review* 1: 62–8.

Whittington, R. (2006) 'Completing the Practice Turn in Strategy Research', *Organization Studies* 27(5): 613–34.

Wilson, D. C., & Jarzabkowski, P. (2004) 'Thinking and Acting Strategically: New Challenges for Interrogating Strategy', *European Management Review* 1: 14–20.

Wood, M. (2005) 'The Fallacy of Misplaced Leadership', *Journal of Management Studies* 42(6): 1101–20.

Chapter 2 ■ Leadership as Practice

Questions for Discussion

1. What paradigm do the authors attempt to question in this article? How do they account for the pervasiveness of these current beliefs? According to their position, what are the problems associated with contemporary views of leadership? What do they propose as an alternative?

2. What evidence is provided to challenge the prevailing notion about leadership? Does their research emphasize paradigm shifts, rather than paradigms?

3. What types of research do the authors cite to dispute the existing leadership paradigm and propose another vision? Do they look to primary or secondary research? Do they analyze models or theoretical work? How persuasive is the research they provide?

4. How might this article help someone who is working on a proposal that contradicts or complicates existing beliefs in another facet of the professional world?

Absolute PowerPoint

Can a Software Package Edit Our Thoughts?

Ian Parker

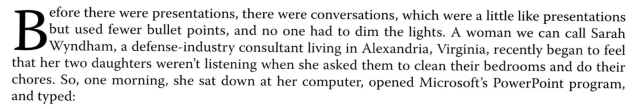

Before there were presentations, there were conversations, which were a little like presentations but used fewer bullet points, and no one had to dim the lights. A woman we can call Sarah Wyndham, a defense-industry consultant living in Alexandria, Virginia, recently began to feel that her two daughters weren't listening when she asked them to clean their bedrooms and do their chores. So, one morning, she sat down at her computer, opened Microsoft's PowerPoint program, and typed:

> FAMILY MATTERS
> An approach for positive change
> to the Wyndham family team.

On a new page, she wrote:

- Lack of organization leads to confusion and frustration among family members.

- Disorganization is detrimental to grades and to your social life.

- Disorganization leads to inefficiencies that impact the entire family.

Instead of pleading for domestic harmony, Sarah Wyndham was pitching for it. Soon she had eighteen pages of large type, supplemented by a color photograph of a generic happy family riding bicycles, and, on the final page, a drawing of a key—the key to success. The briefing was given only once, last fall. The experience was so upsetting to her children that the threat of a second showing was enough to make one of the Wyndham girls burst into tears.

PowerPoint, which can be found on two hundred and fifty million computers around the world, is software you impose on other people. It allows you to arrange text and graphics in a series of pages, which you can project, slide by slide, from a laptop computer onto a screen, or print as a booklet (as Sarah Wyndham did). The usual metaphor for everyday software is the tool, but that doesn't seem to be right here. PowerPoint is more like a suit of clothes, or a car, or plastic surgery. You take it out with you. You are judged by it—you insist on being judged by it. It is by definition a social instrument, turning middle managers into bullet-point dandies.

But PowerPoint also has a private, interior influence. It edits ideas. It is, almost surreptitiously, a business manual as well as a business suit, with an opinion—an oddly pedantic, prescriptive opinion—about the way we should think. It helps you make a case, but it also makes its own case: about how to organize information, how much information to organize, how to look at the world. One feature of this is the AutoContent Wizard, which supplies templates—"Managing Organizational Change" or "Communicating Bad News," say—that are so close to finished presentations you barely need to do more than add your company logo. The "Motivating a Team" template, for example, includes a slide headed "Conduct a Creative Thinking Session":

Ask: In what ways can we . . . ?

- Assess the situation. Get the facts.
- Generate possible solutions with green light, nonjudgmental thinking.
- Select the best solution.

The final injunction is "Have an inspirational close."

It's easy to avoid these extreme templates—many people do—as well as embellishments like clip art, animations, and sound effects. But it's hard to shake off AutoContent's spirit: even the most easy going PowerPoint template insists on a heading followed by bullet points, so that the user is shepherded toward a staccato, summarizing frame of mind, of the kind parodied, for example, in a PowerPoint Gettysburg Address posted on the Internet: "Dedicate portion of field—fitting!"

Because PowerPoint can be an impressive antidote to fear—converting public-speaking dread into moviemaking pleasure—there seems to be no great impulse to fight this influence, as you might fight the unrelenting animated paperclip in Microsoft Word. Rather, PowerPoint's restraints seem to be soothing—so much so that where Microsoft has not written rules, businesses write them for themselves. A leading U.S. computer manufacturer has distributed guidelines to its employees about PowerPoint presentations, insisting on something it calls the "Rule of Seven": "Seven (7) bullets or lines per page, seven (7) words per line."

Today, after Microsoft's decade of dizzying growth, there are great tracts of corporate America where to appear at a meeting without PowerPoint would be unwelcome and vaguely pretentious, like wearing no shoes. In darkened rooms at industrial plants and ad agencies, at sales pitches and conferences, this is how people are communicating: no paragraphs, no pronouns—the world condensed into a few upbeat slides, with seven or so words on a line, seven or so lines on a slide. And now it's happening during sermons and university lectures and family arguments, too. A New Jersey PowerPoint user recently wrote in an online discussion, "Last week I caught myself planning out (in my head) the slides I would need to explain to my wife why we couldn't afford a vacation this year." Somehow, a piece of software designed, fifteen years ago, to meet a simple business need has become a way of organizing thought at kindergarten show-and-tells. "Oh, Lord," one of the early developers said to me. "What have we done?"

Forty years ago, a workplace meeting was a discussion with your immediate colleagues. Engineers would meet with other engineers and talk in the language of engineering. A manager might make an appearance—acting as an interpreter, a bridge to the rest of the company—but no one from the marketing or production or sales department would be there. Somebody might have gone to the trouble of cranking out mimeographs—that would be the person with purple fingers.

But the structure of American industry changed in the nineteen-sixties and seventies. Clifford Nass, who teaches in the Department of Communication at Stanford, says, "Companies weren't discovering things in the laboratory and then trying to convince consumers to buy them. They were discovering—or creating—consumer demand, figuring out what they can convince consumers they need, then going to the laboratory and saying, 'Build this!' People were saying, 'We can create demand. Even if demand doesn't exist, we know how to market this.' SpaghettiOs is the great example. The guy came up with the jingle first: 'The neat round spaghetti you can eat with a spoon.' And he said, 'Hey! Make spaghetti in the shape of small circles!'"

As Jerry Porras, a professor of organizational behavior and change at Stanford Graduate School of Business, says, "When technologists no longer just drove the product out but the customer sucked it out, then you had to know what the customer wanted, and that meant a lot more interaction inside the company." There are new conversations: Can we make this? How do we sell this if we make it? Can we do it in blue?

America began to go to more meetings. By the early nineteen-eighties, when the story of Power-Point starts, employees had to find ways to talk to colleagues from other departments, colleagues who spoke a different language, brought together by SpaghettiOs and by the simple fact that technology was generating more information. There was more to know and, as the notion of a job for life eroded, more reason to know it.

In this environment, visual aids were bound to thrive. In 1975, fifty thousand overhead projectors were sold in America. By 1985, that figure had increased to more than a hundred and twenty thousand. Overheads, which were developed in the mid-forties for use by the police, and were then widely used in bowling alleys and schools, did not fully enter business life until the mid-seventies, when a transparency film that could survive the heat of a photocopier became available. Now anything on a sheet of paper could be transferred to an overhead slide. Overheads were cheaper than the popular alternative, the 35-mm. slide (which needed graphics professionals), and they were easier to use. But they restricted you to your typewriter's font—rather, your secretary's typewriter's font—or your skill with Letraset and a felt-tipped pen. A businessman couldn't generate a handsome, professional-looking font in his own office.

In 1980, though, it was clear that a future of widespread personal computers—and laser printers and screens that showed the very thing you were about to print—was tantalizingly close. In the Mountain View, California, laboratory of Bell-Northern Research, computer-research scientists had set up a great mainframe computer, a graphics workstation, a phototypesetter, and the earliest Canon laser printer, which was the size of a bathtub and took six men to carry into the building—together, a cumbersome approximation of what would later fit on a coffee table and cost a thousand dollars. With much trial and error, and jogging from one room to another, you could use this collection of machines as a kind of word processor.

Whitfield Diffie had access to this equipment. A mathematician, a former peacenik, and an enemy of exclusive government control of encryption systems, Diffie had secured a place for himself in computing legend in 1976, when he and a colleague, Martin Hellman, announced the discovery of a new method of protecting secrets electronically—public-key cryptography. At Bell-Northern, Diffie was researching the security of telephone systems. In 1981, preparing to give a presentation with 35-mm. slides, he wrote a little program, tinkering with some graphics software designed by a B.N.R. colleague, that allowed you to draw a black frame on a piece of paper. Diffie expanded it so that the page could show a number of frames, and text inside each frame, with space for commentary around them. In other words, he produced a storyboard—a slide show on paper—that could be sent to the designers who made up the slides, and that would also serve as a script for his lecture. (At this stage, he wasn't photocopying what he had produced to make overhead transparencies, although scientists in other facilities were doing that.) With a few days' effort, Diffie had pointed the way to PowerPoint.

Diffie has long gray hair and likes to wear fine English suits. Today, he works for Sun Microsystems, as an internal consultant on encryption matters. I recently had lunch with him in Palo Alto, and for the first time he publicly acknowledged his presence at the birth of PowerPoint. It was an odd piece of news: as if Lenin had invented the stapler. Yes, he said, PowerPoint was "based on" his work at B.N.R. This is not of great consequence to Diffie, whose reputation in his own field is so high that he is one of the few computer scientists to receive erotically charged fan mail. He said he was "mildly miffed" to have made no money from the PowerPoint connection, but he has no interest in beginning a feud with an old friend. "Bob was the one who had the vision to understand how important it was to the world," he said. "And I didn't."

Bob is Bob Gaskins, the man who has to take final responsibility for the drawn blinds of high-rise offices around the world and the bullet points dashing across computer screens inside. His account of PowerPoint's parentage does not exactly match Diffie's, but he readily accepts his former colleague as "my inspiration." In the late nineteen-seventies and early eighties, Gaskins was B.N.R.'s head of computer-science research. A former Berkeley Ph.D. student, he had a family background in industrial photographic supplies and grew up around overhead projectors and inks and gels. In 1982, he returned from a six-month overseas business trip and, with a vivid sense of the future impact of the Apple Macintosh and of Microsoft's Windows (both of which were in development), he wrote a list of fifty commercial possibilities—Arabic typesetting, menus, signs. And then he looked around his own laboratory and realized what had happened while he was away: following Diffie's lead, his colleagues were trying to make overheads to pitch their projects for funding, despite the difficulties of using the equipment. (What you saw was not at all what you got.) "Our mainframe was buckling under the load," Gaskins says.

He now had his idea: a graphics program that would work with Windows and the Macintosh, and that would put together, and edit, a string of single pages, or "slides." In 1984, he left B.N.R., joined an ailing Silicon Valley software firm, Forethought, in exchange for a sizable share of the company, and hired a software developer, Dennis Austin. They began work on a program called Presenter. After a trademark problem, and an epiphany Gaskins had in the shower, Presenter became PowerPoint.

Gaskins is a precise, bookish man who lives with his wife in a meticulously restored and furnished nineteenth-century house in the Fillmore district of San Francisco. He has recently discovered an interest in antique concertinas. When I visited him, he was persuaded to play a tune, and he gave me a copy of a forthcoming paper he had co-written: "A Wheatstone Twelve-Sided 'Edeophone' Concertina with Pre-MacCann Chromatic Duet Fingering." Gaskins is skeptical about the product that PowerPoint has become—AutoContent and animated fades between slides—but he is devoted to the simpler thing that it was, and he led me through a well-preserved archive of PowerPoint memorabilia, including the souvenir program for the PowerPoint reunion party, in 1997,which had a quiz filled with in-jokes about font size and programming languages. He also found an old business plan from 1984. One phrase—the only one in italics—read, "Allows the content-originator to control the presentation." For Gaskins, that had always been the point: to get rid of the intermediaries—graphic designers—and never mind the consequences. Whenever colleagues sought to restrict the design possibilities of the program (to make a design disaster less likely), Gaskins would overrule them, quoting Thoreau: "I came into this world, not chiefly to make this a good place to live in, but to live in it, be it good or bad."

PowerPoint 1.0 went on sale in April, 1987—available only for the Macintosh, and only in black-and-white. It generated text-and-graphics pages that a photocopier could turn into overhead transparencies. (This was before laptop computers and portable projectors made PowerPoint a tool for live electronic presentations. Gaskins thinks he may have been the first person to use the program in the modern way, in a Paris hotel in 1992—which is like being the first person ever to tap a microphone and say, "Can you hear me at the back?") The Macintosh market was small and specialized, but within this market PowerPoint—the first product of its kind—was a hit. "I can't describe how wonderful it was," Gaskins says. "When we demonstrated at tradeshows, we were mobbed." Shortly after the launch, Forethought accepted an acquisition offer of fourteen million dollars from Microsoft. Microsoft paid cash and allowed Bob Gaskins and his colleagues to remain partly self-governing in Silicon Valley, far from the Microsoft campus, in Redmond, Washington. Microsoft soon regretted the terms of the deal; PowerPoint workers became known for a troublesome independence of spirit (and for rewarding themselves, now and then, with beautifully staged parties—caviar, string quartets, Renaissance-period fancy dress).

PowerPoint had been created, in part, as a response to the new corporate world of interdepartmental communication. Those involved with the program now experienced the phenomenon at first hand. In 1990, the first PowerPoint for Windows was launched, alongside Windows 3.0. And Power-Point quickly became what Gaskins calls "a cog in the great machine." The PowerPoint programmers were forced to make unwelcome changes, partly because in 1990 Word, Excel, and PowerPoint began to be integrated into Microsoft Office—a strategy that would eventually make PowerPoint invincible—and partly in response to market research. AutoContent was added in the mid-nineties, when Microsoft learned that some would-be presenters were uncomfortable with a blank Power-Point page—it was hard to get started. "We said, 'What we need is some automatic content!' " a for-mer Microsoft developer recalls, laughing. "'Punch the button and you'll have a presentation.'" The idea, he thought, was "crazy." And the name was meant as a joke. But Microsoft took the idea and kept the name—a rare example of a product named in outright mockery of its target customers.

Gaskins left PowerPoint in 1992, and many of his colleagues followed soon after. Now rich from Microsoft stock, and beginning the concertina-collecting phase of their careers, they watched as their old product made its way into the heart of American business culture. By 1993, PowerPoint had a majority share of the presentation market. In 1995, the average user created four and a half presentations a month. Three years later, the monthly average was nine. PowerPoint began to appear in cartoon strips and everyday conversation. A few years ago, Bob Gaskins was at a presentations-heavy conference in Britain. The organizer brought the proceedings to a sudden stop, saying, "I've just been told that the inventor of PowerPoint is in the audience—will he please identify himself so we can recognize his contribution to the advancement of science?" Gaskins stood up. The audience laughed and applauded.

Cathleen Belleville, a former graphic designer who worked at PowerPoint as a product planner from 1989 to 1995, was amazed to see a clip-art series she had created become modern business icons. The images were androgynous silhouette stick figures (she called them Screen Beans), modeled on a former college roommate: a little figure clicking its heels; another with an inspirational light bulb above its head. One Screen Bean, the patron saint of PowerPoint—a figure that stands beneath a question mark, scratching its head in puzzlement—is so popular that a lawyer at a New York firm who has seen many PowerPoint presentations claims never to have seen one without the head-scratcher. Belleville herself has seen her Beans all over the world, reprinted on baseball caps, blown up fifteen feet high in a Hamburg bank. "I told my mom, 'You know, my artwork is in danger of being more famous than the "Mona Lisa." ' "Above the counter in a laundromat on Third Avenue in New York, a sign explains that no responsibility can be taken for deliveries to doorman buildings. And there, next to the words, is the famous puzzled figure. It is hard to understand the puzzlement. Doorman? Delivery? But perhaps this is simply how a modern poster clears its throat: Belleville has created the international sign for "sign."

According to Microsoft estimates, at least thirty million PowerPoint presentations are made every day. The program has about ninety-five per cent of the presentations-software market. And so per-haps it was inevitable that it would migrate out of business and into other areas of our lives. I recently spoke to Sew Meng Chung, a Malaysian research engineer living in Singapore who got mar-ried in 1999. He told me that, as his guests took their seats for a wedding party in the Goodwood Park Hotel, they were treated to a PowerPoint presentation: a hundred and thirty photographs—one fading into the next every four or five seconds, to musical accompaniment. "They were baby photos, and courtship photos, and photos taken with our friends and family," he told me.

I also spoke to Terry Taylor, who runs a website called eBibleTeacher.com, which supplies materials for churches that use electronic visual aids. "Jesus was a storyteller, and he gave graphic images," Taylor said. "He would say, 'Consider the lilies of the field, how they grow,' and all indications are that there were lilies in the field when he was talking, you know. He used illustrations." Taylor esti-mates that fifteen per cent of American churches now have video projectors, and many use Power-Point regularly for announcements, for song lyrics, and to accompany preaching. (Taylor has seen more than one sermon featuring the head-scratching figure.) Visitors to Taylor's site can download photographs of locations in the Holy Land, as well as complete PowerPoint sermons—for example, "Making Your Marriage Great":

Find out what you are doing to harm your marriage and heal it!

- Financial irresponsibility.
- Temper.
- Pornography.
- Substance abuse.
- You name it!

When PowerPoint is used to flash hymn lyrics, or make a quick pitch to a new client, or produce an eye-catching laundromat poster, it's easy to understand the enthusiasm of, say, Tony Kurz, the vice-president for sales and marketing of a New York-based Internet company, who told me, "I love PowerPoint. It's a brilliant application. I can take you through at exactly the pace I want to take you." There are probably worse ways to transmit fifty or a hundred words of text, or information that is mainly visual—ways that involve more droning, more drifting. And PowerPoint demands at least some rudimentary preparation: a PowerPoint presenter is, by definition, not thinking about his or her material for the very first time. Steven Pinker, the author of "The Language Instinct" and a psychology professor at the Massachusetts Institute of Technology, says that PowerPoint can give visual shape to an argument. "Language is a linear medium: one damn word after another," he says. "But ideas are multidimensional. . . . When properly employed, PowerPoint makes the logical structure of an argument more transparent. Two channels sending the same information are better than one."

Still, it's hard to be perfectly comfortable with a product whose developers occasionally find themselves trying to suppress its use. Jolene Rocchio, who is a product planner for Microsoft Office (and is upbeat about PowerPoint in general), told me that, at a recent meeting of a nonprofit organization in San Francisco, she argued against a speaker's using PowerPoint at a future conference. "I said, 'I think we just need her to get up and speak.' " On an earlier occasion, Rocchio said, the same speaker had tried to use PowerPoint and the projector didn't work, "and everybody was, like, cheering. They just wanted to hear this woman speak, and they wanted it to be from her heart. And the PowerPoint almost alienated her audience."

This is the most common complaint about PowerPoint. Instead of human contact, we are given human display. "I think that we as a people have become unaccustomed to having real conversations with each other, where we actually give and take to arrive at a new answer. We present to each other, instead of discussing," Cathy Belleville says. Tad Simons, the editor of the magazine *Presentations* (whose second-grade son used PowerPoint for show-and-tell), is familiar with the sin of triple delivery, where precisely the same text is seen on the screen, spoken aloud, and printed on the handout in front of you (the "leave-behind," as it is known in some circles). "The thing that makes my heart sing is when somebody presses the 'B' button and the screen goes black and you can actually talk to the person," Simons told me.

In 1997, Sun Microsystems' chairman and C.E.O., Scott McNealy, "banned" PowerPoint (a ban widely disregarded by his staff). The move might have been driven, in part, by Sun's public-relations needs as a Microsoft rival, but, according to McNealy, there were genuine productivity issues. "Why did we ban it? Let me put it this way: If I want to tell my forty thousand employees to attack, the word 'attack' in ASCII is forty-eight bits. As a Microsoft Word document, it's 90,112 bits. Put that same word in a PowerPoint slide and it becomes 458,048 bits. That's a pig through the python when you try to send it over the Net. "McNealy's concern is shared by the American military. Enormously elaborate PowerPoint files (generated by presentation-obsessives—so-called PowerPoint Rangers) were said to be clogging up the military's bandwidth. Last year, to the delight of many under his command, General Henry H. Shelton, the chairman of the Joint Chiefs of Staff, issued an order to U.S. bases around the world insisting on simpler presentations.

PowerPoint was developed to give public speakers control over design decisions. But it's possible that those speakers should be making other, more important decisions. "In the past, I think we had an inefficient system, where executives passed all of their work to secretaries," Cathy Belleville says. "But now we've got highly paid people sitting there formatting slides—spending hours formatting slides—because it's more fun to do that than concentrate on what you're going to say. It would be much more efficient to offload that work onto someone who could do it in a tenth of the time, and be paid less. Millions of executives around the world are sitting there going, 'Arial? Times Roman? Twenty-four point? Eighteen point?' "

In the glow of a PowerPoint show, the world is condensed, simplified, and smoothed over—yet bright and hyperreal—like the cityscape background in a PlayStation motor race. PowerPoint is strangely adept at disguising the fragile foundations of a proposal, the emptiness of a business plan; usually, the audience is respectfully still (only venture capitalists dare to dictate the pace of someone else's slide show), and, with the visual distraction of a dancing pie chart, a speaker can quickly move past the laughable flaw in his argument. If anyone notices, it's too late—the narrative presses on.

Last year, three researchers at Arizona State University, including Robert Cialdini, a professor and the author of "Influence: Science and Practice," conducted an experiment in which they presented three groups of volunteers with information about Andrew, a fictional high-school student under consideration for a university football scholarship. One group was given Andrew's football statistics typed on a piece of paper. The second group was shown bar graphs. Those in the third group were given a PowerPoint presentation, in which animated bar graphs grew before their eyes.

Given Andrew's record, what kind of prospect was he? According to Cialdini, when Andrew was PowerPointed, viewers saw him as a greater potential asset to the football team. The first group rated Andrew four and a half on a scale of one to seven; the second rated him five; and the Power-Point group rated him six. PowerPoint gave him power. The experiment was repeated, with three groups of sports fans that were accustomed to digesting sports statistics; this time, the first two groups gave Andrew the same rating. But the group that saw the PowerPoint presentation still couldn't resist it. Again, Andrew got a six. PowerPoint seems to be a way for organizations to turn expensive, expert decision-makers into novice decision-makers. "It's frightening," Cialdini says. He always preferred to use slides when he spoke to business groups, but one high-tech company recently hinted that his authority suffered as a result. "They said, 'You know what, Bob? You've got to get into PowerPoint, otherwise people aren't going to respond.' So I made the transfer."

Clifford Nass has an office overlooking the Oval lawn at Stanford, a university where the use of Pow-erPoint is so widespread that to refrain from using it is sometimes seen as a mark of seniority and privilege, like egg on one's tie. Nass once worked for Intel, and then got a Ph.D. in sociology, and now he writes about and lectures on the ways people think about computers. But, before embarking on any of that, Professor Nass was a professional magician—Cliff Conjure—so he has some confidence in his abilities as a public performer.

According to Nass, who now gives PowerPoint lectures because his students asked him to, Power-Point "lifts the floor" of public speaking: a lecture is less likely to be poor if the speaker is using the program. "What PowerPoint does is very efficiently deliver content," Nass told me. "What students gain is a lot more information—not just facts but rules, ways of thinking, examples." At the same time, PowerPoint "lowers the ceiling," Nass says. "What you miss is the process. The classes I remember most, the professors I remember most, were the ones where you could watch how they thought. You don't remember what they said, the details. It was 'What an elegant way to wrap around a problem!' PowerPoint takes that away. PowerPoint gives you the outcome, but it removes the process."

"What I miss is, when I used to lecture without PowerPoint, every now and then I'd get a cool idea," he went on. "I remember once it just hit me. I'm lecturing, and all of a sudden I go, 'God! "The Wizard of Oz"! The scene at the end of "The Wizard of Oz"!'" Nass, telling this story, was almost shouting. (The lecture, he later explained, was about definitions of "the human" applied to computers.) "I just went for it—twenty-five minutes. And to this day students who were in that class remember it. That couldn't happen now: 'Where the hell is the slide?'"

PowerPoint could lead us to believe that information is all there is. According to Nass, PowerPoint empowers the provider of simple content (and that was the task Bob Gaskins originally set for it), but it risks squeezing out the provider of process—that is to say, the rhetorician, the storyteller, the poet, the person whose thoughts cannot be arranged in the shape of an AutoContent slide. "I hate to admit this," Nass said, "but I actually removed a book from my syllabus last year because I couldn't figure out how to PowerPoint it. It's a lovely book called 'Interface Culture,' by Steven Johnson, but it's very discursive; the charm of it is the throwaways. When I read this book, I thought, "My head's filled with ideas, and now I've got to write out exactly what those ideas are, and—they're not neat." He couldn't get the book into bullet points; every time he put something down, he realized that it wasn't quite right. Eventually, he abandoned the attempt, and, instead of a lecture, he gave his students a recommendation. He told them it was a good book, urged them to read it, and moved on to the next bullet point.

Chapter 2 ■ Absolute PowerPoint

1. Throughout his article, Parker is critical of the way PowerPoint has provided so many pre-formatted presentations through the AutoContent Wizard. Why have business people found this a useful feature of the program? And why does this trouble Parker? What larger problem does he see growing out of PowerPoint's cultural hegemony? And are people in the business world more or less likely to agree with him over time?

2. Do you find Parker's critique of the AutoContent Wizard persuasive? Is it likely to affect the way you use PowerPoint yourself? If yes, how so? For example, are you now more or less likely to use the Screen Beans cartoon characters?

3. Parker's history of PowerPoint can be read as a history of "paradigm formation" (or "paradigm shift") within organizational culture. What drove that shift? What part did technology play in the change? What factors had to come together to make PowerPoint possible? How can it serve as a model for developing other successful products?

4. Parker is especially critical of the culture of active presentation and passive reception that PowerPoint breeds, in his view. Why is this a problem, for example, in a college course? Why should it trouble us, according to Parker, that people seem to deliver and attend more "presentations" than "conversations"? What is the difference between the two, and why is it important to Parker? Do you agree with the assumptions about the way the world should be that his distinction suggests?

5. The experiment involving the high-school student "Andrew" as the subject of a presentation seems an especially interesting example in Parker's article. What conclusions are we expected to draw from this example? How might this example affect the way you watch other students' presentations in this course?

The Résumé
and Cover Letter

Chapter

The Assignment

Prepare a résumé and cover letter in response to a specific, published job posting or advertisement. I recommend you use a posting in a newspaper or on the Internet so that you can offer a print copy. You must bring in a copy of the job listing for peer revision day and hand it in with your final assignment.

Unless your instructor chooses to set forth more specific guidelines, here is the assignment:

- Each document must be one page only (unless your instructor indicates otherwise).

- You must turn in the job announcement with your assignment or it is incomplete.

- These documents should be prepared according to standards discussed in class.

- They should be proofread closely so that there are no errors in either document.

- The assignment and any drafts discussed in class must be turned in according to the schedule set by your instructor. If you fail to turn in the assignment on time or if you fail to have a sufficient draft for peer revision, it will affect your grade for the assignment.

Students must bring the job advertisement on the day of peer revision, since without it peers and instructors cannot judge audience expectations. The résumé should be ordered in a way that best responds to the potential employer's needs, and the cover letter should offer significant details distinguishing the candidate and highlighting aspects of the résumé in a way that clearly responds to those needs. The cover letter should offer a high level of detail and should interpret the résumé for the potential employer.

I am always surprised by the level of error on the résumé, which ought to have absolutely no errors of syntax, grammar, consistency, or sense. Errors in consistency (in spacing, parallel form, layout, and capitalization) are especially prevalent. General sloppiness or failure to adhere to accepted principles (such as using active verbs) will definitely factor into your grade.

Sample Résumés and Cover Letters

The following comments and questions will help you think about the sample résumés and cover letters.

Joel Anderson

Job Advertisement:

INTERNSHIP OPPORTUNITY: Northwestern Mutual Financial Network is looking for interns to work in our Trust Services division. A working knowledge of GAAP and IFRS required. Personal finance experience preferred. Individuals who work well with peers and have leadership potential are encouraged to apply.

After meeting Sara Creighton at a career fair, Joel Anderson submitted this cover letter and résumé. Notice how Joel followed recommended guidelines in organizing his cover letter. The introductory paragraph identifies the position sought and forecasts the letter's content. The second paragraph discusses Joel's qualifications for the internship position. The final paragraph requests an interview and states Joel's phone number and e-mail address. Likewise, Joel's résumé is clearly organized and balanced in format.

However, upon closer examination, we see the substance of Joel's letter and résumé require revision. How might Joel better tailor his letter to his audience? How could Joel more accurately forecast the key points of his letter in the introductory paragraph? How could he be more specific when describing the skills he has developed? Where would transitions help to better show the logic between his ideas? What unnecessary words could Joel eliminate? Which skills do you confidently believe Joel has? Why? How might the concluding paragraph more politely and confidently request an interview? What revisions would you suggest to improve Joel's résumé to make it clearer and more specific? Remember that details lead the reader to conclude that the writer is a terrific job candidate; telling the reader "I am terrific" is unconvincing.

How could the central paragraph of the letter be made more coherent, so that it is not merely additive ("In addition," "Also," "And") but instead makes a coherent statement about what the candidate offers?

Joan Parker

Job Advertisement:

INDUSTRIAL ENGINEER INTERNSHIP: Seeking high-achieving engineering majors to work as summer interns for credit only. Gain valuable hands-on experience at a busy engineering firm. Strong clerical skills and knowledge of design software required.

Joan's experience seems appropriate to the internship. But has Joan's letter emphasized her most relevant experience? What could the writer have done to be more specific in the letter? What abilities is the employer most likely looking for in a job candidate? How might Joan better tailor her letter to highlight these abilities? How could the résumé be improved?

Joan's letter is so general that it could apply to anyone. How can the writer use evidence from the résumé to offer specific details about her abilities? Looking at the résumé, what major problems do you see? What parts of the résumé deserve more emphasis and which deserve less? What part ought to be fleshed out to emphasize her experience with real-world projects even in the classroom?

Lynn Cato

Job Advertisement:

VETERINARY ASSISTANT: Part-time, flexible hours. Must be reliable, self-motivated, people and animal friendly. Good experience for pre-vet students. Call us at 732-555-1234.

Lynn has the benefit of varied experience in the area of animal handling. She runs the risk, therefore, of simply listing her many credentials and missing out on the opportunity to present herself—her motivations and concerns. However, she does a fairly good job responding to items in the job description and presenting her enthusiastic and caring personality. Notice the third paragraph, where she describes her reaction to a problem she saw in the waiting room. Although she does not mention the term "self-motivation," she gives an example of that term in action when she talks about the seminars she developed to teach children about animal care. What better information could she have listed as a bullet under her work for Dr. Morris, rather than the obvious "updated pet records"? One would assume any veterinary receptionist would have to do that.

Gregory Benjamin

Job Advertisement:

FIELD SUPERVISOR: 2–3 years experience with roofing and remodeling required. Ability to speak Spanish a plus. Send résumé and references to: Robbyns' Restoration and Roofing, 197 Essex Street, Hillside, DC 98888. EOE.

Gregory does a nice job balancing his construction experience with his academic experience in his cover letter. Although he has only worked for one company, he stresses his varied work experience and ties it in nicely with his Public Health major. He forestalls any concerns that the owner of Robbyns' Restoration and Roofing might have about his being able to handle both school and work by showing that he has already been doing that very well, and gaining valuable time management skills. He even emphasizes that his organizational skills will help the company stay on schedule and improve customer relations. He presents himself as a superior candidate; that might seem brash, but the details he provides back up his claim. What do you think about the tone of the letter? How might his confidence appeal to or annoy his potential employer? When would this tone be appropriate, and when might it backfire?

Steven S. Adamo

Job Advertisement:

SYSTEMS ENGINEER: We are seeking a diligent and energetic person to develop models to improve manufacturing health-related products. Experience in health technologies and working knowledge of relevant computer software is required. In addition, we are looking for someone with a familiarity with team development and management.

Steven's résumé and cover letter show how a student can tailor coursework to meet an employer's needs. What abilities can we assume the employer is looking for in a job candidate? How does Steven present his coursework as work experience? How might Steven express himself more concisely? In the third paragraph, how do the skills Steven describes give further evidence that he is a good worker? How might Steven shift this paragraph from "telling" the reader he is a problem solver to "showing" the reader he is a problem solver?

Candice Common

Job Advertisement:

MANAGER OF COSMETIC LINE: We are looking for a motivated individual to promote our new line of cosmetic products. Qualified individuals will have a significant amount of experience in sales and/or marketing of beauty products. Evidence of successful implementation of innovative business practices is required.

Notice how Candice's cover letter effectively expands on her résumé, describing key details of her employment history. How does Candice frame these details around a potential employer's interests in the second and third paragraphs? For example, why might an employer be especially interested in the "strong clientele" Candice can build? How does Candice preview these key ideas in her introduction? What transitional phases show the logic between Candice's ideas? Examine how Candice uses these phrases to link the chronology of her employment history and to link her cosmetic abilities to her business skills. What do you think about the letter's tone? Are you convinced that Candice has the abilities she lists in her cover letter and résumé? Why?

Sample Résumés and Cover Letters

11111 RPO Way
New Brunswick, NJ 08901

July 21, 2009

Ms. Sara Creighton
Financial Representative
Northwestern Mutual
New Brunswick, NJ 08901

Dear Sara Creighton,

After briefly speaking with you at the Rutgers Career Fair, I am now interested in an intern position at Northwestern Mutual following the spring semester of 2009. I have carefully read through the information packets that you have given to me, and I think I have the skills that your firm seeks.

Employment as a customer service representative for a commercial bank has allowed me to learn the importance of being a team player. In addition, I've worked at Bloomburg where I had the opportunity to work within a large company doing projects for four different departments. Also, these projects strengthened my computer skills with Microsoft Word, Access, and Excel. And I'd like to add that various times throughout this internship I went beyond what was expected in my duties in order to make sure that projects would succeed.

I am seeking a position that would offer challenge and continued growth opportunity. My passion for doing the job right and taking on responsibilities and challenges make me a strong candidate for this position. I would also strive to make lasting improvements and to work in whatever capacity necessary to succeed. You can contact me at 555-555-5555 and at JLA99@eden.rutgers.edu.

Sincerely,

Joel Anderson

Joel Anderson

Enclosure

JOEL ANDERSON
JLA99@eden.rutgers.edu

CAMPUS ADDRESS
Rutgers University
11111 RPO Way
New Brunswick, NJ 08901
(732) 111-1111

PERMANENT ADDRESS
41 Allen Court
Ramsey, NJ 07013
(201) 111-1111

EDUCATION:

Rutgers University, New Brunswick, NJ
B.A. Marketing, May 2010
G.P.A.: 3.7

EXPERIENCE:

USAA Bank, Ramsey, NJ   *July 2006–Present*
Customer Service Representative
- Participate in weekly meetings.
- Process various financial transactions for customers.
- Resolve customer inquiries and questions about their accounts using CRT System.
- Collect data to create reports in Access and Excel.
- Assist the bank's personal banking representatives and investment specialist to increase sales and profit by promoting the bank's products and services.
- Recognized formally with two appreciation awards.

Bloomburg, New York, NY   *June–August 2005*
Summer Intern
- Provided weekly reports via Access and imported to Excel.
- Presented ways of improving website to managers and implemented those changes by working with other employees and using HTML.
- Researched E-commerce companies on the Internet.

Outback Steakhouse, Edgewater, NJ   *May 2004–Aug. 2004*
Waiter
- Developed good working habits in a fast-paced environment.
- Responsibilities included: making sure weekly schedules were fair and organized, looking after the upkeep of the floor, hosting.

SKILLS:

Microsoft Windows, Microsoft Office, Internet Explorer, HTML
Strong interpersonal skills, superior oral and written communication skills, excellent work ethic.

122 George Street
New Brunswick, NJ 08901

February 4, 2009

Mr. James Barra
Air Cruisers
PO Box 180
Belmar, NJ 07719

Dear Mr. Barra,

I am very interested in working as an Industrial Engineer for your company this summer. I learned of the position from the Internship Guide provided by the Career Services at Rutgers University.

I will be completing my third year as an Industrial Engineering student at Rutgers. I have taken and excelled at manufacturing, work design, and other courses that relate directly to this position and which included real world experience with design projects performed for area businesses. These projects have provided me with knowledge and experience in the practical applications of engineering. I would like to use this knowledge and experience to benefit your company.

I have enclosed a copy of my résumé which further describes my educational background as well as my work experience. I look forward to hearing from you soon. Thank you for your time and consideration.

Sincerely,

Joan Parker

Joan Parker

Joan Parker

CAMPUS ADDRESS
Rutgers University
11111 BPO Way
New Brunswick, NJ 08901
(732) 777-1111

PERMANENT ADDRESS
419 College Avenue
Pittsburgh, PA 88888
(814) 111-1111

EDUCATION:

Rutgers University, College of Engineering. New Brunswick, NJ
B.S. Industrial Engineering, expected May 2010
G.P.A.: 3.29

HONORS:

Dean's List, Fall 2007, Spring 2008 through Fall 2009
Edward Bloustein Distinguished Scholar
Member, Alpha Pi Mu, Industrial Engineering Honor Society

RELEVANT COURSEWORK:

Work Design and Ergonomics—*Fabric Co. Consulting Project,*
Deterministic Models in Operations Research—*Optimization Project,* Manufacturing Processes—*Salt Shaker Design Project,*
Engineering Probability—*Bakery Consulting Project,* Design
of Mechanical Components—*Duplexer Device Design Project,* Accounting
for Engineers, Intermediate Statistical Analysis

EXPERIENCE:

Byers Engineering Co., Somerset, NJ, July 2008–Present
Administrative Assistant
• Aided in the operation of an engineering office.

Six Flags Great Adventure, Jackson, NJ, Summers 2006–2008
Security Officer
• Screened incoming park guests.
• Responsible for the handling and logging in of confiscated materials.
• Maintained appropriate safety and security conditions.
• Trained new officers.

Express, East Brunswick, NJ, June 2006–October 2007
Retail Salesperson
• Provided customer service.
• Assisted with merchandise displays.
• Trained new employees.

COMPUTER SKILLS:

| BASIC | C | SIMON | Word |
| FORTRAN | LINDO | Excel | Symphony |

ACTIVITIES:

Member, Society of Women Engineers.

Campus P. O. Box 867
Forrest Glen, DC 88888

April 20, 2009

Dr. Gilbert Sullivan
Companion Animal Hospital
824 Poplar Street
Hillside, DC 98888

Dear Dr. Sullivan:

I would like to be considered for the position of veterinary assistant. I learned of this opportunity from your advertisement in the *Halcyon Press* of April 19, 2009. I am currently a third year pre-veterinary major attending Halcyon University, and I would love to take advantage of the wonderful learning experience working at your hospital would bring. I feel that I could contribute to your practice and relate to your patients in a caring and professional way.

I have previously worked with veterinarians for both small and large animals at school and during the summers. I have learned valuable customer relations skills in dealing with pet owners at veterinary clinics, and also at the kennel where I work to provide people with calm, well-behaved dogs. Currently, I am enrolled in a class that allows the students to do tests on a group of twelve foals in addition to training them. I have taken blood from these foals for glucose tolerance tests and assisted in ultra-sounding them for body fat. Along with my work with Drs. Morris and Bell, I have also visited the Pennsylvania Equine Center and spent the day with one of their vets, Dr. Josiah Brennan. I assisted in a castration and helped him with the various patients he had that day. In the past few years I have worked with a wide variety of animals including horses, dairy cows, dogs, cats, and sheep. Simply, I enjoy helping all animals in any way I can.

At the last veterinary clinic where I worked, I noticed that the children in the waiting room often did not know how to behave around other people's pets—or even their own! With the support of Dr. Morris, I developed a series of seminars to train children of pet owners how to care for and be affectionate with their animal companions. I also taught them how to behave around a strange animal. These seminars were well-received by the children, their parents, and the clinic staff. I am enclosing a copy of my résumé, which provides more information about my motivation and my ability to work well with people and their animal friends. I can be reached at 888-009-4573 or at lynncato@cl.com. I look forward to hearing from you. Thank you for your time and consideration.

Sincerely,

Lynn H. Cato

Lynn H. Cato

Lynn H. Cato
lynncato@cl.com

Present		**Permanent**
Halcyon University		298 S. 18th Ave.
Campus PO Box 867		Catesville, PA 10324
Forrest Glen, DC 88888		(764)-000-9087
(888) 009-4573		

EDUCATION   Halcyon University, Forrest Glen, DC
Pre-Veterinary Major, Equine Science Minor,
Expected date of graduation: May 2010. GPA: 3.2

HONORS   Halcyon Distinguished Scholar, 2008, 2009

RELEVANT COURSES   Animal Science, Animal Nutrition, Animal Reproduction, Dairy Cow &
Horse Handling, Horse Management, Animal Problems

EXPERIENCE   **Kennel Manager/Dog Trainer, Summer 2008–Present**
Noah's Ark, Brattington, VA
• Responsible for care and exercising of all boarded dogs
• Ran dog obedience classes
• Aided visiting veterinarians and groomers

Volunteer/Assistant, Summer 2007
Dr. Maria Bell, Equine Veterinarian, Owens, VA
• Performed flex tests on horses to check for lameness
• Assisted in ultrasounding mares to check for pregnancy

Barn Manager/Horse Trainer, Summer 2006
Turnaround Farm, Catesville, PA
• Responsible for feeding and exercising of about forty horses
• Trained various horses for hunter/jumper competitions
• Taught beginner lessons
• Assisted visiting veterinarians and farriers
• Groomed at various horse events and shows
• Helped customers find an appropriate mount

Veterinary Assistant/Receptionist, 2005–2006
Dr. Bernard A. Morris, Catesville, PA
• Assisted during small animal surgeries
• Responsible for feeding and bathing dogs and cats
• Wrote letters to clients and updated pet records

SKILLS   Microsoft Word, Microsoft Excel, Access, Internet

ACTIVITIES   **Halcyon Student Safety-Mounted Patrol, Fall 2008–Present**
• Patrol campus on horses and report problems to police

Member, Animal Science Club, Fall 2008–Present

Member, Catesville Equestrian Team, 2004–2008

Halcyon University
Campus P. O. Box 984
Forrest Glen, DC 88888
February 5, 2009

Mr. Howard Robbyns
Robbyns' Restoration and Roofing Co.
197 Essex Street
Hillside, DC 98888

Dear Mr. Robbyns:

I am writing to express my interest in the position of field supervisor for your company. I learned of the opening from the February 4, 2009, *Washington Post* classifieds and feel that I am a superior candidate for this job. I can offer you my knowledge of onsite safety and my hand-on experience in construction, as well as my ability to work well with a variety of people.

For several years I have been a supervisor for Herb Chundley Construction, a company handling the remodeling and renovations of homes and modular units. I have worked on several large projects as well as smaller scaled jobs and have dealt with the completion of several projects at the same time. The leadership qualities I have learned over the years will be invaluable in a supervisory position. Both on the job and as a member of Labor Union #934, I have learned how to deal with a diverse group of people at many levels: labor, management, and customer. In addition to having a working knowledge of Spanish, I am fluent in Polish. Most of the projects I have worked on involved either remodeling or installing and repairing different kinds of roofing, both shingle and tar. Being quite familiar with the tools and machinery needed for tasks at hand, I will be able to inform and assist workers with any difficulties they may encounter.

My on the job experiences have led me to a firm commitment to providing a safe working environment, something which my coursework in Public Health and Environmental Science at Halcyon University has reinforced. My experience and training will aid in the prevention of job-site accidents. In order to work fulltime and take a fulltime courseload, I have had to develop my organizational and scheduling skills, something which will further help me complete all site-work on time. As I have learned, staying close to or ahead of schedule is one of the best ways we can promote customer satisfaction and increase repeat business.

I have enclosed a copy of my résumé that shows my work and academic experience. Please contact me at handygreg@cl.com to set up an interview. Larry Anthony of Local # 934 (888-541-5893) and Herb Chundley (888-541-7032) have offered to provide references for me. Feel free to call them. I look forward to hearing from you.

Sincerely,

Gregory J. Benjamin

Gregory J. Benjamin

GREGORY J. BENJAMIN

handygreg@cl.com | (888) 009-4708

Halcyon University, Campus P. O. Box 983, Forrest Glen, DC 88888

OBJECTIVE: Seeking a supervisory position in the field of construction with emphasis on roofing and exterior remodeling.

ABILITIES:

- Skilled at organizing projects and estimating time of completion.
- Speak Spanish and Polish.
- Knowledge of all types of excavation and remodeling techniques.
- Experience in organizing productive crews for job sites.
- Skill with all types of saws and tools needed for repair and remodeling.
- Proficient knowledge of Microsoft Excel and Microsoft Access.
- Experience in customer relations.
- Certified in CPR and Lifesaving since 2006.

EXPERIENCE: **Member of Labor Union #934, District of Columbia**

Herb Chundley Construction: *Fall 2008–Present*

- Remodeled homes and modular units, including the interior, exterior, and roofing.
- Organized separate projects according to time, amount of labor, and cost of materials and labor.
- Developed time-saving techniques in a safe working environment.
- Organized extremely large project including the renovation of five multifamily homes.
- Organized large projects at multiple mobile home complexes.
- Supervisor of several large projects dealing with roofing and siding on several different style homes and other types of buildings.

EDUCATION: **Halcyon University, Forrest Glen, DC**   *Fall 2007–Present*

Public Health Major. GPA: 3.5 Major GPA: 3.92

- Courses in Environmental Science and Public Health
- Courses dealing with environmental hazards and precautions and also public safety and awareness.
- Attended several work safety seminars including jobsites located at DC Civic Center, Capitol Hill Complex, and Metro Recycling.

21 Cedarville Ave.
Piscataway, NJ 08940

May 7, 2009

Newton Manufacturing, Inc.
178 Technology Plaza
Fairfield, NJ 65746

Dear Director of Human Resources:

A posting in *The Star Ledger* on March 3, 2009 attracted my attention. I saw that your company desires to hire a systems engineer to develop models for more efficient manufacturing of products for the health industry. I believe my education and work experiences make me a strong candidate for the position, and I hope you will concur.

Later this month I will graduate from Rutgers University, School of Engineering with a B.S. degree in Industrial and Systems Engineering. During my four years at Rutgers, I have completed the full range of courses needed to begin a career. For your needs, two courses have special relevance. Production Control was a course where I learned that perfection is essential when the manufactured product is intended to remedy life-threatening illnesses. Simulation Modeling was another course of significant importance. In that class and lab, we developed prototypes to prepare for actual manufacturing.

In conjunction with my course work, I have been working part-time for Audio Hearing Instruments for the past two years. The tasks I have been responsible for have given me practical experience in solving problems relating to worker efficiency and attention to details.

I hope this letter and the attached résumé persuade you that I am a strong candidate for the systems engineer position. An opportunity to meet with you for an interview for the position would be greatly appreciated. You can contact me by phone at (732) 555-1234 or by email: sadam@eden.rutgers.edu. Thank you for you consideration.

Sincerely,

Steven S. Adamo

Steven S. Adamo

Steven S. Adamo
21 Cedarville Ave.
Piscataway, NJ 08940
(732) 555–1234
sadam@eden.rutgers.edu

Objective	To obtain an entry-level position requiring strong analytical and organizational skills in a manufacturing engineering environment.
Education	*Rutgers University, School of Engineering* B.S., Industrial and Systems Engineering, May 2009 GPA 3.65

Relevant Coursework

Manufacturing Processes	Production Control
Design of Engineering Systems	Manufacturing Facility Layout
Engineering Probability	Computer Controlled Manufacturing
Simulation Modeling	Quality Control/Design of Experiments

Computer Skills

Software:	Microsoft Word, Excel, Access, PowerPoint Micrografx, Stat-grahix, Arena/SIMAN, TK Solver
Languages:	Fortran, C++

Experience

Dec. 2007 to Present

Audio Hearing Instruments, Manufacturing Support Group, Manville, NJ
Industrial and Systems Engineer Intern
• Perform time studies for floor-plan design and assembly line layouts
• Designed fixture/tools for process improvement
• Manage process database
• Provide support to international facilities

Sept. 2006 to Dec. 2006

International Rope Connector
Senior Project
• Group leader of four person engineering team
• Design/constructed/tested universal connector
• Determined facility layout and process for mass production

May 2005 to Sept. 2006

Williams Lumber Company, Sussex, NJ
Truck Driver
• Delivered lumber and other building supplies to construction sites
• Developed communication skills

Awards and Affiliations

N.J. Science Scholar Award 2007
School of Engineering Scholar 2006
Association of Industrial Engineers

123 Castlepoint Terrace
Hoboken, NJ 07030

March 19, 2009

P.O. Box 221
New York, New York 10002

Re: Job ID#23344

To whom it may concern,

I saw your ad at *Monster.com*, and I noticed that you are requiring a responsible yet out-going individual to oversee your new cosmetic line in New York. Launching a new line requires an individual who is capable of dealing with the multiple responsibilities, such as make-up artistry, a willingness to learn new information, mathematical knowledge for placing orders and budgeting, managerial experience, sales experience, and sociability to help build the client base. I feel that I have the skills and experience that will be required of launching your line in New York.

Currently the counter manager for "Poppy," a budding Australian cosmetics line at Barneys, I have seen the initial difficulties that can come with launching an international cosmetic line, but I also know of the great satisfaction that eventually comes with overseeing the rise of success. With "Poppy" I have not only built a strong clientele for the line by proving my abilities with the customers, but also with being personable. I am not only their make-up artist providing a service but also a friend. Having worked with cosmetics for a year and a half-now, I have gone from being a novice to an expert in the field—from working as a sales person, to working on movie sets, photo shoots and weddings. As in my résumé, my mathematical skills were also put to the test with the two inventories I had to execute, as well as maintain an accurate stock book. I also assisted with the launch of another new cosmetics line at Barneys—"Cargo." As their resident make-up artist, I coupled my enthusiasm with my artistic ability to boost sales by 45%, as well as create a niche for a once unknown cosmetic line in New York.

My skills in cosmetics as well as business are a unique combination that would prove useful in launching and overseeing your line in New York. I would like to have the opportunity of interviewing in person, so that I may show you a photo-portfolio of my work. I will contact you tomorrow to set up a date at your convenience. Thank you for your time and consideration.

Sincerely,

Candice Common

Candice Common

Objective	Seeking a fulfilling account executive position for a budding cosmetic company.
Experience	*February 2007–Current* <u>Poppy Cosmetics Inc.</u> New York, NY Poppy Counter Manager • Maintained a cosmetic counter at Barneys NY. • Acted as a liaison between store buyers and cosmetic vendors. • Established a strong niche for the new line by building a strong clientele list. • Produced special events to promote sales and knowledge of the line throughout the department as well as with clients. • Organized, prepared and executed the last two inventories. • Responsible for a 30% increase in projected sales through makeovers. *October 2004–February 2007* <u>Cargo Cosmetics Inc.</u> New York, NY Resident Make-up Artist • Responsible for the professional application of make-up for all of Cargo's clientele at Barneys NY. • Increased sales by over 45%. • Built an extensive clientele list. *July 2002–October 2004* <u>Estee Lauder</u> Seattle, WA Sales Associate • Consistently ranked first as part of the sales staff at Nordstrom's. • Assisted in cosmetic training and promotions throughout the department. • Worked well in a team atmosphere. *March 2002–May 2002* <u>Warranty and Financial Products Inc.</u> Seattle, WA Customer Satisfaction and Verification Officer • Maintained customer satisfaction for this budding corporation. • Ensured quality content of all sales from the sales staff through verification and data entry of customer information. • Assisted in the training of 15 new individuals weekly.
Education	*Fall 2006–Present* <u>Rutgers University</u> *New Brunswick, NJ* • Currently a pre-business majors. *Fall 2005–Spring 2005* <u>Southern Methodist University</u> Dallas, TX

Chapter 3 ■ Peer Review: Résumé and Cover Letter

Please fill out the following form for your partner. Feel free to write comments on the drafts as well.

Does the cover letter . . .
1. directly address the employer?   _____ yes _____no
2. respond to a specific, published job posting?   _____ yes _____no
3. explain why the job candidate is best suited to **this job?**   _____ yes _____no
4. include a high level of detail concerning the strengths
   of the job candidate?   _____ yes _____no
5. appear in full block form and include all six elements
   (return address, date, recipient's address, salutation, body, closing)?   _____ yes _____no

Is the cover letter . . .
1. signed?   _____yes _____no
2. free of all grammatical and typographical errors?   _____yes _____no
3. no more than one page in length, in 12 point
   Times New Roman font with one-inch margins?   _____yes _____no

Does the résumé . . .
1. catch the attention of the reader?   ✓ yes _____no
2. include specific, active language?   ✓ yes _____no
3. list and describe relevant work and/or academic experience?
   list and describe relevant extracurricular   _____yes ✗ no
4. interests and/or activities?   ✓ yes _____no
5. provide appropriate contact information?   ✓ yes _____no

Is the résumé . . .
1. visually appealing and appropriately formatted?   ✓ yes _____no
2. free of all grammatical and typographical errors?   ✓ yes _____no
3. no more than one page in length, in a professional font
   size and style?   _____yes ✗ no

What parts of the drafts did you like the most?
The bordering for sections

What parts of the drafts need the most improvement?
2 pages

Additional Comments/Suggestions:
Calm down champ. you can't do everything

Chapter 3 ■ Peer Review: Résumé and Cover Letter

Please fill out the following form for your partner. Feel free to write comments on the drafts as well.

Does the cover letter . . .
1. directly address the employer?   _____ yes _____no
2. respond to a specific, published job posting?   _____ yes _____no
3. explain why the job candidate is best suited to **this job?**   _____ yes _____no
4. include a high level of detail concerning the strengths
   of the job candidate?   _____ yes _____no
5. appear in full block form and include all six elements
   (return address, date, recipient's address, salutation, body, closing)? _____ yes _____no

Is the cover letter . . .
1. signed?   _____yes _____no
2. free of all grammatical and typographical errors?   _____yes _____no
3. no more than one page in length, in 12 point
   Times New Roman font with one-inch margins?   _____yes _____no

Does the résumé . . .
1. catch the attention of the reader?   _____yes _____no
2. include specific, active language?   _____yes _____no
3. list and describe relevant work and/or academic experience?
   list and describe relevant extracurricular   _____yes _____no
4. interests and/or activities?   _____yes _____no
5. provide appropriate contact information?   _____yes _____no

Is the résumé . . .
1. visually appealing and appropriately formatted?   _____yes _____no
2. free of all grammatical and typographical errors?   _____yes _____no
3. no more than one page in length, in a professional font
   size and style?   _____yes _____no

What parts of the drafts did you like the most?

What parts of the drafts need the most improvement?

Additional Comments/Suggestions:

Chapter 3 ■ Peer Review: Résumé and Cover Letter

Please fill out the following form for your partner. Feel free to write comments on the drafts as well.

Does the cover letter . . .
1. directly address the employer?   _____ yes _____no
2. respond to a specific, published job posting?   _____ yes _____no
3. explain why the job candidate is best suited to **this job?**   _____ yes _____no
4. include a high level of detail concerning the strengths
   of the job candidate?   _____ yes _____no
5. appear in full block form and include all six elements
   (return address, date, recipient's address, salutation, body, closing)?   _____ yes _____no

Is the cover letter . . .
1. signed?   _____yes _____no
2. free of all grammatical and typographical errors?   _____yes _____no
3. no more than one page in length, in 12 point
   Times New Roman font with one-inch margins?   _____yes _____no

Does the résumé . . .
1. catch the attention of the reader?   _____yes _____no
2. include specific, active language?   _____yes _____no
3. list and describe relevant work and/or academic experience?
   list and describe relevant extracurricular   _____yes _____no
4. interests and/or activities?   _____yes _____no
5. provide appropriate contact information?   _____yes _____no

Is the résumé . . .
1. visually appealing and appropriately formatted?   _____yes _____no
2. free of all grammatical and typographical errors?   _____yes _____no
3. no more than one page in length, in a professional font
   size and style?   _____yes _____no

What parts of the drafts did you like the most?

What parts of the drafts need the most improvement?

Additional Comments/Suggestions:

Researching Your Topic

Chapter

Research work is like any other work students encounter: a little basic knowledge makes the process more efficient. There are basically five things students need to know to be successful doing research for this course:

- When to use **primary** and **secondary** sources.
- How to judge among **scholarly**, **professional**, and **popular** publications.
- How to research **patrons**, **problems**, and **paradigms**.
- How to find **books**, **journal articles**, and other library resources.
- The proper way to cite sources according to **MLA style**.

These five aspects of research are covered in the paragraphs that follow.

Primary and Secondary Sources

How will you show that your topic is important and needs to be addressed? It will not be enough to rely on an emotional appeal or to expect people to take you at your word. Research will be required to demonstrate the nature and extent of the problem in a logical way. Your instructor may require primary research as well as secondary research, but knowing how and when to use them is important.

Primary Research

Primary research, sometimes called fieldwork, is data that you personally collect about the topic. Experiments, surveys, questionnaires, direct observations with note keeping, and interviews are typical examples of primary research. Data you collect in experiments, observations, and surveys can be presented in charts or graphs to quantify the problem. Questionnaires and interviews can be helpful when opinions are important.

Secondary Research

Even if you do collect your own research, you will need other research to interpret your data for others. That is why it is necessary to look at published sources. Secondary research is the term used to describe the search for published information, which you must take at secondhand. The value of secondary sources depends a lot on their credibility.

For your proposal, you might do both primary and secondary research to introduce the problem, but you must do secondary research for the literature review (or paradigm) that helps interpret the problem and explain your solution. Each proposal stands or falls on the quality of its research, and all need a solid foundation of published and authoritative research to support their claims. Without published sources you will be very hard pressed to develop a justification for your plan of action.

Scholarly, Professional, and Popular: Evaluating Secondary Sources

If there is one thing that students should learn in college, it is that not all information is equally valid or credible. When evaluating sources, students need to keep in mind the types of sources they are, since that will greatly affect the power they have to persuade the reader. Three terms are key: scholarly, professional, and popular.

Scholarly Sources

Scholarly sources are articles and research studies published in peer-reviewed journals or books. They show what scholars in a particular discipline are thinking about topics based on their research. In the scholarly journals, you will see that discussions reference accepted concepts and models. These readings can be difficult because the contributors to these journals use specialized vocabulary that someone outside of or fairly new to the discipline may not quickly comprehend. Realizing that these sources are the strongest authorities you will have for your proposal should help you persevere even when the reading is challenging. Scholarly sources are found in college and university libraries. Many journals are now in electronic form and accessible on the Web, but many are still only in print form. When you access the Rutgers Libraries, you will see whether articles you need can be downloaded or whether you need to go to the library and photocopy or take notes on the information.

Professional Sources

Newsletters, journals, magazines, and websites that are used by the practitioners of a given profession or discipline are known as professional sources. They include up-to-date information about existing and new products, business applications, and commonplaces of the profession. You might find articles there about successful companies or methods written by respected people working in that field. These sources have some authority and can be excellent places to look for models of success. But because the writers of these publications often do not do research themselves and because they often do not take a critical perspective on their specialty or on companies in their industry (where these writers might be employed), professional sources are not considered quite as authoritative as scholarly sources. These publications can often be found in the Rutgers Libraries or through Internet sources.

Popular Sources

Newspapers, magazines, and websites that are readily available to the public and written to a broad audience are generally called popular sources. While they are the easiest sources to find, they have the least value when authority is being established for a proposal that requests funding. Popular sources can, however, supplement the scholarly and professional sources and show how your topic is of general social interest. Many Internet sources would fall under the category of popular.

Based on this brief discussion of the three types of sources, you can see that often the more easily obtained the information is, the less authority it has. The most authoritative sources are generally written for a specialized audience. Recognize the category of the sources you use so you can judge how well they bolster your own authority. Each proposal stands or falls on the quality of its research, and all need a solid foundation of published and authoritative studies, theoretical works, and other documents.

Researching the Patron, Problem, and Paradigm

Often when students begin their research, they see their job as finding out as much as they can about the problem that they want to address. While this can be a good way to start your research, you need to recognize that finding information about the problem is only part of your task. You will also have to do research on funding sources (the patron) and ways of solving the problem (the paradigm). Each part of the project will require different types of research.

Patron

How will you find a funding source? And how will you pitch your project to them? You will have to do research to find the best patron for your project and to learn more about what interests them. Often this research is not directly cited in your paper, but it is among the most important in making your paper realistic.

Even if the organization that will be funding your project is the company you currently work for or the school you attend, you will still want to do some research to find out how your project fits with their mission and values. Look at your company website. Look at what is online about your school or about the specific department in your school you are going to ask for funding. How can you connect your project with the issues and problems that concern them?

If there are no local sources of funding for your project, you will need to do some research to see what organizations (including government agencies, private philanthropies, and corporations) share your interests. Here are three good methods for getting started finding a funding source:

Method 1: Go to the Library

The Rutgers Libraries has a wealth of print sources that can help you find funding. These sources are often more complete than sources you find on the Web, though they might not be as current or quick to browse. Ask the reference librarians for help getting started.

Method 2: Check Out Online Clearinghouses

There are a number of grant clearinghouse websites, where you can quickly access many groups that provide funding for projects. Some good websites to start your search for funding include the following:

The Foundation Center
http://foundationcenter.org/ and http://foundationcenter.org/findfunders/
This is the best clearinghouse for charity and private philanthropy information.

Catalogue of Federal Domestic Assistance
http://www.cfda.gov/
The official government clearinghouse for all sorts of funds.

Grants.gov
http://www.grants.gov/
A clearinghouse for different granting agencies of the U.S. government.

Community of Science
http://www.cos.com/
A clearinghouse for science-related projects.

National Science Foundation
http://www.nsf.gov/funding/
The NSF sponsors theoretical research in the sciences.

Environmental Protection Agency
http://www.epa.gov/epahome/grants.htm
The EPA sponsors environmental projects.

National Institutes of Health
http://grants1.nih.gov/grants/oer.htm
The NIH sponsors health and health education grants.

U.S. Department of Education
http://www.ed.gov/fund/landing.jhtml

Method 3: Browse the Web

Since most organizations who might fund your project probably have a website or are listed on the Web, a search engine, such as *Google,* is not a bad initial search tool. Try entering your keywords for your topic, perhaps along with the words "grants" or "funding," and you should at least get some hints about who is interested in your subject area. This method involves a lot of trial and error, and you are better off starting with Method 1 and Method 2. However, when looking for some initial guidance, doing a general Web search should at least give you a better sense of your topic and who is interested in it.

Problem

How can you prove that there is a problem? And how can you emphasize its importance? To make a good case, you will have to do some research on your topic with the goal of finding numbers or of defining your problem well enough to understand its scope.

Before you begin your research on the problem, it's a good idea to think about the specific information that would be useful to your case. Some questions to consider:

- What are the most important numbers needed to convince your patron that this problem is important to address? How can you quantify its scope and scale?

- Can you conduct some of this research yourself, or use research that you have already done? Or will you need to rely on secondary sources of research?

- In order to quantify the problem, what are your best sources of documented evidence? What secondary sources might have information that can help your case?

- Which groups or organizations might have already studied the problem? And where might they publish their findings?

If you can get good numbers, you will be able to make especially powerful visual aids.

When You Can't Find the Numbers You Need

- *Keep trying.* Often, especially with online research, key information is hidden behind the keywords that you haven't tried. For instance, say you are writing a project on making a community service project mandatory at a local high school. You need to find information about teens and community service or volunteering. A search in *Statistical Universe* using the keywords "teens" and "community service" or "volunteerism" will get you nowhere. The perfect graph for your project can only be found under "surveys—opinions and attitudes, by age." Start early and be persistent. Don't do your research when you are pressed for time.

- *Try extrapolating.* Often it is possible to take percentages from national studies and use them to make educated guesses as to how many people will be affected by an issue on a local level. In order for this to work well, your local population must be entirely typical with the rest of the larger area. For instance, if you absolutely can't find rates of smoking for your town, you could use state or local averages and then work out the equation. If 30 percent of people in New Jersey smoke, one might assume that 30 percent of people in Paterson smoke. However, if your local area is different in some significant way from the larger population, you should not rely on extrapolation.

    A town populated by a significant number of young families cannot be compared to a town with several senior citizen retirement villages. If you are reduced to documenting your local problem by extrapolating from national statistics, you must be honest about it and clearly show how you have arrived at the figures you are using.

- *Fill in the gaps with primary research.* Sometimes a problem is so new or so local that there is not a large amount of hard data to draw from. In that case, you will have to do some surveys or other primary research. Make sure that your surveys are legitimate and convincing. Your sample size must be large enough and varied enough to be representative. The fact that twenty of your friends say they dislike Economics 101 is not good evidence that a university should drop the course. As you survey, keep track of what day and time you did the survey, how many people responded, how many of each gender, age, and so on, depending upon the subject of the survey. You should also ask your survey questions in such a way that they will generate good statistical responses. If you conduct your surveys well and present them carefully, they can enhance your credibility. For example, which of the following two statements seems most convincing and why?

    - Fifty percent of the people I surveyed disliked Economics 101.

    - Out of 1,000 students, 50% stated that they ranked Economics 101 (on a scale of 1–10, 1 being the lowest) at 3 or below.

- *Use uncertainty to your advantage.* Sometimes a lack of knowledge is the best evidence you have that a problem exists. Scientists use uncertainty all the time in order to show that more research must be done. If you are writing a research proposal, you should use the lack of statistical information as part of your documentation of the problem. Be sure to discuss the possible dangers or lack of opportunities that result from "not knowing." Perhaps a central part of your project could be to gather data.

Paradigm

How do you support your claim that your plan is the best way to address the problem? A paradigm gives you that support. You should think of it as the research-based rationale for your plan. It authorizes your claims about the problem and justifies your methods.

If you are doing a scientific research project in any given field, your paradigm will derive from previous research. That previous research offers you both examples of practice (what experimental methods did they use?) and a way of understanding the results (how did the experiment support the hypothesis based on previous theory?) Defining your paradigm outside of the hard sciences is not as straightforward, because there is usually not as strong a consensus as there is in the sciences about which methods and theories are best. However, you can still use the model of the sciences to guide you in researching support for your plan.

You need to think of paradigms as ideally having two parts, along the scientific model: a **theoretical frame** and **models of success**. A model of success is an example of how others have successfully addressed the problem in some other context. A theoretical frame is a language for explaining how a certain solution will work.

Searching for a Theoretical Frame

Let's say that you wanted to take on the problem of crime on campus. To find research to justify a plan of action, you would want to find a theoretical frame and search for models of success. Both parts of your paradigm must be developed through the use of scholarly research.

If you were studying sociology or law enforcement, it would be logical for you to take on the problem of campus crime since your previous studies had already prepared you for the issue. You might already have an idea, in fact, of what theoretical frames might relate to the issue. If you don't, then at least you would know where to look to find out. You could talk to professors. You could look in your textbooks (especially in their bibliographies). Ultimately, though, you will need to do some research to see what others have written in journal articles and in books about ways of addressing the problem. That's where you will find your theoretical frame and the language you will need to explain it.

To address the problem of campus crime, you would want to look at what researchers have written in the areas of sociology or law enforcement (the fields that seem most applicable to your problem—though other fields might offer ideas as well). One theory of crime you might encounter in your reading is the "broken windows theory," which suggests that if you address small crimes (such as broken windows) you will be addressing the larger issue because, for one thing, small crimes and big crimes are committed by the same group of offenders.

Searching for Models of Success

If you wanted to address the problem of crime on campus, you would logically look at programs at other schools that helped to reduce crime. You would probably also want to look at towns and cities, since they are also potentially good models. You could look for these models in a number of ways.

- You might look in professional or popular sources, such as college journals or newspapers and magazines, which might have stories about successful crime stopping initiatives.
- You could look on the Web, where schools might have posted information about their programs (especially those that proved successful).
- You might ask experts in law enforcement who they look to for models, and then try to interview people involved with the programs they suggest.
- If you have already begun your theoretical research, you may have come across some examples in scholarly sources that you can then try to find out more about.

Once you found those models of success, you would want to repeat the research process to see what specific information you could turn up about how and why those programs worked. The more information you could turn up the better, since you will need that research to justify your own choices in constructing a plan.

Merging Theory and Practice

To construct a coherent project, you will need to merge theory and practice so that your theoretical frame explains the model of success you are using to justify your plan. A good example of this merging of theory and practice in the case of campus crime would be to use the model of the New York Police Department who made their city the safest in the nation by cracking down on low-level street crime (from petty theft to vandalism), following the logic of the broken windows theory. You could use the NYPD as your model and draw examples of good practice from them and explain them using the language of theory.

White Paper Assignment

A white paper is a document which describes a current problem. Your white paper will help you begin documenting and quantifying an actual problem in anticipation of the midterm letter. In addition, you will have the opportunity to present information in light of the needs of your chosen funding source.

The white paper should help you collate and organize information and test the viability of your topic. Pay close attention to the **scope** of your potential project. This is the time when you should be aware of your ability to fully address the problem identified. Upon further review, if the problem still requires additional narrowing or framing, this is the time to consider the possibilities. Your white paper should be brief (one to two pages) and include a significant amount of **fieldwork**. When drafting your white paper, consider whether a possible proposal does all of the following:

1. **Identifies with people**: Does the writer have a particular reader (or funding source) in mind? Does the writer's approach seem appropriate to the reader's concerns? Should the writer imagine a different reader for the idea or find out more about the reader's concerns? Does the project address the needs of a particular population? Might the interests of the reader differ from those of the population to be served? How so?

2. **Points to a problem**: Does the writer demonstrate a need for this proposal? Has he or she discussed a problem that could be researched and documented? How might the writer find out more about the problem? What sources of information might be helpful? What types of evidence would help illustrate the problem better?

3. **Faces complexity**: Is the idea of sufficient complexity to require a detailed proposal? If not, can you suggest ways to develop the project so that it would be adequately complex? Has the writer considered all the major problems here, or is there something he or she is avoiding?

4. **Suggests lines of research**: Does the topic lend itself to library research (a course requirement)? What other kinds of research should the writer consider? How might the writer support his or her claims about the problem suggested by the proposal?

5. **Positions the work within a paradigm**: Does the writer have a definite approach to the problem or issue? How might the writer position him or herself within a discipline or field of study in approaching the topic? What disciplines might be helpful? What research might the writer pursue in developing the paradigm?

6. **Demonstrates originality**: Is the specific work proposed at least somewhat original? Has this idea been tried before? What could make this idea more innovative? Are there other ways of approaching the problem?

7. **Stays within reach**: Is the proposed idea manageable? In other words, is the scope of the proposed work something that can be done well, given the time frame and resources? Is the student remaining within his/her reach, if not his/her grasp? Is the idea focused enough in terms of population, location, or issue? Is it something that could actually get done? Can you see this student actually taking on such a project now or being able to do so within the next few years?

Follow your instructor's directions about format and use of sources for this assignment.

Finding Books, Journal Articles, and Other Sources at the Library

Today there can never be the excuse that you "couldn't find any research" on something. You will see, in fact, that there is usually too much information on any topic. Just try a search on the Index called *Business Source Premier* (from the Rutgers Libraries home page, http://www.libraries.rutgers.edu/, click on "Indexes and Databases" and click on *Business Source Premier* which is listed near the top in alphabetical order). Enter keywords about your topic and you should find that there is lot of information out there (much of which is accessible online in full-text format). And if you try a search at *Google*, it is likely you will get too many hits to look through in a sitting. You must learn to be selective, have confidence in your ability to analyze what you read, and just simply get to work.

The best place to start is the Rutgers Libraries home page, http://www.libraries.rutgers.edu. If you are using a computer off campus, it can be set up to access the Rutgers Library: on the library's home page, click "Off-Campus Support" for instructions. The library home page is set up for easy use, listing the Library Catalog (listing all book and periodical holdings at all Rutgers Libraries), "Indexes and Databases" (offering expansive bibliographic references, and sometimes full text, of articles in various fields), and "Research Guides" (offering links to library resources and quality websites reviewed by Rutgers librarians).

The only way to learn how to use the library or its home page is by using it. But if you have trouble getting started, there are tutorials online (click "Learning Tools"). Your class will also have a library tour to familiarize you with the resources available at Rutgers, so be prepared to ask questions of the reference librarians. Remember the reference librarians can be the best teachers of library skills; the library is their classroom, and you are their students. Show them what you have done; ask them questions; seek their advice whenever you get stuck looking for information. The more specific your question, the better the help you will receive.

If you can't locate a source at Rutgers, you can order any book or journal article through interlibrary loan, usually very quickly (no more than two weeks). If you start your research early, you should be able to get all the information you need. Be careful, however, to continue your research efforts while awaiting sources you have ordered. The deadline for completing an assignment will not change if your ordered source does not arrive on time or proves less than helpful.

Some Advice on Searching the Internet

You should never rely upon general Internet searching as your main source of information. Internet sources tend to be too simplified and too much driven by self-interest to serve as the basis for your research. You should always seek a wide variety of sources, using books for depth of coverage, peer-reviewed journals for thinking in your field, and periodicals for timely coverage of recent events. The Internet should be only a supplement to these sources. These suggestions are therefore intended to give you some ideas about using the Internet as an assistant rather than a crutch.

- Often web searches can help you most in developing a list of keywords that you can use later in searching through databases and books. Try putting quotes around specific phrases, like "binge drinking" rather than binge AND drinking, since this will help narrow your search to only sources that use those words together. Remember the basics of Boolean logic: use "and" to narrow and "or" to expand categories.

- If you are beginning with a broad subject (cancer, AIDS, alcohol, guns), try starting with the "course guides" prepared by Rutgers Librarians (accessible from the Rutgers Libraries home page at http://www.libraries.rutgers.edu). Use the guides to help narrow your topic and to get ideas.

- An increasing number of statistical sources are available online. You can also use *Statistical Abstracts of the United States* and *Statistical Reference Index,* which are available in the reference section of most campus libraries. If you are seeking government statistics, check out "thomas," the government center for information at http://www.thomas.gov/. For New Jersey information, try http://www.state.nj.us/. For census information, go to http://www.census.gov/. If you were looking for statistics on campus crime (as in our example above), you would definitely need to visit the Office of Postsecondary Education's Campus Security Statistics Website at http://ope.ed.gov/security/.

- If you find a good website, see if it contains links to others or lists of references you can find in the library. Often, Web sources are abstracted versions of much better journal articles or books. Go to the original source!

A Brief Guide to Using MLA Style

The following guidelines are not intended to be all-inclusive but merely to help you avoid typical pitfalls in citation. For the purposes of this class, you should use citation style as given by the Modern Language Association. You will need to know MLA style for both in-text citation and your Works Cited page. The following are guidelines based on current MLA recommendations. For more information on the intricacies of MLA citation, consult the *MLA Handbook for Writers of Research Papers* (available in the reference section of all campus libraries). For the latest recommendations on electronic references, go to the frequently updated MLA website at <http://www.mla.org/>. The following examples of format are all based on those sources.

In-Text, Parenthetical Citation

MLA citation format tries to simplify references by eliminating footnotes and replacing them with short parenthetical citations that are elaborated in your Works Cited. The main purpose of in-text citation therefore is to link information in your text with entries on your Works Cited page. For that reason, you need to make the connection between citations and sources clear by using the same primary name in your text as the primary identifying reference in your Works Cited.

Unlike scientific citation formats, which emphasize author and date of publication, MLA emphasizes author and page number. The two pieces of information you should have in a textual reference are the last name of the author and the page number (if the text is paginated). Page references are especially important when you are using a direct or indirect quotation from the text. If you mention the author(s) in your sentence, then it is not essential to put the name(s) into your parenthetical citation. Two examples:

> According to James Q. Wilson and George Kelling, "at the community level, disorder and crime are usually inextricably linked, in a kind of developmental sequence" (33).

> According to the classic study of the "broken windows" phenomenon, disorder leads inevitably to crime (Wilson and Kelling 33)

In parenthetical or in-text citation with up to three authors, you should include all of the names; with four or more authors you should cite the primary author and indicate others with "et al." For example:

One author: (Jordan 98)

Two authors: (Jordan and Slinkoff 98)

Three authors: (Jordan, Slinkoff, and Presser 70)

Four or more: (Jordan et al. 78).

In-text citations for four or more authors would look like this:

> Jordan et al. found an increased cancer rate in overweight mice (78).

Sometimes page numbers are not available, especially when dealing with electronic sources. In this case, the MLA suggests that you use paragraph numbers for reference, especially when quoting. Otherwise, simply use the author's name in your parenthetical citation. And in the case of quoted material not spoken by the author, be sure to indicate that the line was quoted in (abbreviated "qtd. in") the source you used and was not an original citation. For example:

> The case of Abner Louima is the exception that proves the rule in Siegel's view: "'the lesson of the 'broken windows' applies to cops as well as to criminals. With 'broken windows' you say, if you allow the small things to get out of hand, the big things will be worse'" (qtd. in Skelley 10). According to Siegel, the 70th precinct commander did not enforce rules vigorously, which allowed disorder and, eventually, criminality among his officers (Skelley).

If the source has no discernable author, then use the title (or the first few words of longer titles, followed by ellipses). And be sure to use the title for reference both parenthetically and in your works cited:

> *Parenthetical citation for unpaginated, non-authored source:*
> Safir's first action was to focus on the seemingly "trivial" crime of jumping subway turnstiles to avoid paying the fare ("Commissioner describes NYPD 'success story'").

> *Works Cited listing for unpaginated, non-authored web source:*
> "Commissioner describes NYPD 'success story.'" *Yale Bulletin and Calendar*, 28 Jan. 2000. Web. 3 March 2009.

Non-Accessible Sources

Since the whole purpose of including citations and references is to provide your reader with the means of using the same sources themselves for future research, you should consult with your instructor about which sources you can and cannot use on your Works Cited page. The MLA does offer style formats for citing e-mail messages, postings to a Listserv, and personal interviews. Original research that you have done to find information about your project (for example, survey results that you have gathered) should not be recorded on your Works Cited page, but should be explained clearly in your text.

> A survey of 45 Busch campus students conducted at the Busch Student Center on April 1, 2003, showed an overwhelming number avoided taking Friday classes.

> In an interview on January 12, 2003, Robert Spears, the Director of Parking and Transportation for the Rutgers, New Brunswick campus, discussed some of the problems that made additional parking spaces on College Avenue Campus impractical.

> In a March 10, 2003 e-mail response to my inquiries, Professor Dowling said that he thought student evaluations "put pressure on faculty to do the popular thing rather than the right thing" and therefore ought to be replaced by another system.

Your Works Cited Page

Your Works Cited page is just that: it reflects the works that you have actually used in your text, not works that you consulted for background information but did not use for reference. According to the latest guidelines, it should be double-spaced consistently throughout, even within entries. Do not skip extra space between each entry. You must list your sources in alphabetical order, either by the author's name or the title. If you have two or more sources by the same author, list them in alphabetical order by title and replace the author's name with "---." in the second entry. Do not number your entries on the page—alphabetical order and indentation will separate one entry from the next.

The following examples will give you some idea of format; for more complete information, consult with your instructor or the *MLA Handbook*.

A book:

> Jacobs, Jane. *The Death and Life of Great American Cities.* New York: Random House, 1961. Print.

> Wilson, William H. *The City Beautiful Movement.* Baltimore: Johns Hopkins UP, 1989. Print.

A book with two or three authors:

> Wilson, James Q. and Richard Herrnstein. *Crime and Human Nature: The Definitive Study of the Causes of Crime.* New York: Simon and Schuster, 1985. Print.

A book chapter:

> Wilson, James Q. and George Kelling. "Broken windows: The police and neighborhood safety." *Thinking About Crime.* Ed. J. Q. Wilson. New York: Vintage, 1985. 77–90. Print.

Periodicals:

If the periodical is paginated continuously throughout the year, only the volume number is needed. If each issue begins with page 1, include the issue number after the volume number separated by a period. For example, for "volume 17, issue 4," use 17.4.

> Brown, Lawrence and Wycoff, M.A. "Policing Houston: Reducing Fear and Improving Service." *Crime and Delinquency* 33.1 (1987): 71–89. Print.

> Strecher, Victor (1991). "Revising the Histories and Futures of Policing." *Police Forum* 1.1 (1991): 1–9. Print.

Newspaper:

> Campbell, Geoffrey. "Crime Is Down All Over." *New York Times* 11 October 1997, late ed.: B14+. Print.

Government documents and other reports:

> Federal Bureau of Investigation. *Crime in the United States, 2000.* Washington, D.C.: U.S. Government Printing Office, 2001. Print.

Web references:

Just as with print sources, web sources should be cited in the order of author, title, source. Differences arise because of the impermanence of web sources and the fact that many do not have clear authors or titles on their pages. The impermanence of web sources makes it necessary to add your date of access. In the case where there is no listed author, then use the title as your main listing, and only if there is no author or title should you merely list the source. In any case, be sure to list the actual article or page you are using, not simply the address of the website you accessed first. Do not expect your reader to be able to follow all of the links you followed to find the article.

> "Capitalism." World Book Online. Vers. 3.2.6. Nov. 2008. *World Book.* Web. 3 Dec. 2009.

> Muzzey, Elizabeth H. "Biochemical Reactions in Toddlers." *Journal of Northeastern Medicine* 36, 2001. Web. 17 Apr. 2009.

E-mail:

> Samson, Dolores. Message to the author. 3 May 2009. E-mail.

> Samson, Dolores. "Re: Customer Service." Message to the author. 3 May 2009. E-mail.

Interview:

> Vandeen, Harry. Interview with Jon Stewart. *The Daily Show.* Comedy Central, Los Angeles. 8 Aug. 2009. Television.

> Sansevarius, Buran. Telephone interview. 7 Dec. 2008.

> Jorge, Eric. Personal interview. 1 May 2009.

Sample Annotated Bibliography

An annotated bibliography is simply a preliminary Works Cited page to which notes or "annotations" have been added after each entry. The main information required would be a few sentences summing up what the source says and how it will be useful to your project. You might also want to say whether you will be using the source to quantify the problem or to set up the research paradigm for your project.

Works Cited

Boccacio, Frank. "Improving Customer Service." *Entrepreneur's Weekly* 14 (2001): 5–8. Print.

This article will help support my customer service improvement plan and offers models of success. The author gives several examples of the beneficial results companies experienced when they adopted better customer relations strategies. I can use it to help set up a paradigm of successful models.

Fiegel, Darla and George Kartin. *Starting Your Own Small Business: A New Guide.* New York: Cornell UP, 1998. Print.

Although this book is a guide to setting up a business, it includes valuable information about the importance of a well-thought-out customer relations plan. It also gives a guide on how to train new employees in good customer service that I can modify for use in my project to improve customer service at our auto service.

Sensenig, Becca, et al. "Customer Dissatisfaction at Major Auto Dealerships." *Wall Street Journal.* 9 Oct. 2000: D6. Print.

Sensenig lists the major complaints that customers seeking auto service have, and she shows that major dealerships are not paying attention to the levels of dissatisfaction in their clientele. I can use this article to show that the problems I see at Sharlene's are common among auto service centers. I could also use it as part of my argument that paying attention to customer complaints will give us a marketing advantage over dealerships.

"Taking Time to Listen." *CNBC Online.* 1999. CNBC, New York. Web. 8 Sept. 2002.

This is a transcript of a program on CNBC about the benefits of listening to customer complaints in a genuine way. The advantages of listening carefully to customers before their auto service and following up after the service has been completed are shown. The disadvantages of some current methods, like bribing customers to give a good report by giving them a free oil change or tank of gas, are clear from the client interviews. I can use quotations from some of the clients to show Sharlene's that there is a problem with their current methods.

■ Peer Review: Annotated Bibliography

Please fill out the following form for your partner. Feel free to write comments on the draft as well.

1. Is the document clearly labeled as a list of references
   at the top of the page?   _____ yes _____ no

2. Does the document contain a minimum of six sources?   _____ yes _____ no

3. Are there various types of sources represented (books to develop a
   theoretical framework, scholarly journals for detailed models, etc.)?   _____ yes _____ no

4. Are at least 50 percent of the references cited from scholarly sources?   _____ yes _____ no

5. Is the document formatted in proper MLA citation style
   (alphabetized, indented after first line, publication elements
   ordered correctly, etc.)?   _____ yes _____ no

6. Is the document correctly spaced, in 12 point
   Times New Roman type, with one-inch margins?   _____ yes _____ no

7. Is each entry annotated and detailed in describing how the
   corresponding source would be useful to the plan?   _____ yes _____ no

8. Is each annotation 100–150 words in length, single-spaced,
   and presented in a clear, readable form?   _____ yes _____ no

9. Do the bibliographic entries suggest a theoretical framework
   for the plan?   _____ yes _____ no

10. Do the bibliographic entries include models of success appropriate
    to the plan?   _____ yes _____ no

11. Based upon the entries, is there evidence of a recognizable
    paradigm (or rationale) for the plan?   _____ yes _____ no

12. Is the document free of errors in grammar, usage
    and/or sentence structure?   _____ yes _____ no

What is the one part of the draft you liked the most?

What is the one part of the draft that needs the most improvement?

Additional Comments/Suggestions:

■ Peer Review: Annotated Bibliography

Please fill out the following form for your partner. Feel free to write comments on the draft as well.

1. Is the document clearly labeled as a list of references at the top of the page? _____ yes _____ no

2. Does the document contain a minimum of six sources? _____ yes _____ no

3. Are there various types of sources represented (books to develop a theoretical framework, scholarly journals for detailed models, etc.)? _____ yes _____ no

4. Are at least 50 percent of the references cited from scholarly sources? _____ yes _____ no

5. Is the document formatted in proper MLA citation style (alphabetized, indented after first line, publication elements ordered correctly, etc.)? _____ yes _____ no

6. Is the document correctly spaced, in 12 point Times New Roman type, with one-inch margins? _____ yes _____ no

7. Is each entry annotated and detailed in describing how the corresponding source would be useful to the plan? _____ yes _____ no

8. Is each annotation 100–150 words in length, single-spaced, and presented in a clear, readable form? _____ yes _____ no

9. Do the bibliographic entries suggest a theoretical framework for the plan? _____ yes _____ no

10. Do the bibliographic entries include models of success appropriate to the plan? _____ yes _____ no

11. Based upon the entries, is there evidence of a recognizable paradigm (or rationale) for the plan? _____ yes _____ no

12. Is the document free of errors in grammar, usage and/or sentence structure? _____ yes _____ no

What is the one part of the draft you liked the most?

What is the one part of the draft that needs the most improvement?

Additional Comments/Suggestions:

■ Peer Review: Annotated Bibliography

Please fill out the following form for your partner. Feel free to write comments on the draft as well.

1. Is the document clearly labeled as a list of references at the top of the page?   _____ yes _____ no

2. Does the document contain a minimum of six sources?   _____ yes _____ no

3. Are there various types of sources represented (books to develop a theoretical framework, scholarly journals for detailed models, etc.)?   _____ yes _____ no

4. Are at least 50 percent of the references cited from scholarly sources?   _____ yes _____ no

5. Is the document formatted in proper MLA citation style (alphabetized, indented after first line, publication elements ordered correctly, etc.)?   _____ yes _____ no

6. Is the document correctly spaced, in 12 point Times New Roman type, with one-inch margins?   _____ yes _____ no

7. Is each entry annotated and detailed in describing how the corresponding source would be useful to the plan?   _____ yes _____ no

8. Is each annotation 100–150 words in length, single-spaced, and presented in a clear, readable form?   _____ yes _____ no

9. Do the bibliographic entries suggest a theoretical framework for the plan?   _____ yes _____ no

10. Do the bibliographic entries include models of success appropriate to the plan?   _____ yes _____ no

11. Based upon the entries, is there evidence of a recognizable paradigm (or rationale) for the plan?   _____ yes _____ no

12. Is the document free of errors in grammar, usage and/or sentence structure?   _____ yes _____ no

What is the one part of the draft you liked the most?

What is the one part of the draft that needs the most improvement?

Additional Comments/Suggestions:

The Midterm
Sales Letter

Chapter

The Assignment

Write a four- to five-page business letter or memo, single-spaced, not including the list of references, that accomplishes the following:

- Represents the initial correspondence to your patron
- Addresses a specific person by name
- Explains a current problem
- Explains at least some of your initial research toward a solution (your paradigm)
- Cites your research clearly (according to MLA style)
- Gives a sense of your plan of action and associated costs
- Closes with an invitation to your oral presentation
- Appends a list of Works Cited of at least eight sources, cited in MLA style (remember, though, that at least ten sources are required for the final proposal)

The midterm sales letter should be written as a **letter of persuasion,** and as such it carries the added burden of addressing a particular reader and using some of the means of persuasion available to you for appealing to him or her (with special attention to rational or logical appeals).

Requirements

The midterm paper will be graded according to how well it does the following:

- Adheres to proper letter or memo format
- Discusses, documents, and quantifies the problem
- Highlights the reader's concerns about that topic
- Cites specific facts and examples from your research

- Briefly proposes a plan and provides a rationale for it
- Convinces your reader to hear more
- Provides a list of Works Cited in MLA style
- Is proofread for errors and appearance

Purpose

The midterm sales letter serves the following purposes:

- As a draft of the final proposal, it provides you an opportunity to organize your research toward a practical goal and to begin presenting your information clearly.
- As an evaluative tool, it allows you to receive feedback on your work thus far, so you can have a sense of where you stand with your proposal and in the class.
- As an exercise in persuasive writing, it gives you practice in the most valuable form of writing for business.

Typical Pitfalls and Problems

Students typically go wrong with the midterm paper in the following ways:

- They do not address a specific person capable of funding the project.
- They fail to provide evidence of the problem or trend they seek to address.
- They fail to explicitly cite their research.
- They assert things without evidence.
- They fail to attach a list of references.
- They use insufficient or inappropriate sources.
- They are poorly proofread for errors and appearance.

Some General Advice, or "14 Steps to a Strong Sales Letter"

You have already gained some practice in writing the letter of persuasion when you wrote the cover letter with your résumé. Here you are also making a sales pitch, but in a much more detailed way. There are fourteen things you will want to consider as you write it. Obviously, each situation should dictate the type of approach you take. Also, these ideas should not limit your creativity. Remember that the audience should always direct your approach. Who will read your letter? What are your reader's concerns and interests? How can you appeal to this reader most powerfully? How can you explain your evidence? The answers to these questions should guide the way you write the sales letter, and they will always vary from situation to situation. What follows, generally speaking, are fourteen essential elements to a persuasive sales letter:

1. **Know your audience.**

   Knowing your audience will require some preliminary primary research, or fieldwork. If you are responding to a specific request for a proposal (commonly called an RFP), then you will know some of what your audience expects. You will usually be addressing someone you do not know very well at all. Find out what you can. What is the corporate culture like at your reader's organization? What is their motto or corporate philosophy? What image do they project in their advertising? What recent endeavors have they undertaken? What problems are they facing? What is their competition up to? Find out about your reader's general interests so that you can know better how they might fit with your idea. What specific benefits can the individual or organization you plan to address gain from solving the problem or responding to the trend you are considering?

2. **Get the right name, and get the name right.**

Address your letter to a specific person. How many times have you seen a letter that opens, "Dear Sir or Madam"? Does that inspire much interest in you? Not only is a letter addressed to a specific person bound to generate a more positive response, it will more certainly be read—and it will more likely be read by that specific person capable of making a decision on your project. (The success of annoying ads like Publisher's Clearinghouse is due in no small way to the appearance of personal interest: even the most cynical readers are unconsciously and unavoidably flattered by the fact that Publisher's Clearinghouse knows their name).

How do you find out the person to whom you should address the letter?

This is another one of those "legwork" things, but fortunately these days it doesn't require any walking around: usually a simple telephone call or a "visit" to the company website is all you need. This is part of the fieldwork, or primary research, discussed in Chapter Four.

When in doubt, just ask! Call up the company and ask a receptionist. Talk to a few people—maybe even speak to the person you plan to address (that will give you a better sense of his or her style and will provide a good introduction to your letter). Just ask, and be nice about it. Who would handle the sort of project you have in mind? What department? What person in that department?

Once you know who you should address, find out how you should address that person. How do you spell his or her name? For purposes of the oral presentation, you will want to know how it is pronounced. Does he or she have a title? Does she prefer Ms., Mrs., or Dr.? Is there a middle initial? A Jr., Sr., or Roman numeral? Find out.

3. **"Dear" is never wrong as an address.**

"Dear" is the expected mode of address. Though you may have struggled in personal correspondence over whether or not to write "Dear" to your reader, in business correspondence it is simply a standard formality.

4. **Make a strong first impression.**

How you open your letter will depend upon the specific audience and the specific appeal you want to make. If you know the addressee, you will likely want to remind him or her of that fact and allude to your most recent or most positive interaction. If you don't know the addressee personally, you'll have to be more creative. You can rarely go wrong by trying to open with a confident and definitive statement, and you should open emphatically whenever possible. Point to the problem or need you seek to address, or state the sort of vision you will provide in responding to this need. Get this person to read further.

5. **Show that you identify with your reader's concerns.**

Explicitly state what you know about your audience's interest in the idea you will propose or the problem you seek to solve. Explain why this person is the most appropriate addressee. Show that you can see things from the reader's perspective, and that you see the proposal as a win-win situation. Your funding source will want to know what is in it for them.

6. **Specify and quantify the problem or need you seek to address.**

If you can quantify the problem, you can show its magnitude and importance. Alternately, you might give an anecdote or example that helps highlight the importance of this problem to your audience.

7. **Get to the point.**

There are some cases where you may wish to enigmatically string your reader along before revealing your specific project. Usually, though, readers in business don't have time to read a mystery novel. So don't keep your reader waiting too long for your discussion of how you intend to solve the problem or respond to the recent trend you have identified. If you offer a deal, be up front about it. What are you offering? What do you want in return? Give your reader a forecast of what to expect.

8. **Provide evidence and examples.**

This is the key to a successful letter for this course. You must cite your research. You must also show that you can use the information you have collected to construct an effective argument for action. You might say that it requires putting information into action. Evidence is always logically persuasive.

9. **Activate your reader's imagination.**

Invite your reader to engage with your idea, perhaps by using rhetorical questions. Get your reader to participate in your text.

10. **Encourage empathy.**

Now that you have shown your reader that you see things from his or her perspective, start to turn the tables a bit. Get the reader to identify with your reasons for being involved in this project, and present your reasons in the best light possible. If your ethos is key to your appeal, you may consider highlighting it earlier in your letter.

11. **Close with a call to specific action and further contact.**

Make sure that the reader sees this as a pressing need, with a deadline for action. For the purposes of your sales letter for the class, you must invite your reader to hear your presentation, listing the specific date, time, and location.

12. **Make contact easy.**

It is always a good idea to provide a way for your reader to contact you easily, either by phone or e-mail. Don't forget to put that down, usually in the last paragraph—especially if it isn't clearly printed on the stationery you use.

13. **Sign off "Sincerely."**

Don't get fancy with the closing address, unless it is especially appropriate to offer "Best wishes." Like "Dear" at the outset, "Sincerely" is the standard close.

14. **Follow up and be persistent.**

Many times you will discover that your letter has languished in the wrong department or that a busy addressee has failed to take any action because the letter has gotten buried under more pressing work. Follow up your letter after a reasonable interval, perhaps with a phone call or another method of contact. Don't give up.

Midterm Sales Letters

The sample papers that follow are rather typical of the work that students turn in at midterm. Generally, they are competent samples. However, in line with the chronology of assignments, they all need to be improved to make them more coherent and turn them into fully developed projects.

Since the Six P's represent the process of writing the proposal, in order, it is not surprising that most midterm papers do a good job of identifying an appropriate patron to fund the project, defining a population to be served, and trying to understand the problem they want to address, but that they also might be rather vague about their paradigm and the plan. Of course, the price can never be definitive until the plan is sufficiently detailed. Some vagueness is natural, but the better midterm papers will still suggest a more coherent sense of project and will do more not only to describe a paradigm but also to show how that paradigm informs the plan. Since each element of the plan must be justified by published research, you can't possibly have all of the parts of your plan in place until you have identified and integrated all of your sources. However, in the midterm sales letter all of the Six P's must be represented in some way.

The following papers are representative examples of student submissions. They are intended for discussion purposes only and should not necessarily be taken as models of strong work.

Margaret Simms
52 Xavier Drive
New Brunswick, New Jersey 08901

October 19, 2011

C. Travis Webb
Chairperson
Young Americans Center
3550 E. 1st Avenue
Denver, Colorado 80206

Re: Achieving Personal Financial Success for Rutgers Students

Dear Mr. Webb,

Young Americans Center is a leader in providing financial education to America's youth. Recently, the project known as Young Ameritowne, is impacting the lives of children as young as fifth grade. CEO Richard Martinez says that "every transaction is an educational opportunity," exemplifying the Young Americans Center's commitment to improving children's financial future ("Teaching Kids About Money"). Through the program in Denver, the children are learning, in real "town" scenarios, how to budget and effectively manage money. This is something even adults today can benefit from, says Fox Denver anchor Joana Corals. In fact, college students can also greatly benefit from financial education, specifically personal finance.

College students are an important group, as they are America's youth on the verge of entering "our free enterprise system" (yacenter.org). Specifically for the college students of today, economic climates and job markets are more challenging to deal with, as "the recession drags painfully on," which places these students on high priority for financial knowledge (*mybudget360.com*).

I hope you will agree that Young Americans Center can make a big difference in the lives of the large number of college students who may not have had the chance to participate in a program like Ameritowne. With better financial knowledge, college students, whom we may call the future of America, can create a better world for themselves and others who follow, such as the fifth graders in Denver.

The Broader Issue

Today, the average American college student struggles with personal finance, and limited knowledge is a main culprit. "Financial literacy is the ability to make informed judgments and effective decisions regarding the use and management of money," which is where college students fall short and may be called "financially illiterate" (Gavigan 24). A study at Texas A&M University, indicated that college freshmen "are unable to balance a checkbook and most have no insight into the basic survival principles involved with earning, spending, saving and investing" (Avard 334). Another study done using questionnaires among 1,800 students in fourteen different American colleges concluded that, "college students are not knowledgeable about personal finance," and accounted one reason as higher education institutions' lack of emphasis on students' personal finance education (Avard 332). Personal finance is an everyday function, and a skill for life, making the absence of such knowledge in students extraordinarily problematic. Some scholars agree that "When individuals cannot manage their finances, it becomes a problem for society," expanding the scope of this problem from students to nationwide (Avard 332).

In particular, students have trouble with "concepts dealing with investing, saving and risk," risk also including credit card use (Avard 334). Students are "constantly accumulating debt, through student loans and credit cards," while they're in school, and "may not realize how their current debt can negatively affect their future credit rating," and even hinder their financial goals (Henry). Credit cards may be a useful tool in building a solid credit history, increasing credit power in the future, and learning payment responsibility. However, when misused, credit cards can accumulate an overwhelming debt. "Lack of personal financial knowledge place students at a greater financial risk for having large and perhaps unmanageable, debt burdens," and will make life post-graduation even more difficult (Lawrence, et al. 5). Students also may have limited knowledge about the specifics of credit cards, such as limits or interests, and further, may not realize the damage they could be doing to their future credit rating. A credit rating will influence your situation in life, as it pertains to getting a home, a car, and even a job. "Increasingly, students with high credit card debt are having trouble getting good jobs because employers are reviewing credit reports," which is an aspect of job hunting students may be unaware of (Lawrence, et al. 5).

Students also have a problem with budgeting; a majority of them do not have one, and others do not understand the term (Henry). Most students entering college do not have a financial plan, which is crucial during this period of transition "from financial dependence to independence" (Lawrence). Statistics have heightened concern for this problem. It is reported that, "this year's freshmen will likely emerge with average debt well above 2011 grads: $4,138 in credit-card debt atop their $22,900 in student loans" which is a heavy burden to walk away from college with (Chatzky 23). To make matters worse, "the number of bankruptcies among young people under age 25 has grown by 50% since 1991" exemplifying the lack of personal finance knowledge even after college graduation (*njaes.rutgers.edu*). Moreover, we are living in what many economists are calling "the worst financial crisis since the Great Depression," giving this problem a true sense of urgency (Gavigan 24). *Newsweek* exaggerates students' financial ignorance by stating, "By the time they graduate, they'll be well-versed in Faulkner, microbiology, or Mandarin—but chances are, they won't have even a basic command of financial tasks like living on a budget," and by then, students will face even bigger challenges such as buying a house or having children.

It is found that "people with low financial literacy are more likely to have problems with debt, less likely to participate in the stock market, less likely to accumulate wealth, and less likely to plan for retirement," which gives students today, with low financial literacy, a grim future; one they hoped not to have after attending college (Lusardi 3). A 2009 study revealed 84% of students admitted they need more education on financial management ("Study finds rising number"). Today, the students at Rutgers University are included in the vast number of students who are "financially illiterate." Rutgers Cooperative Extension states that "Many of New Jersey's young adults are leaving school without the knowledge and skills necessary to make critical life decisions (e.g., wise use of credit, developing a spending plan, purchasing auto insurance)" and 86% of Rutgers students are from the state of New Jersey (njaes.rutgers.edu).

The Problem at Rutgers

Most recently, Rutgers University's tuition was raised by 4.0% (*news.rutgers.edu*). A student member of the Rutgers Board of Governors spoke for her peers explaining that students are "working multiple jobs, accruing debt and, in one case, relying on a grandfather's second mortgage to afford school" (Mulvihill). Such cases exemplify the great lengths to which students go, to afford going to Rutgers. According to a Rutgers Financial Aid report, students graduating in four years accumulate $17,411 in loan debts alone. This amount only increases when a student takes longer than expected to graduate. A report from the Rutgers University Student Affairs Committee also stated, "Student Financial Management and Credit-Card Debt are important issues facing students at Rutgers," and they were appalled by how easy it was for students, with blank credit history, to obtain one or more credit cards ("Report"). The Consumer Federation of America has found "about 70 percent of undergraduates at four-year colleges possess at least one credit card" and accumulating the above-mentioned debt of $4,138 (njaes.rutgers.edu). The rising debt, from loans or credit cards, is a serious concern for the Rutgers student community, and they must be prepared to manage and understand their finances.

The students at Rutgers University have access to a highly reputable education, ranking 58th in the Association of American Universities. Among such an education, personal finances should be a top priority before sending graduates out into the world. How well students do in life, with high regard to finance, will reflect on Rutgers, and the future of America.

Supporting Theory and Models of Success

The work of Amartya Sen has long impacted public policy and social sciences, specifically, his theory known as "capability theory" may be applied here. To Sen, a "capability" is a freedom that a person has to lead one kind of life or another. Based on one's capabilities, we may "judge how well someone's life is going," as we often call one's "well-being" (Robeyns 60–61). The theory has also helped many scholars in "comparing how well two persons (or societies) are doing," which brings us back to college students reflecting Rutgers and America. If we improve a student's "capability" to manage and understand money, we have done our job, as according to Sen it is part of society's job to develop these capabilities in citizens, one way being through a formal education (Johnson 123). "This relates to the need to educate students on personal finance," they need to develop this capability in order to secure their well-being in the world (Johnson 124). A student's life will be made much easier with the understanding of money and how to easily manage it, rather than "have it be a stressful (and foggy) task" and it often can be (Johnson 124).

Junior Achievement Program, Dallas, Texas

Some programs have already begun to improve this "capability" in students through experiential financial education, such as the Junior Achievement Program (JA) in Dallas, Texas. The JA program, known as "JA Personal Finance," is taught at the high school level over several weeks, and involves real-world stimulations and role-play. All the stimulations and role plays set out to show students how they might generate wealth in the real world, and to follow, how to manage that wealth effectively. They focus mainly on concepts in the banking industry and get the students to stimulate running a bank. The program was successful in increasing students' financial knowledge, particularly in tracking expenses, saving money, and feeling confident making their own financial decisions. After the program, 46% of the students said that saving their money in a savings account was the most important thing they had done. However, the criticism of this program is lack of access to financial institutions, as many of the students are low-income. Perhaps more than 46.5% of the students would have opened a savings account, if they had access to one (Johnson 128).

Banking at School, Illinois

Another program is the Banking at School program, which "has regained popularity as concern about financial literacy has grown" and the program continues to grow and develop (Johnson 129). One such example took place in Illinois, initiated by the State of Illinois Treasurer's Office, for students in the fourth to the eight grades. Also part of Sen's theory is a "capability" being a freedom, and with freedom there should be a "real opportunity to accomplish what we value" and although individual students may not deem "money" as a value, it is certainly a value in society, and its power allows one to participate in the world, which is also part of Sen's theory, to be a full social person (Robeyns 62). Turning back to financial education, students therefore must have the "real opportunity" to begin managing money, which is part of what Banking at School does. They match a school with a participating bank or credit union, and a representative collects deposits once a month from the school, in addition to the teacher adding financial education to the curriculum. Now, "Illinois reports over 200,000 students participating in the state's bank-at-school program," and the students have been given access to save money, improving their capability (Johnson 129). This may be concluded from their chapters that are as follows: "What is money?, Why do people save?, What are banks for and how do they work?, Where does money come from?, and The World of Work," none of which include a money management lesson (*lba.org*). A drawback to this program may be the lack of emphasis on money management. Once they reach eighteen years of age, they can withdraw the money, and some at that point may be headed off to college where many students still don't have such a "capability" to manage money.

Initial Plan

Young Americans Center can have their representatives, or elect representatives already part of Rutgers (qualified student or staff) to advertise the initial visit. Rutgers often hosts seminars, information panels, and workshops that have, depending on the advertising, a good student turnout. I have personally gone to workshops with well over fifty students. These presentations or workshops are presented by a vast number of sources, including career services, specific departments, student clubs, and even large companies or corporations like Johnson & Johnson. The Young Americans Center can establish recognition on campus, and start to show students that financial literacy is a vital skill for the real world, and that this organization has helped students understand finances as young as fifth grade.

Frequent workshops may be held at any one of the student centers, aimed at enhancing students' capability to understand and manage money, and ultimately, become financially literate. "Experience plays a role in learning," which is something the Junior Achievement program adopted through their role-play and simulations (Johnson 130). During the workshop, Rutgers should also engage in "real-world" experiences, like the ones they will face very soon like paying their loans off, managing their current income, dealing with credit cards, saving for a house, or even retirement.

Given enough of these workshops, perhaps Rutgers can require that students go to at least one. Perhaps undergraduate curriculum will soon require a personal finance course, as many colleges are now starting to do, with the growing concern of this issue.

I hope that you have enjoyed reading my letter, and that you will strongly consider Rutgers for your next project. I am confident that we can significantly improve Rutgers students' financial literacy, and that they will go on to use this "capability" to be successful in the world. I would like you invite you and your staff to an oral presentation of this proposal on October 24 at 6:10 p.m., at the New Brunswick Campus in Scott Hall 202. Feel free to contact me at any time via e-mail at msimms@rutgers.edu or by phone at 732-632-8876. Thank you for your time. It is greatly appreciated.

Sincerely,

Margaret Simms

Margaret Simms

Works Cited

Avard, Stephen, et al. "The Financial Knowledge of College Freshmen." *College Student Journal* 39.2 (2005): 321–39. Print.

Chatzky, Jean. "The Student Financial Crisis." *Newsweek* 158.10 (2011): 2 Print.

Gavigan, Karen. "Show Me the Money Resources: Financial Literacy for 21st-Century Learners." *Library Media Connection* 28.5 (2010): 24–7. Print.

Henry, Reasie A., Janice G. Weber, and David Yarbrough. "Money Management Practices of College Students." *College Student Journal* 35.2 (2001): 244. Print.

Johnson, Elizabeth, and Margaret S. Sherraden. "From Financial Literacy to Financial Capability among Youth." *Journal of Sociology & Social Welfare* 34.3 (2007): 119–46. Print.

Lawrence, Frances C., et al. *Credit Card Usage of College Students: Evidence from Louisiana State University* (Research Information Sheet #107). Baton Rouge, LA: Louisiana Agricultural Center (2003): 1-27. Print.

lba.org. Web. 2011.

Lusardi, Annamaria. "Financial Literacy among the Young." *Journal of Consumer Affairs* 44.2 (2010): 358–80. Print.

"Making the Case for Financial Literacy– 2010." Jumpstart.org. Web. 26 November 2011.

Mulvihill, Geoff. "Rutgers Raises In-state Tuition by 1.8% after Board Cuts Planned Hike in Half." *The Associated Press* 14 Jul. 2011. Print.

Mybudget360.com. Web. 2011.

njaes.rutgers.edu. Web. 2011.

"Report of the Rutgers University Senate Student Affairs Committee and Executive Committee: Student financial management and credit card debt." Web. 5 November 2011.

Robeyns, Ingrid. "Sen's Capability Approach and Gender Inequality: Selecting Relevant Capabilities. *Feminist Economics* 9.2-3 (2003): 61-92. Print.

"Study finds rising number of college students using credit cards for tuition." salliemae.com. Sallie Mae, April 2009. Web. 2 December 2011.

"Teaching Kids about Money." Fox News. Denver, Colorado. 6 Oct 2011. Television.

YAcenter.org. Web. 2011.

Christine Redmond
466 Oak Street
Metuchen, New Jersey 08840

June 19, 2012

Brian Colvin
Associate Athletic Director of Finance and Administration
Louis Brown Athletic Center
83 Rockafeller Road
Piscataway, New Jersey 08854

Re: Rutgers Softball Facilities Proposal

Dear Mr. Colvin,

Since its inception in 1979, the Rutgers softball team has certainly had a unique story. From losing seasons to championship berths, not much has stayed the same over the years for this program. However, one issue has prevailed and become mainstream for the organization: the Rutgers softball team does not generate revenue. Instead, it has sub-par facilities that don't come close to competing with its Big East counterparts. It is understandable in these tough economic times to overlook what seems to be a minor issue, but in fact by fixing a problem like this, the university's athletic department should realize that it is alleviating some of its own financial stresses. Impending budget cuts put the spotlight on spending issues within the department, and the future of a non-revenue sports program like the softball team depends on a plan of action. I am calling this issue to your attention because a project of this scale would need some funding from the department, and as the Director of Finance, I understand that you would oversee the financial aspect of a project of this scope. I would also like to bring my proposal to the attention of Mr. Douglas Kokoskie the Senior Athletic Director for Facilities, Events, and Operations, who would play an essential role in carrying out a proposal involving an athletic field at Rutgers.

The Problem of Spending within the Athletic Department

The profits that have been generated within the athletic department have been deemed insufficient. According to Bloomberg News, it is costing the average student nearly $1,000 in student fees to support Rutgers' sports teams (Bloomberg). In other words, when a student pays his or her tuition bill for the year, $1,000 goes solely to the athletic department. If that wasn't enough, out of fifty-four surveyed schools, Rutgers' athletics took the most money ($28.5 million) from its university budget last year. According to financial reports filed with the National Collegiate Athletic Association ("NCAA.com"), Rutgers was one of thirty-three schools that lost money and subsequently increased its university financial support budget from the previous year (Bloomberg).

The current revenue that is being generated from our sports teams isn't enough to reduce funding from the school. If funding isn't reduced, budget cuts will begin to effect non-revenue sports at Rutgers, leaving the softball program at a clear disadvantage.

The Rutgers faculty council has recently weighed in on the issue at hand, and rightfully so. The council believes that academics are losing out because of the massive amount of money flowing into the athletic department. Subsequently, on March 30 they voted in demand of "$5 million of cuts in university funding of athletics by fiscal 2016 and a referendum on sports fees required of students" (Bloomberg). This has been a continuing debate among faculty and administration, and it certainly promises to give the athletic department a tough time avoiding yet another budget cut. However, a stable revenue-generating plan of action would certainly point the university in the right direction to at least put a dent in the debt caused by Rutgers' sports teams.

As previously mentioned, Bloomberg surveyed fifty-four public institutions including Rutgers University. Schools that were successful in reducing university funding had a major similarity attributing to their success. The athletic budget funds nineteen non-revenue sports here at Rutgers (taking out football, men's basketball, and women's basketball), something that no other school does.

Currently, the softball program brings in zero dollars in revenue. Not a single penny. It does not charge admission to games. It does not offer a concession stand. In fact, the softball program does not offer but one single reason for any fan to attend a game and support the program. Bleachers holding a capacity of only about 150–200 people are the only form of seating. The "press box" is a tarp thrown over some metal poles. When music does come out of the dated speakers, it is hardly recognizable. What this program does, on the other hand, is use hundreds of thousands of dollars of department resources to fund scholarships, trips, equipment, and salaries.

This is not to take credit away from the team. For its third consecutive season, the softball program made it to the Big East championship in 2012. It had a few individual record-setting performances along with several notable victories this past season including wins over Texas State (43), Notre Dame (29), and Syracuse (22). The team finished its 2012 campaign ranked 70th overall out of 289 Division 1 teams ("NCAA Division 1 Softball Rankings").

While the softball team at Rutgers continues to make remarkable accomplishments, it still does not have the facilities to show for all its success. By updating these facilities, the program will have the ability to generate revenue and not rely so heavily on the athletic budget for support.

Research to Support Updating the Rutgers Softball Facilities

Profit maximizing behavior is essential for any serious sports team or organization to stay afloat. It is reasonable to assume that a private firm, or in this case the athletic department, "is interested in [its] profits and that higher profits are better than lower profits" (Bradley). Aju Fenn proposes in his article entitled, "Sports Economics," that like any other business, there are two sides to the profit equation when it comes to sports economics: revenues and costs. One of the most basic forms of revenue (and consequently the simplest to calculate) is from admission. It is calculated by multiplying the average cost of admission by the number of attendees present at a competition (Fenn). In order to start making money, the Rutgers softball program will have to begin by charging admission to the games.

However, as noted by Hoye et al. in "Unique Aspects of Managing Sport Organizations," simply charging admission is not enough. Fans are encouraged to attend competition based on what the experience offers. While external factors such as the weather might be important in determining attendance at a game (Fenn), these circumstances are not controllable. On the other hand, the athletic department does have control over creating an atmosphere that is enjoyable for teams, the officiating crew, and fans alike. Attending a sports competition can be related to a consumer purchasing a product. These consumers, or in this case the fans, develop emotional attachments to the product, or team, they support. Ultimately, they experience psychological motivations that drive them to attend games (Hoye et al.).

According to Michael Silk in his article "Sports Stadiums," building these facilities "has become a central component of revitalization...and stadiums have become among the most effective vehicles for advancement [within an organization]" (Silk). By "revitalizing" the softball field, the program will make strides toward generating revenue. In addition to the money spent by fans to attend sporting events, "there are also millions of dollars spent each year on sports memorabilia—clothing, hats, collectibles, and so forth" (McDonald). While this trend is most prevalent at a professional level, creating a facility that sells merchandise still has the opportunity to bring in money for the softball program.

According to Hoye et al., "A sports venue will attract more fans if it provides attractive and comfortable facilities, good views of play, easy accessibility, and a large scoreboard. Other external factors that may influence fans' decisions are the price; special promotions; and even what other leisure alternatives are offered" (Hoye et al.). It is not surprising, then, that notable Big East programs, specifically the University of South Florida, the University of Louisville, and the University of Notre Dame offer most, if not all, of the aforementioned amenities.

Models of Success within Other Big East Softball Programs

After speaking in a telephone interview with Chris Paras, the Assistant Athletics Director of Facilities at the University of South Florida, it became evident as to why USF made it to the Women's College World Series in the 2012 season. As Mr. Paras pointed out, the formula is simple. His state-of-the-art facilities attract the top recruits in the nation. These recruits produce wins for the program. And as this organization has shown, fans will support a winning program.

It was clear to the athletic department at USF that the time had come for change. So as part of a revitalization plan to update a number of athletic facilities on site, the softball program received a brand new, state-of-the-art stadium. Previously, what they had was in need of maintenance. The life expectancy of certain facilities was up, and some teams didn't even have buildings to use. As Mr. Paras put it, when it came to the department's facilities the athletic program was "really limited with potential as far as being a Big East contender." Though the NCAA puts a limit on how much a program can charge to enter a game, increasing numbers in attendance have certainly made an impact. With the new updates the stadium can accommodate more fans, expanding from only a couple hundred seats to about 750. As a result of having larger facilities, the program has seen a definite increase in revenue.

The USF softball field is not only used for practice and competition within the organization. The program runs camps, as well as doing some internal sharing within the university. In fact, the stadium has been turned into a movie theatre where people are able to pay a small admission fee to sit in the stands and enjoy a movie on the big-screen scoreboard. The program has been able to enjoy a steady profit by renting out the stadium for outside activities.

At the University of Louisville, a similar scheme is used to produce profit within the organization. Ulmer Stadium "can accommodate up to 2,200 fans, features field lighting, home and visiting bullpens, and a climate-controlled press box and a video board" ("Ulmer Stadium"). The ten-year-old venue offers state-of-the-art upgrades that attracted a large crowd for the 2011 Big East Championship. More recently, the stadium was selected as a host site for the 2012 NCAA Softball Regional as it was three years earlier in 2009. Similarly to USF's field, Ulmer Stadium is used not only for practice and competition, but also for high school softball games, tournaments, and team camps ("Ulmer Stadium"), all of which are revenue-generating events for the university's athletic department. The facility also has a stand set up along the bottom level of the stadium that sells Louisville softball merchandise.

Melissa Cook Stadium at the University of Notre Dame is yet another example of an update that has given back to the organization in more ways than one. According to my correspondence with Assistant Athletics Director of Event Management Monica Cundiff, there was a laundry list of reasons for creating the new stadium such as, "allowing more fans to attend games and being able to host post-season, conference, and NCAA tournaments." The list goes on and the stadium serves other purposes including, "giving the student-athletes a better experience by playing in a nicer stadium and having a locker room and team room on-site so the student-athletes have somewhere else to go for down time as well as studying."

According to Ms. Cundiff, since the stadium was built in 2008, there has been a tremendous growth in fan attendance and revenue. The program has also made a more extensive marketing effort toward the promotion of the Notre Dame softball team in order to "build a fan base and promote the games." Most of the program's profit comes from ticket revenue and group sales.

Similar to Rutgers, Notre Dame's previous facility, Ivy Field, did not charge admission to games. Ms. Cundiff indicated that on a typical Saturday or Sunday when the weather was nice in South Bend, the crowd at Ivy Field ranged from about 150 to 200 fans, which is about the maximum capacity of Rutgers' current softball field. Now, on the other hand under those same conditions, between 500 and 750 people will buy tickets and attend a game. "You can say the stadium has something to do with it for sure," Ms. Cundiff confirmed, "and the increase in marketing efforts is instrumental."

Notre Dame hosted the 2012 Big East Championship tournament just four years after the stadium's unveiling in 2008, attesting to its success as a leading Division I facility. While the stadium has several features benefitting players and coaches for both the home and visiting teams, it also boasts "Wi-Fi capabilities, a family picnic lawn, chair back and bleacher seating, a concessions area, interior restrooms, and a common area which make the new Cook Stadium a very fan friendly place to enjoy a softball game" ("Melissa Cook Stadium"). The stadium can accommodate 850 fans and its primary use is practice and competition ("Melissa Cook Stadium").

The Cost of Updating the Rutgers Softball Facilities

Melissa Cook Stadium at the University of Notre Dame features a $4.9 million state-of-the-art field equipped with four batting cages, a maximum capacity of 850, Hilltopper Stabilizer synthetic dirt, and bluegrass sod. The stadium was partially funded by a $3 million donation in memory of Melissa Cook, class of 1994 ("Melissa Cook Stadium"). The University of South Florida updated its softball facilities as part of a department-wide, $35 million project ("USF Softball Stadium").

Certainly, neither of these plans serves as a strict financial blueprint for Rutgers. However, the point is that building facilities that will last long and be put to good use will cost a sufficient amount of money. It is a risk, but a necessary one for the betterment of the softball program and, more importantly, the athletic department as a whole.

Things that will need to be taken into account for a project like the one proposed include: the cost of hiring an architectural company, construction costs, equipment costs, the cost of labor, and facility maintenance for the updated field. Surely, the department would have to employ staff to work ticket sales and a concession area during events.

The Plan to Update the Rutgers Softball Facilities

Clearly, in order for the softball team to even attempt to create profit, its facilities must be up to par with its revenue-generating counterparts in the Big East. By adding stadium seating that replaces the bleachers currently in place, the field will be easily accessible, hold more fans, and the program can begin to charge admission for the games. Aesthetic changes made to the field such as replacing the infield dirt and outfield grass, reconstructing the dugouts, and improving the bullpens and batting cages will attract both fans and prospective recruits. As the research has shown, both of these parties are equally important in the process of generating revenue. Finally, by having newly updated facilities, it will not be difficult to rent the stadium out for other uses, such as high school games, camps, or even campus events.

I appreciate you taking the time to read my proposal. I hope that you will consider this plan to improve the softball facilities here at Rutgers where we are a leading university, and our facilities should represent us as such. I would also like to invite you to attend an oral presentation of this proposal on Thursday, July 12, 2012, at 4:00 p.m. in Loree 007. Please feel free to contact me by phone at (732) 890-4326 or by e-mail at credmond@rutgers.edu if you have any questions.

Sincerely,

Christine Redmond

Christine Redmond

Works Cited

Bradley, Michaele. "Profit MaxiMization." *21st Century Economics: A Reference Handbook.* Ed. Rhona C. Free. Thousand Oaks, CA: SAGE, 2010. 110–25. *SAGE Reference Online.* Web. 20 Jun. 2012.

Eichelberger, Curtis, and Elise Young. "Rutgers Football Fails Profit Test As Students Pay $1,000." *Bloomberg News.* Bloomberg, 06 May 2012. Web. 13 Jun. 2012.

Fenn, Aju. "Sports Economics." *21st Century Economics: A Reference Handbook.* Ed. Rhona C. Free. Thousand Oaks, CA: SAGE, 2010. 533–42. *SAGE Reference Online.* Web. 13 Jun. 2012.

Hoye, Russell, Matthew Nicholson, and Aaron Smith. "Unique Aspects of Managing Sport Organizations." *21st Century Management: A Reference Handbook.* Thousand Oaks, CA: SAGE, 2007. 502–10. *SAGE Reference Online.* Web. 13 Jun. 2012.

McDonald, Becky. "Sports Promotion." *Encyclopedia of Public Relations.* Thousand Oaks, CA: SAGE, 2004. 807–09. *SAGE Reference Online.* Web. 20 Jun. 2012.

"Melissa Cook Stadium." *The Official Site of Notre Dame Athletics.* University of Notre Dame. Web. 13 Jun. 2012.

"NCAA.com." *NCAA Division 1 Softball Rankings.* NCAA. Web. 20 Jun. 2012.

Silk, Michael. "Sports Stadiums." *Encyclopedia of Urban Studies.* Ed. Ray Hutchison. Thousand Oaks, CA: SAGE, 2009. 763–67. *SAGE Reference Online.* Web. 20 Jun. 2012.

"Ulmer Stadium." *University of Louisville Official Athletic Site- Facilities.* Louisville Athletics. Web. 13 Jun. 2012.

"USF Softball Stadium." *Official Athletics Website of the University of South Florida.* USF Athletics. Web. 13 Jun. 2012.

Chapter 5 ◼ Midterm Sales Letter Workshop

Please fill out the following form for your partner. Feel free to write comments on the draft as well.

Does the document . . .

1. directly address the funding source?   ____ yes ____ no
2. catch the attention of the reader?   ____ yes ____ no
3. discuss why the reader is appropriate?   ____ yes ____ no
4. include specific and descriptive headings to help guide the reader?   ____ yes ____ no
5. express a clear command of population and problem?   ____ yes ____ no
6. adequately *document* a problem for a specific location and population?   ____ yes ____ no
7. appropriately *quantify* the problem?   ____ yes ____ no
8. argue in a way that would *appeal* to the audience?   ____ yes ____ no
9. refer to specific *evidence*?   ____ yes ____ no
10. offer *examples* and/or *details* from sources?   ____ yes ____ no
11. cite each source in-text according to MLA format?   ____ yes ____ no
12. describe a particular *paradigm*?   ____ yes ____ no
13. offer a researched *rationale* for the plan?   ____ yes ____ no
14. present a plan which follows logically from the *research*?   ____ yes ____ no
15. include the *suggestion* of a budget?   ____ yes ____ no
16. invite the reader to his/her presentation
    (including date, time, and location)?   ____ yes ____ no
17. include a list of *Works Cited* prepared according to MLA standards
    with a minimum of eight published sources and at least 50% cited
    from scholarly work?   ____ yes ____ no
18. appear in full block form and include all six elements
    (return address, date, recipient's address, salutation, body, closing)?   ____ yes ____ no

Is the document . . .

1. signed?   _____ yes _____ no

2. free of all grammatical and typographical errors?   _____ yes _____ no

3. four to five pages in length, not including the Works Cited page(s),
   in 12 point Times New Roman font with one-inch margins?   _____ yes _____ no

What parts of the draft do you like the most?

What parts of the draft need the most improvement?

Additional Comments/Suggestions:

Chapter 5 ■ Midterm Sales Letter Workshop

Please fill out the following form for your partner. Feel free to write comments on the draft as well.

Does the document . . .

1. directly address the funding source? _____ yes _____ no
2. catch the attention of the reader? _____ yes _____ no
3. discuss why the reader is appropriate? _____ yes _____ no
4. include specific and descriptive headings to help guide the reader? _____ yes _____ no
5. express a clear command of population and problem? _____ yes _____ no
6. adequately *document* a problem for a specific location and population? _____ yes _____ no
7. appropriately *quantify* the problem? _____ yes _____ no
8. argue in a way that would *appeal* to the audience? _____ yes _____ no
9. refer to specific *evidence*? _____ yes _____ no
10. offer *examples* and/or *details* from sources? _____ yes _____ no
11. cite each source in-text according to MLA format? _____ yes _____ no
12. describe a particular *paradigm*? _____ yes _____ no
13. offer a researched *rationale* for the plan? _____ yes _____ no
14. present a plan which follows logically from the *research*? _____ yes _____ no
15. include the *suggestion* of a budget? _____ yes _____ no
16. invite the reader to his/her presentation (including date, time, and location)? _____ yes _____ no
17. include a list of *Works Cited* prepared according to MLA standards with a minimum of eight published sources and at least 50% cited from scholarly work? _____ yes _____ no
18. appear in full block form and include all six elements (return address, date, recipient's address, salutation, body, closing)? _____ yes _____ no

Is the document . . .

1. signed? _____ yes _____ no

2. free of all grammatical and typographical errors? _____ yes _____ no

3. four to five pages in length, not including the Works Cited page(s), in 12 point Times New Roman font with one-inch margins? _____ yes _____ no

What parts of the draft do you like the most?

What parts of the draft need the most improvement?

Additional Comments/Suggestions:

Chapter 5 ■ Midterm Sales Letter Workshop

Please fill out the following form for your partner. Feel free to write comments on the draft as well.

Does the document . . .

1. directly address the funding source?   _____ yes _____ no

2. catch the attention of the reader?   _____ yes _____ no

3. discuss why the reader is appropriate?   _____ yes _____ no

4. include specific and descriptive headings to help guide the reader?   _____ yes _____ no

5. express a clear command of population and problem?   _____ yes _____ no

6. adequately *document* a problem for a specific location and population?   _____ yes _____ no

7. appropriately *quantify* the problem?   _____ yes _____ no

8. argue in a way that would *appeal* to the audience?   _____ yes _____ no

9. refer to specific *evidence*?   _____ yes _____ no

10. offer *examples* and/or *details* from sources?   _____ yes _____ no

11. cite each source in-text according to MLA format?   _____ yes _____ no

12. describe a particular *paradigm*?   _____ yes _____ no

13. offer a researched *rationale* for the plan?   _____ yes _____ no

14. present a plan which follows logically from the *research*? _____ yes _____ no

15. include the *suggestion* of a budget?   _____ yes _____ no

16. invite the reader to his/her presentation
    (including date, time, and location)?   _____ yes _____ no

17. include a list of *Works Cited* prepared according to MLA standards
    with a minimum of eight published sources and at least 50% cited
    from scholarly work?   _____ yes _____ no

18. appear in full block form and include all six elements
    (return address, date, recipient's address, salutation, body, closing)?   _____ yes _____ no

Is the document . . .

1. signed? _____ yes _____ no

2. free of all grammatical and typographical errors? _____ yes _____ no

3. four to five pages in length, not including the Works Cited page(s), in 12 point Times New Roman font with one-inch margins? _____ yes _____ no

What parts of the draft do you like the most?

What parts of the draft need the most improvement?

Additional Comments/Suggestions:

The Oral Presentation

Chapter 6

The Assignment

The oral presentation is a ten- to fifteen-minute spoken proposal addressed to your patron (i.e., the person or people who might fund your idea). The ten- to fifteen-minute parameter does not include time spent setting up and breaking down the materials. This limit also does not include the time required for questions from the audience. This is a formal presentation, and you must use visual aids to help convey information clearly and effectively. The point of the presentation is to make a leadership statement for a specific audience that puts information into action by proposing a research-justified solution to a well-defined problem.

The oral presentation is both a useful step in the process of developing your project and a unique assignment for which you will receive a grade. It therefore serves two sometimes competing purposes:

- As an "oral draft" of the final project, it's an opportunity to rehearse your audience-awareness, to organize your research, to develop your plan, and to get feedback from the class and the instructor on how to improve your project. A significant amount of your grade will be based on how well you have researched your project and how well prepared you are to put together the final proposal.

- As an exercise in public speaking, it's a chance to practice the arts of oral persuasion. Part of your grade will be based on how well you perform as a speaker.

While instructors will generally focus their grades and their remarks on the strength of your content, offering advice on revision, they will also take notice of your form and poise. Usually, those students who have the strongest content do best overall.

The basic parts of the presentation are laid out in the sections that follow. I suggest that you carefully read over the advice offered here, especially if this is the first time you have ever spoken before a group.

The Basic Parts of the Presentation

Every presentation will have to take its own form, based on the situation and the topic. If you are addressing a potentially resistant audience, for example, you may have to begin by winning them over or addressing possible objections they might have to your idea. Therefore, you should recognize that you cannot always adhere to a single form for the talk, and the outline below may have to be adapted to your particular needs.

As part of the drafting process of your proposal, the oral presentation gives you a chance to firm up your project and work out all of the parts. You should therefore keep in mind the Six P's of the project proposal: patron, population, problem, paradigm, plan, and price. Each of the Six P's should be represented in your presentation. Your talk should suggest the basic form of the final paper and should do these nine basic things:

1. Announce your topic with a "title slide," which should display your name and the title of your talk. This corresponds to your title page in your proposal.

2. Begin by addressing your specific audience, explaining why they should be interested in your project. This corresponds to the letter of transmittal in the final paper, where you address the Patron.

3. Give your audience some sense of how you'll proceed, perhaps with an outline, or presentation agenda. This corresponds to the table of contents in the final paper. This could be presented on a slide, in a handout, or both.

4. Define the problem and try to quantify it in some way. This corresponds to your introduction section of the final paper, where you will generally lay out the Problem.

5. Present your research, being sure to cite sources in the proper format. This will correspond to the research or literature review section of the final paper, which is where you develop your Paradigm.

6. Describe your plan of action. This corresponds to your plan or procedures section, where you set forth the Plan.

7. Tell us about your budget and explain the Price.

8. Close with a call to action, which might correspond to your discussion section of the final paper.

9. Along the way, be sure to use visual graphic aids, just as you will in your final paper.

The two main differences, then, between the oral presentation and the final paper is (1) that the oral is spoken and (2) that it is missing a list of references. You must, however, cite any published material used in your presentation.

How to Prepare

As with all assignments, you will have to prepare in the ways that have worked for you in the past. But here is some advice if you don't know where to start:

- **Research your imagined audience.** Who do you imagine might come to your talk? What is their degree of prestige and power? What level of knowledge or technical sophistication do they possess? What are their names? Many people like to begin their talk by welcoming the people in the imagined audience and thanking some of them by name for coming. This could appear on the title slide, as well. The more specifically you can imagine your audience the better your talk will be.

- **Plan ahead.** You can't wait until the last minute to prepare for a talk, and the sooner you start the better. The most important things to work on ahead of time are your visual aids, especially any visual graphic aids you want to use, such as PowerPoint slides, video and/or audio. The sooner you begin putting your materials in order, the more secure you will feel about the presentation itself.

- **Focus your talk around key points or examples.** Remember that you can't cover everything in your talk, but you will be able to cover the major points of your argument and the chief examples that support you (which you should be able to discuss in detail). If you can establish these points on paper, you will be able to focus your work.

- **Prepare an outline.** You will definitely want to prepare an outline for yourself, and you likely will want to provide your audience with an outline as well so they can follow you more easily. As you outline, pay attention to the logic and flow of your talk.

- **Develop solid visual graphic aids.** Remember one rule of thumb: if it can be represented visually, then it should be. You should have at least three visual graphic aids (visual representations of numerical information), but if your talk will cover technical information or you will be referencing numerical information you may need to use more than that. These should be effective and useful to your talk.

- **You might prepare notecards for details.** You shouldn't read your talk, but you may need to write some things down for reference. You may want to use notecards to remember numbers, names, and key details you want to cover. Number your notecards so you can keep them in order, and try to key them to your outline for easy use.

- **Know your information and examples so you can talk about them freely.** One of the best ways to prepare for the talk is just to read over your research so that you know your topic well. If you can talk about your key examples off the cuff, then you will do fine. This skill will prove to be vital in the question-and-answer part of the presentation.

- **Rehearse the talk out loud.** The key to preparing any fine performance is a dress rehearsal. Practice in front of the mirror or, better, in front of a friend. Time your talk to make sure it will not run over 15 minutes (you will be surprised how easy that is to do), and so you have a better sense of time management. If you are especially nervous about speaking in a classroom, rehearse your talk in an actual classroom.

- **Get some sleep the night before.** A good night's sleep may be the best preparation for any situation where you will be the center of attention.

- **Double-check everything.** Make a checklist for yourself. Are your slides in order? Do you have your notecards? Make sure you have everything covered. Arrive early to test and set up any equipment you plan to use.

- **Back up all software**. You can't afford delays due to fumbling with technology. Most likely, you won't get an opportunity to reschedule your presentation.

The Question of Delivery

Delivery is all about ethos. Do we believe you? Do you impress us? Do you know what you are talking about? Like the way you package and present your final paper, the way you present your information will go a long way toward keeping their interest and attention. Here is some general advice on delivery:

- **Dress the part.** Students always ask, "Do we have to dress up for our presentation?" I usually respond, "It depends on your imagined audience." If you research your patron properly, you will know what they expect. You should definitely wear clothes that are appropriate to the context. If you want to make a good impression, it's generally a good idea to break out some of your better clothes. Sweatpants will not reflect well on you in any situation. For men, a tie is always best, but an outfit you would wear on a casual Friday at an office job might do. For women, any outfit you would wear to an office job should be sufficient. Ask your instructor for specific guidelines.

- **Create the context.** Clothes are only part of setting the stage for your talk. You will also want to indicate your imagined audience and acknowledge their interests whenever possible. Highlight the fact that you know your imagined audience well and make sure that you keep them in mind throughout.

- **Use a tone appropriate to your imagined audience.** One way of keeping the audience in mind is by using the same language and tone that you'd use if they really were in the room. If you are asking university officials for money, for example, you wouldn't want to talk about "the RU Screw."

- **Enunciate and speak clearly.** This doesn't always mean speaking loudly, but you should speak clearly enough so that everyone can hear you.

- **Make eye contact.** Try to make eye contact with everyone in the room at some point during your talk.

- **Don't rely too much on notes.** Organize your presentation around an outline and use notecards, but *do not write out or read the presentation*. In other words: speak it, don't read it. You should know your information well enough at this point to be able to speak with confidence and knowledge using only an outline and visual aids to support and guide you. If you need to write down facts, figures, names, or an outline, use notecards because they are relatively unobtrusive. Try not to put too much between yourself and the audience … and NEVER read the slides to your audience.

- **Project energy and "sell" your idea.** If I have one major criticism of student presentations, it's that they rarely give off much energy. Imagine that you are really asking someone for money. You have to sell them on your plan. Turn any nervousness you have about the talk into energy and put a little bit of performance into your presentation. It will count for a lot with your audience and will keep them interested.

- **Ignore distractions and mistakes.** Everyone slips up here and there. Don't draw attention to mistakes, but move on so that both you and your audience can leave them behind.

- **Move for emphasis only—don't pace.** Everyone has tics and idiosyncratic actions that come out when they speak before a group. One person I know always holds a cup of water between himself and the audience as a sort of shield. Odd tics are usually an unconscious way of defending yourself from the people you're addressing. Pacing, for example, presents your viewers with a moving target so they can't hit you if they start to throw vegetables or bricks. Try to recognize these actions ahead of time and work through them. You have nothing to fear from your listeners, so try generally to stand still. Just don't stand in front of the screen too often or you'll be blocking people's view of your visual aids.

- **Be careful with humor.** Many guides to giving oral presentations will tell you to begin with a joke to loosen up your audience. What if you're talking about an especially serious topic? Use humor in moderation and only where appropriate.

Advice on Using PowerPoint Slides

Since most students rely almost exclusively on PowerPoint for their visual aids, here is some advice on preparing and using them:

- **Begin with a title slide**. Be sure to have a title slide that sets the stage for your talk and introduces yourself and your topic. It also helps to make a good first impression—especially if it is well prepared. The title slide, like a title page, should display your title, your name, and your organization. Welcome your patron and make him/her/them comfortable. Use white space, graphics, color, or design elements that are consistent with your other slides to make it attractive.

- **Use a slide for each section of your talk.** Each section of your talk—or even every topic you cover—should have its own slide. This way you can mark the turns in your argument by changing the visual image, and you can help guide your audience through each part.

- **Have one theme per slide.** Remember not to crowd too much information onto each slide. It's best to just try to cover one theme on each one. Be wary of **text-heavy** slides.

- **Give each one a header (and number them if it helps you).** Each of your slides should have its own head line or header, indicating the topic it covers. You might want these headers to correspond to the outline you presented earlier to make your talk easier to follow. Headers should have a consistent style and form and should give a good idea of what you'll cover in that section of your talk.

- **Be sure to cite sources on charts, graphs, paraphrases, or quotes.** Each visual graphic aid that uses information derived from a source should have a "source" reference at the bottom, fully visible to your audience.

- **Use large letters and a clear font.** Remember that your slides have to be seen in the back of the room as well as the front. Make them as clear and as large as possible, yet strive for an attractive appearance.

- **Maintain a consistent font and style.** All of your slides should have the same font and if you use a border it should be the same on each one. Often it is less important to follow any rule than it is to be consistent in the styles you choose. Such consistency helps to project a sense of unity to your presentation.

- **Try a unifying border or logo.** To help further project that image of unity, you can use a logo or border on each slide. This is especially useful when you are representing a company, where you may want to have your company logo or a border with colors or a style consistent with your company image.

- **Jazz it up with color if you can.** There is no question that people are impressed by color, and your presentation will stand out more if you use color in your slides and in your visual aids. However, if expense is an issue you may want to stick to black and white.

- **Strive for active voice.** Use active voice forms in your slides whenever possible, just as in all business writing.

- **Put numbers in a visual graphic form.** Remember that if something can be illustrated it probably should be illustrated. A picture is not always worth a thousand words, but it will usually keep you from using a thousand words to say the same thing. If a number or an idea or a definition or a procedure can be illustrated, it probably should be.

- **Let the audience absorb each slide.** Too often students don't leave their slides up long enough, often because they are hurrying through the presentation. Try to manage your time well and use a slide for each section of your talk, leaving each one on the screen until you raise a new topic.

- **Point to your slides for reference.** Draw your audience's attention to key aspects of your slides by interacting with them. You can do this in several ways—on screen, with the mouse, with a shadow, or with a light pen.

Some PowerPoint Slide "Don'ts"

- **Don't use all caps.** Studies show that people can distinguish words and parts of sentences more easily if you use both lowercase and capital letters. Readers also perceive text written in all capital letters as shouting.

- **Don't put too much information on each slide, or use long sentences, because viewers cannot absorb it all.** Try to put no more than short phrases on each slide, and don't overcrowd them. If you find yourself putting a lot of information on a slide, then likely you need to break that information up to fit on several.

- **Don't use characters smaller than 20 point.** Remember that the people in the back of the room will have trouble with small text.

- **Don't violate the rule of parallel form.** Each slide should have information that fits together in such a way that you can list it using phrases in parallel form. This helps the audience to see connections and to organize information.

- **Don't be inconsistent in capitalizing words.** In fact, don't be inconsistent about anything.

- **Don't forget to proofread for typos.** Typos on a presentation slide are like an unzipped fly: they destroy your ethos and make you look silly.

Final Words of Advice

Recognize that it's normal to be nervous.

Most people feel a bit nervous whenever they have to speak before an audience, especially the first few times they have to do so. Remember that this is normal. If fears persist, though, here are a few thoughts that might help you get past your fears:

- Remember that you know more about your topic than anyone in the room. Just try to make yourself clear and you will automatically have something to offer the audience.

- Your listeners take your nervousness for granted. In fact, since most student listeners are not used to giving presentations themselves, they expect everyone to be nervous and will either overlook or identify with your situation.

- This might be the friendliest audience you will ever face. As fellow students, your listeners are on your side and generally want to give you high marks: I often notice that student reviewers generally see the most positive aspects of individual talks and tend to overlook problems (even after I have urged them to offer critical comments).

- Recognize that if this is your first talk it is a necessary rite of passage. The more practice you have giving presentations, the easier they will get and the less nervous you will feel each time.

- Turn fear into motivation. Nervousness can be a spur to greater preparation. Fear is not necessarily a negative thing, but the way you respond to it has to be positive. One common negative response to fear is procrastination, which is merely avoidance behavior (a variation on running away). The best response to fear is work, which can only help you in developing your project and bolstering your confidence in your subject knowledge.

If you still have worries or fears, talk them over with your professor or with friends. The more you face your fears, the better off you'll be in the long run.

Don't talk down to your audience, but challenge them to follow.

The biggest mistake that students make in presenting a technical subject is trying to get their audiences "up to speed" by giving lots of background information, usually in the form of textbook knowledge, before they begin the presentation itself. Background information should not be presented at the start, for several reasons:

- It destroys the fiction you are trying to create that you are speaking to a knowledgeable audience. Right away, you have confused your listeners as to who your audience really is. Chronologically speaking, your audience has read your midterm letter and are there to hear more.

- It sets the wrong tone, making your audience feel like they are being talked down to by a schoolmaster. Treat your audience as equals and they will prick up their ears in order to become equal to your conception of them.

- It underestimates your audience's intelligence. Because you are speaking to a college-educated audience, most of your listeners will already possess much of the basic knowledge needed to follow your talk. There may even be some audience members as expert as yourself in your field of study. Listeners will feel insulted by your explanations of "osmosis," for example, and will tune you out. Challenge them to tune in instead.

- It wastes time that you will need to present your idea. Remember that you only have a maximum of 15 minutes to give your talk. How can you present everything you learned in your core curriculum in such a short time? You can't, so don't try.

- It mistakenly tries to anticipate questions that are best left to the question-and-answer period. Remember, if someone in the audience doesn't understand something they can always ask about it afterward. And what question is easier for you to handle than the most basic questions where you get to show off the breadth of your knowledge?

- It will not make sense in the abstract. Because information is never useful except in context, audiences have a very difficult time understanding definitions, explanations, or lessons offered in report form apart from the flow of argument.

- It is unnecessary. If a presentation is organized logically, your audience will follow your argument even if they do not understand all of the details. If you feel it is necessary to explain certain technical ideas, remember that it is much more useful to offer such explanations briefly in the context of your argument (or in the question period after) than it is to give them ahead of time. Just do your thing with confidence and your audience will be impressed, especially if they don't understand all the details.

Logic should govern above all.

This point was brought home to me once while listening to a student presentation on training co-op students to use proper care and technique in recording information in the field so as to comply with government regulations. Basically, these students were making many small mistakes (such as recording temperatures in Fahrenheit instead of Centigrade) that were destroying the integrity of whole projects. What could be more understandable? Yet the speaker began by presenting "background information" about the types of studies the students were doing and the specific data they were collecting. By the time she had finished offering that long explanation, she had to rush through her plan to train these students in better data-collecting techniques. As one reviewer in the audience noted, "I had no idea what she was talking about until she said that these students were using felt-tipped pens on rainy days to write down information." Basically, the audience did not need to know what was being written down with that felt-tip pen to understand that such pens posed a problem in the field.

State your argument up front; don't keep your audience in the dark.

You will never have your audience's attention more than you do at the outset of your talk. So tell them as much as you can up front. Someone once said that the best advice for giving a talk is to do three things: "One: tell your audience what you're going to say; two: say it; and three: tell them what you said." While following that advice literally will lead you to an overly formulaic presentation, it does suggest the importance of leading your audience clearly through your argument with all of the forecasting statements and signposts you can muster. As I suggest above, one of the easiest ways of helping your audience to follow your talk is to provide an outline at the outset and then use slides to signal your transitions (just as you should use strong topic sentences to signal your transitions at the opening of a new paragraph in writing).

Focus on your evidence.

The most important aspect of the presentation is that you show that you have the evidence and research to support your assertions. Just as you would do in a written form, be sure to cite your sources. Name the authorities who inform your paradigm. Name the sources for all statistical data you cite. Name the authors of studies or experiments that you reference. Describe examples or models you reference in specific detail. Emphasize that there is a wide array of evidence to support you in your claims.

Illustrate your budget with a pie chart.

As part of your plan, you must include a budget, since it is one of your imagined audience's biggest concerns. Since this is one place you will always have numbers to work with, why not use a nice pie chart or other visual aid to sum up your budget? A pie chart is most appropriate because it lets you enumerate both the total and the parts.

Close with a polished call to action.

The closing of your presentation should sum up the plan you have in mind and urge your audience to act upon it. Hence the content of your close should focus on what needs to be done, and it should take a form that tries to influence your audience to act. Use whatever rhetorical powers you can muster to get them to listen. Listeners tend to remember best what comes at the beginning and at the end of a presentation more than anything in between. Therefore, in the same way you should strive to make a good first impression, you should close your talk with words that reflect well upon you as a speaker and offer up the "take home" message of your talk in a memorable way. Some speakers actually write out their closing words in order to polish and hone their form and tone. A strong close also signals clearly the end of your talk and lets the audience know it is time to applaud.

Graphic Aids Assignment

Visual aids are an important part of both your oral presentation and your final project. They can provoke an immediate response in your audience in a way that a paragraph of statistics may not. In preparation for your oral presentation, bring in at least three visual aids with written commentary.

For the purposes of this assignment, these three visual graphic aids should be taken from popular sources, such as newspapers or magazines, or printed out from online sources (e.g., *Google* images). They could be ones that you are considering using for your oral presentation and project proposal, but they could also just be interesting examples of graphics. Please do not bring in pictures or photographs; I would much rather have you find images which are visual representations of statistical information, as in charts, tables, graphs, and so on. You may find certain graphics that you find misleading, or would like to show the class possible "sneaky" tactics used by the presenters. To help you develop good, informative, attractive visual aids, we will look at your examples and some others in a peer review/class presentation session.

Using PowerPoint to Develop a Presentation

You are required to use visual aids in your presentation, including at least three visual graphic aids (such as graphs or charts). While there are a number of computer programs that can help you do this, no program is as effective as PowerPoint in helping you put together a coherent slide show that combines words and images.

Why Use PowerPoint?

Transparencies can be just as effective as PowerPoint slides and may be your only choice if you are not in a Smart Classroom. However, PowerPoint slides can easily be made into transparencies. In addition, PowerPoint offers both the graph-making abilities of Excel and the text-making abilities of Word while giving you powerful tools for keeping your slides consistent in layout and design.

What to Include on Your Slides

Do not try to put everything you want to say on your slides or you will overwhelm your audience with information. Instead, your slides should emphasize the major points and primary evidence that you want your audience to remember. Focus your PowerPoint slides around key points or examples. Ideally, you should try to limit each slide's content to four to five bulleted points (never more than seven) that are about five words each (the sound-byte version of your talk). This way your audience will be able to focus on what you are saying rather than focusing on reading the slides.

Getting Started

Open PowerPoint. You will automatically see this screen once the program loads:

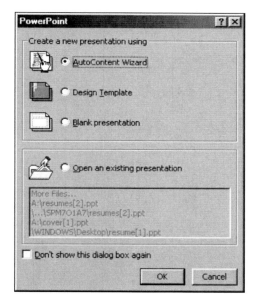

Because writing and presenting is an active decision-making process, the best presentations will usually begin by selecting either the "Design Template" or "Blank Presentation" option. This way you can control the content-making process so that your presentation best suits your audience's needs. The design template offers you a professional-looking presentation. However, these templates are somewhat generic and are usually recognized by business professionals, so you might consider creating your own template by selecting "Blank Presentation."

For a blank presentation, *select "Blank Presentation" and click OK.* Now you can see the slides that are available to create a presentation.

Creating a Title Slide

You should begin your presentation with a title transparency that sets the stage for your talk and introduces you and your topic. A good title slide will also help you make a good first impression. The title slide, like a title page, should display your title, your name, and your organization. Use white space, graphics, color, or design elements that are consistent with your other slides to make it attractive. Any of the blank presentation slides will work as a title slide, but the first slide choice is most commonly used.

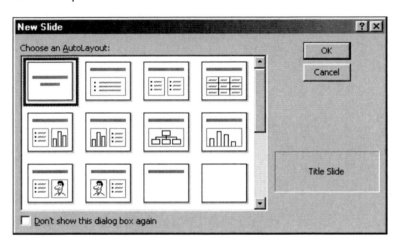

Highlight the type of slide you would like to use. Click OK. Now you can edit the slide.

When you have finished, *be sure to save your work!* Once you have saved, *start a new slide by clicking on "Insert" and then scrolling to "New Slide."*

Organizing the Rest of Your Presentation

Before you select the blank slides for the rest of your presentation, think about the logical progression of your talk. You might find the Six P's a useful basic outlining tool, moving in order through Patron (why did you choose this audience?), People (who needs help?), Problem (what evidence do you have of a problem?), Paradigm (what research informs your solution?), Plan (how will your plan be implemented?), and Price (how much will it cost?). Try to chunk major ideas together on each slide, outlining your talk so that the audience can remember its most important points and understand the parts of your argument. For each section, ask yourself what the key ideas are and develop bullet points to represent each one. And spend some time thinking about what visual graphic aids will be the most powerful in persuading your audience.

You should especially try to use visual graphic aids to help quantify the problem, since a picture can be a powerful persuader early on in your talk.

Inserting Tables

Tables are used to show a large amount of numerical data in a small space. They provide more information than a graph with less visual impact. Because of the way they organize information into vertical columns and horizontal rows, tables also permit easy comparison of figures. Be sure to use concise, descriptive table titles and column headings. In addition, arrange the rows of the table in a logical order. When putting dollar amounts into tables, be sure the decimals are aligned for easy addition or subtraction. *To create a table, click on the fourth slide.*

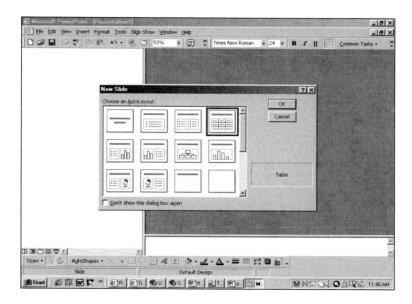

Before PowerPoint will insert a table, it asks you to enter the number of columns and rows you need. *Enter the number and click OK.*

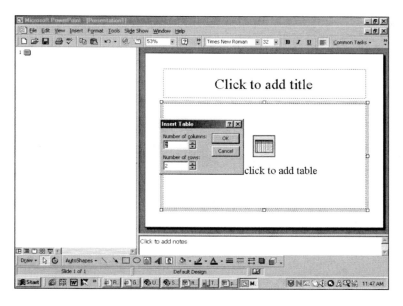

Through the Tables and Borders toolbar, PowerPoint enables you to align text with the top or bottom, center text vertically, change the border color, change the cell color, and manually split cells with the "draw table" button.

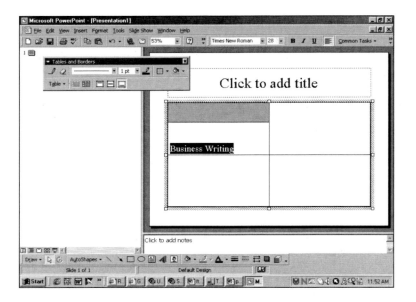

Inserting and Editing a Graph

Before you make a graph, think about the information you want to convey. Draw a picture by hand and think about whether there is room for text on the page as well. *Choose a new slide that has a graph where you want it (with text or without)*; you will see a spreadsheet and a preformulated graph. If you don't see the spreadsheet, double-click on the graph and it will appear.

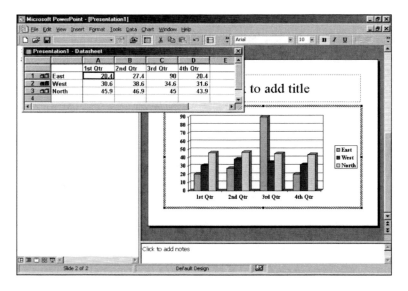

PowerPoint's graph-making layout is like that of Excel. You do not draw the graphs yourself. Rather, you change the data in your spreadsheet and then PowerPoint draws the graph you need automatically. However, you can change the appearance of your graph directly. Click on any part of the graph to change its size, shape, or color.

To change the type of chart you are using, click on "Chart" and scroll to "Chart Type." You will see the following menu where you can choose several different graphing options, including bar graphs, pie graphs, line graphs, and even bubble graphs. *Select the graph that is best suited to conveying your data.* For instance, line charts are generally used to show changes in data over a period of time and to emphasize trends. Bar charts compare the magnitude of items, either at a specific time or over a period of time. Pie charts compare parts that make up the whole. With pie charts, you should start at the 12 o'clock position with the largest unit and work around in descending order.

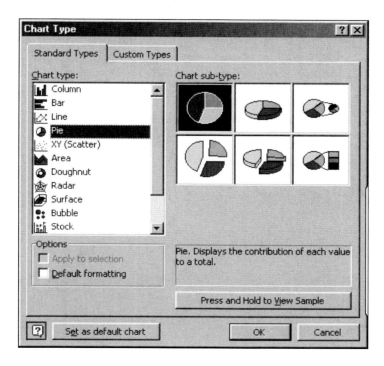

Whatever chart you choose, be sure to keep it simple. Your goal is to focus the reader's attention on the data in the chart rather than on the chart itself. In addition, you will want to label all charts as figures and assign them consecutive numbers that are separate from table numbers. This way if your audience has a question about a specific image later, they can refer to it by name and number.

Using Photos and Graphics

The "power" of PowerPoint comes from the way it allows you to seamlessly integrate text and images. Images can be a powerful support for your message, though they can also distract from what you want to say if they are not well chosen. Ideally, you will want to develop your own original images to use in your presentation. But sometimes noncopyrighted graphics and images can be useful. *To insert clip art, simply double-click on the image field and follow the screen instructions to choose items from the Microsoft Clip Art Gallery. To add an image you have saved on your computer, click on "Import Clips" and navigate to where you saved it. To include photos or graphics from a website, you can first save them on your computer or simply right-click on the object and then click on "Copy."*

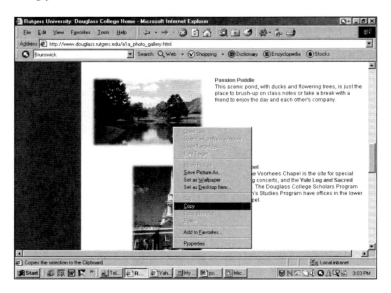

Return to your PowerPoint presentation. Right-click on the slide where you want the object and select "Paste."

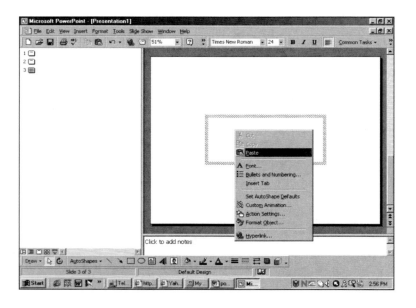

Making a Master Slide

You can also make any graphic or photo into a background for all of your slides. *To create a background go to "View," scroll to "Master," and click on "Slide Master."*

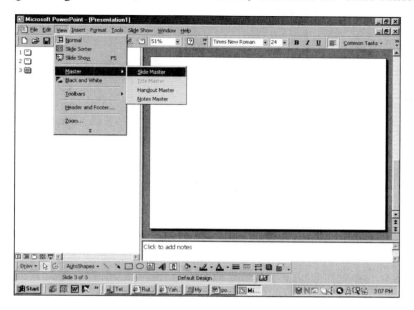

Right click on the center of the slide and select "Paste."

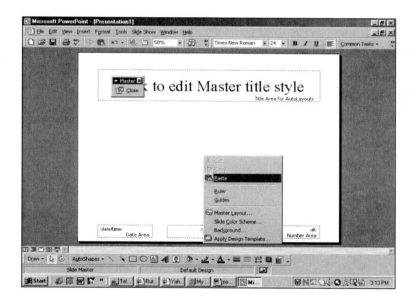

Click on the graphic. Grab a corner of the graphic and stretch the object across the screen so that it will fill the background of your master slide.

Sometimes it is hard to see text against an image background. But if the image is well chosen or especially appropriate to your topic it can help you to create an original background that breaks from the familiar generic backgrounds that most presenters use. Also, there are ways to make a background image fade into the background so that your text and support graphics can take center stage.

To blend your image into the background of a master slide, try the following:

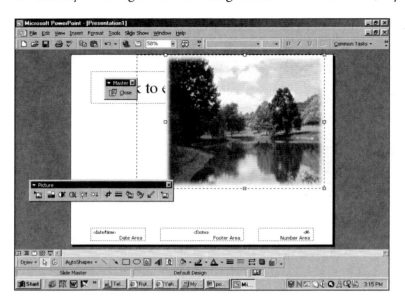

Click on "View." Scroll to "Toolbars." Check "Picture" and "Master." Alternate between clicking on "Less Contrast" and "More Brightness" until your background is light enough so your audience can read the text on your PowerPoint slide.

Click on "Close" on the Master toolbar to apply this background to all of your slides.

Adding Text

Once you have the basic visual layout of your talk you can add your text. This part is easy. *To make a slide with bullet points select the second slide from the New Slide menu.*

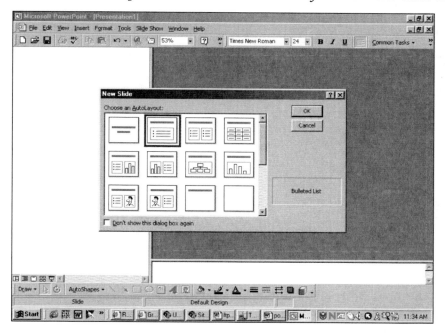

Add the text that you want.

Viewing Your Presentation

To view your presentation, go to "View" and click on "Slide Show." Press the right arrow key to advance your slides. *To exit, press the Esc key on your keyboard.*

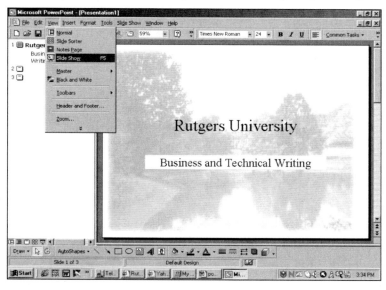

You are now ready to give a PowerPoint presentation!

Creating Your Own PowerPoint Template

This brief tutorial will guide you through the process of creating your own template for your PowerPoint slides, which will help individualize your presentation and help it stand out from others.

STEP 1: Find, create, or modify an image using Adobe Photoshop.

Unless you have a lot of experience with Photoshop, you will most likely want to find and modify an image to serve as your background. Therefore, I will focus on that option.

1A. Use *Google* Image Search to find something suitable.

In my own search, I went to *Google* Image Search (http://images.google.com/) and tried the term "leukemia." I quickly located an interesting image here: http://www.stanford.edu/group/cleary/leukemia.jpg

WARNING: Be sure to pick an image that is not too busy and will not distract from the information you present. Try out your template image on other people before you commit to it. Also, if you are doing a presentation in a professional setting, you may want to find noncopyrighted images or create your own images to avoid problems of copyright infringement.

1B. Save the image to your My Pictures folder.

1B1. Get the best version of the image onto your computer's browser window.

1B2. Right-click on the image and choose "Save Picture As . . ."

1B3. Save the image to your My Pictures folder (usually the default setting) or anywhere you can easily find it and work with it later. The My Pictures folder, by the way, is located in your My Documents folder.

1C. Modify the image with Photoshop to create an 800 x 600 pixel .jpg or .gif file.

1C1. Open Adobe Photoshop.

Go to Start → Programs → Adobe Photoshop CS.

1C2. Use Photoshop to open your image.

In Photoshop, go to File → Open → My Pictures → and navigate to your image. If you have the image open on your desktop, you can also simply drag and drop it into Photoshop directly.

1C3. Change the width or height of your image to > 800 × 600 pixels.

Go to Image → Image Size and change the width or height accordingly. In my case, I had to modify the width to 800 pixels and the height was greater than 600 automatically.

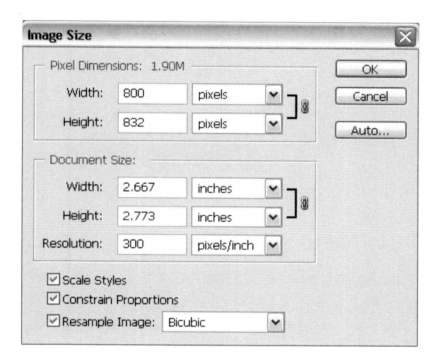

1C4. Create a New file 800 × 600 pixels.

Go to File → New and use the New window to create an 800 × 600 pixel background.

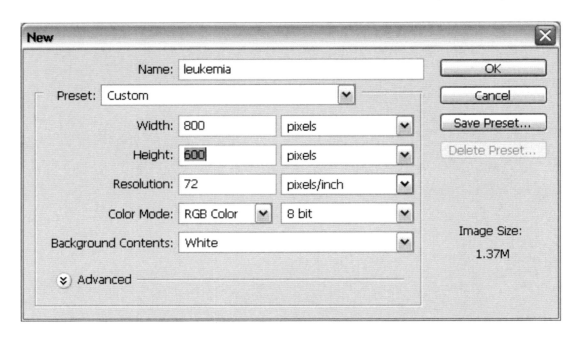

WARNING: Be sure to adjust the background and Color Mode accordingly. You will probably want to use "RGB Color."

1C5. Drag the ">800 × 600" image from its pane over to your new 800 × 600 file pane.

Be sure that the image is placed properly. You can also now modify the image further, as I will discuss. For example, to make an area where your text will display well, you can use the Eyedropper tool to pick the dominant color of your image and then the Paint Brush tool (with a large-sized brush, and the opacity set to about 50%) to dim your image slightly and make it fade into the background. This way your text will be easier to see later. There are other ways to modify your image, including the Clone Stamp and other tools. But painting an opaque layer over it is the easiest and fastest way to get a more simplified background to help your text stand out.

1C6. Save for Web.

Go to File → Save for Web. Save the image as a .jpg or .gif file to the My Pictures folder or wherever you will be able to find it easily later. This is the image you will use as your background.

WARNING: Be sure to select either .gif or .jpg in the Save for Web dialog box. Also, using Save alone will not work for you since Adobe will only save your working file as a PSD file, which you cannot use later. Be sure you are saving a .jpg or .gif file.

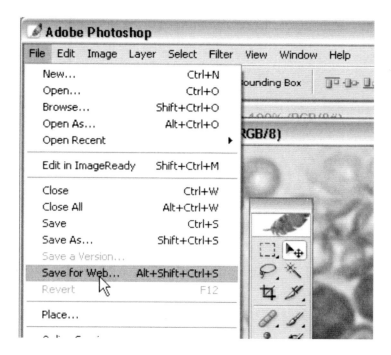

Save for web.

1C7. Close Photoshop and Save your work files (.PSD) just in case.

STEP 2: Create the PowerPoint Template

2A. Open PowerPoint.

2B. Begin a new Blank presentation.

Choose File → New. The New Presentation task pane appears. Click the New → Blank presentation option on the right of the screen.

2C. Open the Slide Master.

Choose View → Master → Slide Master.

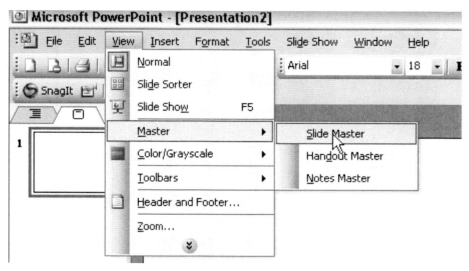

2D. Choose Insert → New Title Master.

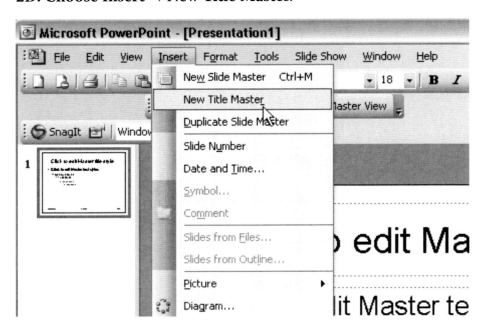

You will see two slide previews in the left pane. Both previews are linked through a connector. The top preview represents the slide master and the bottom preview represents the title master. Any elements you place within these masters show up on all of the slides based on them. The title layout slides are based on a title master. All of the other slide layouts are influenced by the slide master. (PowerPoint has more than 26 slide layouts, which you will find in the Slide Layout task pane.)

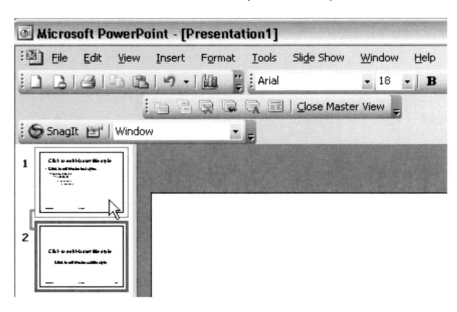

2E. Add your background image.

Choose Format → Background.

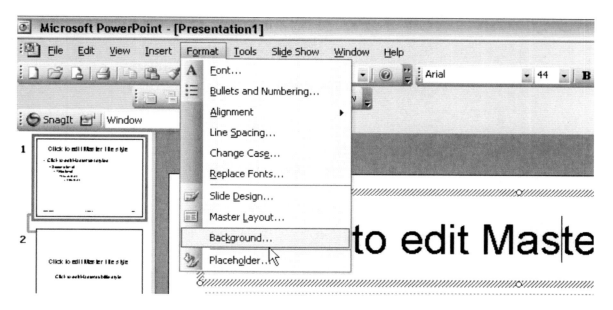

2E1. In the Background dialog box, click the downward-pointing arrow and click "Fill Effects."

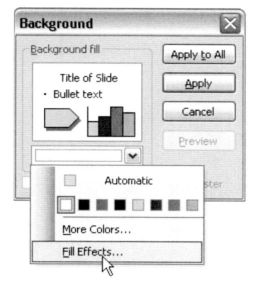

2E2. Select the Picture tab.

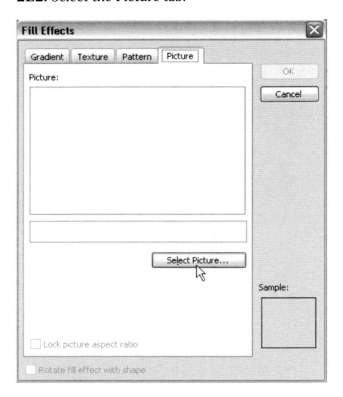

2E3. Find your picture (probably in My Pictures) and insert it.

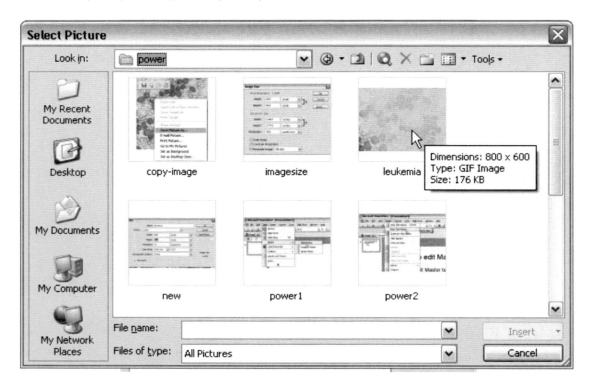

2F. Save Your Template

It's a good idea to save your template before we go further as a .pot (Design Template). Go to File → Save and be sure to select "Designer Template" or "PowerPoint Template" (.pot) from the "Save as type" part of the dialog as shown.

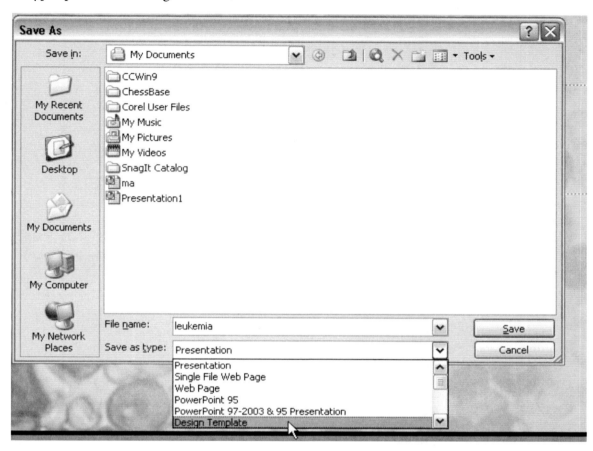

Once your design template is saved, you can create a new presentation using it.

Adapted from:

http://www.computorcompanion.com/LPMArticle.asp?ID=197

See the rest of that tutorial for additional help.

Beyond Bullet Points:

How to Unlock the Story Buried in Your PowerPoint

Cliff Atkinson

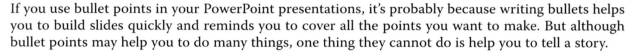

If you use bullet points in your PowerPoint presentations, it's probably because writing bullets helps you to build slides quickly and reminds you to cover all the points you want to make. But although bullet points may help you to do many things, one thing they cannot do is help you to tell a story.

Some of the world's largest organizations have adopted the word "story" as their new mantra for corporate communications. Marketing messages should tell a story, corporate strategy should tell a story, mission statements should tell a story, and even Web sites should tell a story. Why the sudden interest in stories? For one clue, look no further than the approach you may be applying to your own PowerPoint slides, which locks out the possibility of telling a story in the first place.

Bullet Points

The origin of bullet points in presentations is actually clearly visible on most PowerPoint slides—a type of outlining approach that everyone uses, yet no one questions. This approach always begins by placing a category heading at the top of a slide—such as Our History, Challenges, Outlook and Lessons Learned. It is remarkable that you see exactly the same headings in every presentation, across organizations, professions and even cultures.

These headings do nothing more than establish a category of information, which you then explain with a bulleted list below it. Although this approach can help you create slides quickly, it also guarantees that you never do anything more than present a series of lists to an audience. When the primary way we communicate is by presenting lists to one another, it is no wonder that the phenomenon of story is gaining momentum, because a story is the opposite of a list. Where a list is dry, fragmented and soulless, a story is juicy, coherent and full of life. Presented with the choice, any audience will choose life.

So, that leaves us with the essential problem: If we can agree that the era of the story is dawning, and that bullet points are standing in our way, how do we unlock the power of a story in our PowerPoint presentations? This is becoming an issue of strategic concern to major players by large organizations where PowerPoint has replaced the written word as the predominant way of communicating information.

What Kind of a Story?

The concept of a story may be new to the boardroom, but storytelling is at least as old as the person who defined it as an art 2,400 years ago: Aristotle. If you think Aristotle's ideas on story are no longer relevant, look no further than a movie screen. Hollywood screenwriters still credit Aristotle with writing the definitive elements of story, including action, a plot, central characters and visual effects.

But even Aristotle knew that not all stories are created equal. So, the natural question arises, "Exactly what kind of story is appropriate for a presentation?" For example, a story can take the shape of a Hollywood blockbuster meant to entertain, or a story can be a colorful anecdote about something that happened on vacation. Although both are stories, neither is complete enough to fulfill the complex needs of presenters and audiences today, both of which need much more than entertainment or personal anecdotes in order to make fully informed decisions.

Instead, we now need a specific type of story that blends a classic story structure along with classic ideas about persuasion. Again, Aristotle adds a great deal to the discussion, because he wrote the book on persuasion, in addition to the book on storytelling. In order to bring Aristotle's ideas up to date in a media-savvy world, you need to blend one part storytelling, one part persuasion and one part Hollywood screenwriting to create a powerful approach for your PowerPoint presentations.

Unlocking the Secret Code of a Persuasive Story

A persuasive story uses the structure of a story, but spins the story in a particular way that ensures it aims at achieving results we need in presentations: by using persuasion. You can apply this fundamental structure to any type of presentation. Using a visual medium such as PowerPoint gives you additional levels of communicative power, the same ones that Hollywood shows us every day.

For example, let's see how a persuasive story looks in the form of the first five slides in a PowerPoint presentation to a board of directors, where the presenter is seeking approval for a new product. Instead of using a category heading, the top of each slide features a simple statement that addresses each category of information that the board needs to know about, as described here.

Slide 1: Establish the setting. The headline of Slide 1 reads: Our sector of business is undergoing major change. The subject of this headline establishes the common setting for the presentation and relates the "where" and "when" for everyone in the audience.

Slide 2: Designate the audience as the main character. The headline of Slide 2 reads: Every board faces tough decisions about what to do next. The subject of this headline establishes the members of the board as the main characters in this story, establishing the "who" of the story.

Slide 3: Describe a conflict involving the audience. The headline of Slide 3 reads: Six new products have eroded our market share. The subject of this headline describes a conflict the board faces that has created an imbalance. This explains "why" the audience is there.

Slide 4: Explain the audience's desired state. The headline of Slide 4 reads: We can regain profitability by launching a new product. The board doesn't want to stay in a state of imbalance, so the subject of this headline describes the board's desired state, describing "what" the audience wants to see happen next.

Slide 5: Recommend a solution. The headline of Slide 5 reads: Approve the plan to build Product X, and we'll reach our goals. This final headline recommends a solution, describing "how" the audience will get from its current state of imbalance to its desired state of balance.

Reading these five headlines in succession reveals an interesting and engaging story that will be sure to capture the board's attention. And when you add an illustration to each of these headlines, you open up the power of projected images, including full-screen photographs, clip art, or even simple animated words.

The Rest of the Story

The five slides in this example form the backbone of Act I of a persuasive story structure. Act II then spins off of the pivotal fifth slide, explaining the various reasons why the audience should accept the solution. Act III frames the resolution, setting the stage for the audience to decide whether to accept the recommended solution.

With the solid structure of your first five slides in place, your presentations will move well beyond the stale world of bullet points, and into the lively world of a persuasive story. By blending together the classic concepts of story and persuasion with your PowerPoint software, you are sure to engage your audience and make things much more interesting—and productive—for both you and your audience.

Organizing Data in Tables and Charts: Different Criteria for Different Tasks

Jane E. Miller

Introduction

Tables and charts are efficient tools for organizing numbers. Too often, however, students and quantitative analysts do not give much consideration to the order in which they present data in tables or charts. This lack of thought means that the sequence of items may not be compatible with the author's objectives, whether testing a hypothesis, describing a pattern or reporting data for others' use. The appropriate criteria for arranging data in tables or charts often differ depending on whether they are to be used primarily with or without a prose description. Tables or charts intended to present numbers as evidence to address a specific question or to accompany a description of a pattern are usually best organized so that they coordinate with the associated narrative. On the other hand, tables intended to present data for reference use such as periodic series from the Bureau of Labour Statistics or a national census might work better if structured so that readers can find the numbers of interest to them with little written guidance. These two broad objectives suggest very different considerations for organizing variables or response categories.

No one of these purposes is inherently more important than the other, but in many cases a particular objective can be identified for reporting numbers in a given type of document. For example, numbers presented in a science laboratory report or a history essay are usually being applied as evidence for a particular hypothesis or to illustrate a trend or other pattern. In such cases, empirical or theoretical criteria are frequently a sensible basis for arranging the data because that is how they will be discussed in the accompanying prose. In contrast, detailed reference data on population or income for each of a dozen or more dates or places might not come with a written description, so using a self-guiding convention is well-suited to such tasks. This article uses data from the U.S. Consumer Expenditure Survey to illustrate four approaches to organizing data within tables and charts, discussing the situations for which each approach might be preferred.

Table 1 presents data on major categories of expenditures from the 2002 Consumer Expenditure Survey (CEX).

Item	Expenditures ($)
Average annual expenditures	42,557
Food	5612
Alcoholic beverages	415
Housing	13,481
Apparel and services	1872
Transportation	7984
Health care	2410
Entertainment	2167
Personal care products and services	562
Reading	145
Education	771
Tobacco products and supplies	334
Miscellaneous	846
Cash contributions	1366
Personal insurance and pensions	4593

Table 1   Average annual expenditures by major expenditure category, a U.S. Consumer Expenditure Survey, 2002

Source: U.S. Department of Labor, Bureau of Labor Statistics, 2004a. Table 1.

aFor all households with complete income reporting.

The CEX is conducted annually by the Bureau of Labor Statistics (BLS) using a diary survey form to collect detailed information on expenditures (U.S. Department of Labor 2004a). The information is then coded into the standard categories shown in Table 1, which retains the original order of major expenditure categories from a standard BLS report (U.S. Department of Labor 2004b).

Organizing Data To Accompany A Prose Description

When testing hypotheses or portraying trends or other patterns, it is helpful to organize your data in tables or charts in the order you will describe them. For such purposes, alphabetical order and the sequence of items from the original data source are poor organizing principles because they rarely correspond to substantively interesting or empirically relevant patterns. Consider Figure 1, which presents the information from Table 1 in chart form, again preserving the order of expenditure categories from the BLS report. The heights of the bars and the conceptual content of adjacent categories vary erratically, requiring readers to zigzag back and forth across the axes to identify the rank order of expenditure categories by dollar amount or to compare categories of necessities to one another or to non-necessities.

For similar reasons, Figure 2—which sequences the expenditure categories alphabetically—would also be a poor choice to accompany a description of empirical rankings or a discussion of necessities versus non-necessities.

Instead, to complement a prose description of a pattern, it is often sensible to arrange your data so that the audience can

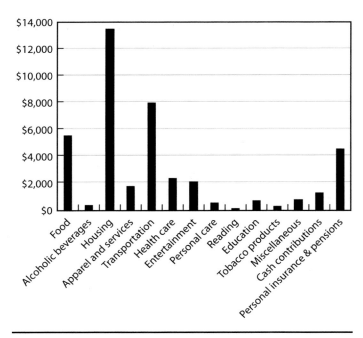

Figure 1 Major categories of expenditures, BLS ordering, 2002 U.S. Consumer Expenditure Survey

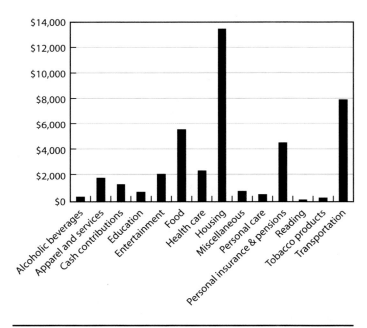

Figure 2 Major categories of expenditures, alphabetical order, 2002 U.S. Consumer Expenditure Survey

easily follow the associated narrative using the well-established conventions of tracking left-to-right and top-to-bottom within the table or chart. Before creating the table or chart or writing the associated prose, consider which of the organizing principles described below best matches the main point you wish to make. Arrange the rows and columns (or axes and legend) accordingly, and then describe the numbers in the same order as they appear in the table or chart.

Which organizing criterion to use depends largely on the type of variables in question. When reporting results for ordinal variables such as age group or income quintile, the sequence of items in rows, columns or axes will be obvious. Likewise, it makes sense to follow the natural order of values for interval or ratio variables such as date, age in years or income in dollars or pounds.

For tables or charts that present nominal variables such as favourite flavour of ice cream, or items such as categories of consumer expenditures, the categories or variables lack an inherent order. In those instances, either empirical criteria or theoretical principles usually provide a good basis for deciding how to organize them.

Empirical Ordering

For many tables or charts presenting distributions or associations, an important aim is to show which items have the highest and the lowest values and where other categories fall relative to those extremes. If this is your main point, it is often suitable to organize the categories in ascending or descending order of frequency or value. For example, figure 3 shows major categories of consumer expenditures in descending order of dollar value.

Theoretical Grouping

Arranging items into conceptually related sets can be very effective. For example, Duly (2003) reports statistics on consumer expenditures for necessities, which she defines as housing (including shelter and utilities but excluding other categories of housing-related expenses), food and apparel. To present the associated numbers, figure 4 groups the expenditure categories into necessities on the left-hand side of the x-axis and non-necessities on the right-hand side, with axis titles to identify those classifications. A table version would comprise separate panels for necessities and non-necessities, each with rows reporting the respective component categories. The accompanying description could then contrast the relative shares of necessities and non-necessities without requiring the audience to meander all over the table or chart to find the pertinent numbers.

Using Multiple Organizing Criteria

For tables or charts that present more than a few variables, a combination of approaches is often useful. For instance, consider grouping items theoretically and then arranging them within those groups in order of descending frequency or other empirical consideration. Figure 4 divides categories of consumer expenditures into necessities and non-necessities, and then organizes them in descending order of dollar value within each of those classifications, providing a useful structure for pointing out key patterns in the data.

Sometimes it makes sense to apply the same criterion sequentially, such as identifying major theoretical groupings and then minor topic groupings within them. Among the necessity categories of consumer expenditures are items related to housing, food and apparel, each with a major heading. Within each of those major categories would be minor categories and subcategories, such as shelter and utilities as subcategories under housing.

For charts or tables organized into several theoretically or empirically similar groups of items, alphabetical order can be a logical way to sequence items within those groups. For example, data on all the nations of the world might be grouped by continents, and then listed alphabetically within each continent. Alphabetizing within conceptual or empirical groupings also works well if several items have the same value of the statistics reported in the table (e.g., mean value or frequency).

Writing a Narrative to Accompany the Table or Chart

Having created a table or chart that presents data in empirical or theoretical order, it is usually helpful to write the narrative to coordinate with that pattern, mentioning the organizing principle as you refer to the associated table or chart. For example, to describe the empirical pattern across categories of consumer expenditures, you might write:

> Figure 3 presents average consumer expenditures for the United States in 2002 in descending order of dollar value. Housing was the highest single highest expenditure category, followed by transportation, food and personal expenditures and pensions . . .

An analysis that compares necessities and non-necessities could read:

> Figure 4 shows average consumer expenditures for necessities and non-necessities in the U.S. in 2002. Among necessities, shelter was the highest. . . . Among non-necessities, transportation . . .

Organizing Data for Reference Use

Reference documents typically include little if any prose description, so using a familiar convention or standard sequence is a sensible way to help readers find specific information quickly.

Alphabetical Order

Alphabetical order is a widely understood organizing principle, commonly used in a variety of settings. For example, the daily stock market report of opening, closing, high and low prices effectively organizes thousands of numbers in a predictable format that readers can use without guidance.

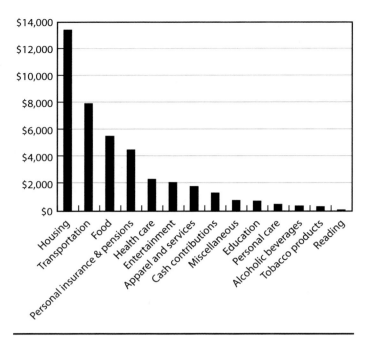

Figure 3 Major categories of expenditures, descending dollar value, 2002 U.S. Consumer Expenditure Survey

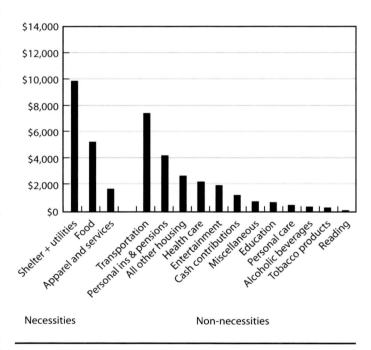

Figure 4 Descending dollar value of expenditures, necessities/non-necessities, 2002 U.S. Consumer Expenditure Survey

Order of Items from a Standard Document

Reference data from periodic surveys, censuses or surveillance systems are frequently best organized using the order of items from the original data collection instrument or following a standard coding or reporting scheme for that data source. People wishing to use those data often locate the variables of interest using original documentation such as the code book, survey instrument or census form, or by consulting copies of earlier volumes of the same reference publication. Using that standardized approach to organize tables or charts of reference data facilitates users' collection efforts by maintaining consistency across sources. Table 1 above employs such an approach, presenting the expenditure categories in the standard order used in many BLS reports (U.S. Department of Labor 2004b). Having collected the data of interest to them, users can then organize those numbers to suit to their objectives, whether summarizing trends for a report or testing a hypothesis about relationships among variables.

Summary

Using appropriate organizing principles can significantly enhance the efficacy of a quantitative description or increase the accessibility of reference data. Readers of this article who would like to go further into the issues explored here may find it useful to refer to Miller (2004).

References

Duly, A. (2003). Consumer spending for necessities. *Monthly Labor Review,* **126**(5), 3. Available online at http://stats.bls.gov/opub/mlr/2003/05/art1full.pdf. Accessed June 2007.

Miller, J.E. (2004). *The Chicago Guide to Writing about Numbers.* The Chicago Guide to Writing, Editing, and Publishing. Chicago: University of Chicago Press.

U.S. Bureau of Labor Statistics (2004a). *Consumer Expenditure Survey, Diary Survey Form.* Available online at http://stats.bls.gov/cex/csx801p.pdf. Accessed June 2007.

U.S. Department of Labor, Bureau of Labor Statistics (2004b). *Consumer Expenditures in 2002.* Report 974. Available online at http://stats.bls.gov/cex/csxann02.pdf. Accessed June 2007.

Sample PowerPoint Presentations

Slide 1

Slide 2

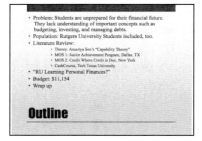

Slide 3

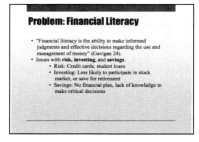

Slide 4

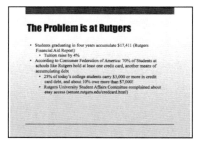

Slide 5

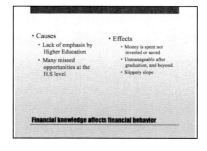

Slide 6

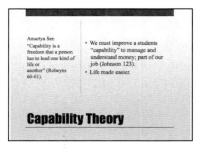

Slide 7

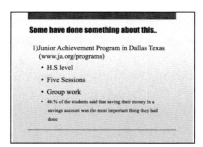

Slide 8

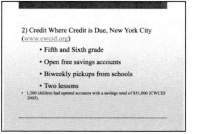

Slide 9

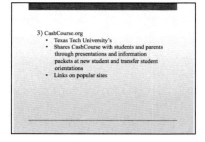

Slide 10

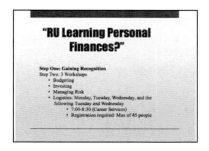

Slide 11

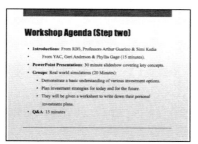

Workshop Agenda (Step two)

- **Introductions**: From RBS, Professors Arthur Guarino & Simi Kedia
- From YAC, Geri Anderson & Phyllis Gage (15 minutes).
- **PowerPoint Presentations**: 30 minute slideshow covering key concepts.
- **Groups**: Real world simulations (20 Minutes):
  - Demonstrate a basic understanding of various investment options.
  - Plan investment strategies for today and for the future.
  - They will be given a worksheet to write down their personal investment plans.
- **Q&A**: 15 minutes

Slide 12

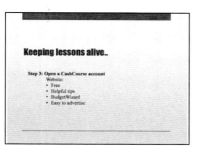

Keeping lessons alive..

Step 3: Open a CashCourse account
Website:
- Free
- Helpful tips
- BudgetWizard
- Easy to advertise

Slide 13

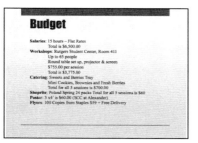

Budget

Salaries: 15 hours -- Flat Rates
Total is $6,500.00
Workshops: Rutgers Student Center, Room 411
Up to 65 people
Round table set up, projector & screen
$755.00 per session
Total is $3,775.00
Catering: Sweets and Berries Tray
Mini Cookies, Brownies and Fresh Berries
Total for all 5 sessions is $700.00
Shoprite: Poland Spring 24 packs Total for all 5 sessions is $60
Poster: 3 x4' is $60.00 (SCC at Alexander)
Flyers: 100 Copies from Staples $59 + Free Delivery

Slide 14

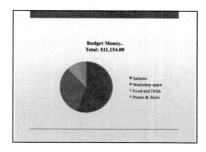

Budget Money..
Total: $11,154.00

- Salaries
- Workshop space
- Food and Drink
- Poster & flyers

Slide 15

Young Americans Center

MISSION STATEMENT: As experts in financial education, we are committed to developing the financial literacy of young people through real-life experiences and hands-on programs purposefully designed to enable them to prosper in our free enterprise system.

YoungAmeritowne - award-winning educational program offered to 5th and 6th grade teachers to help teach students about business, economics and free enterprise in a fun and hands-on way.

Slide 16

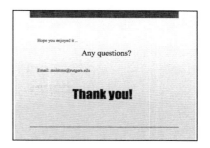

Hope you enjoyed it ..

Any questions?

Email: msimms@rutgers.edu

Thank you!

Slide 1

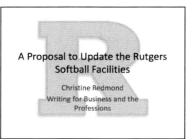

A Proposal to Update the Rutgers
Softball Facilities

Christine Redmond
Writing for Business and the
Professions

Slide 2

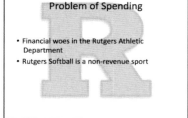

Problem of Spending

• Financial woes in the Rutgers Athletic
  Department
• Rutgers Softball is a non-revenue sport

Slide 3

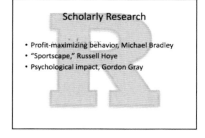

Scholarly Research

• Profit-maximizing behavior, Michael Bradley
• "Sportscape," Russell Hoye
• Psychological impact, Gordon Gray

Slide 4

UNIVERSITY OF
SOUTH FLORIDA

Source: University of South Florida www.gousfbulls.com

Slide 5

CARDINALS

Source: University of Louisville www.uoflsports.com

Slide 6

UNIVERSITY OF
NOTRE DAME

Source: University of Notre Dame www.und.com

Slide 7

Plan to Update Facilities

• Seating
• Concessions
• Aesthetic Changes
• Marketing

Slide 8

Cost of Updating Facilities

Costs

■ Construction and
  Labor- 25%
▨ Equipment and
  Supplies- 70%
▨ Maintenance- 5%

Slide 9

A Call to Action

• Instrumental to financial health
• A worthy cause
• Pride!

Slide 10

Go RU!

Chapter 6 ■ Oral Presentation Evaluation

1. **Audience**: How well did the speaker address the funding source?

   1   2   3   4   5   6   7   8   9   10

2. **Eye Contact**: How well did the speaker acknowledge and address those actually present?

   1   2   3   4   5   6   7   8   9   10

3. **Delivery**: How were the speaker's volume, enunciation, posture, appearance, and body language?

   1   2   3   4   5   6   7   8   9   10

4. **Evidence**: Did the speaker support claims, give examples, reference facts, and cite sources?

   1   2   3   4   5   6   7   8   9   10

5. **Organization**: Was the presentation easy to follow? Were all Six P's represented, in the correct order?

   1   2   3   4   5   6   7   8   9   10

6. **Visual Aids**: Were there sufficient, attractive, and useful visual graphic aids?

   1   2   3   4   5   6   7   8   9   10

7. **Preparation**: Did the presentation show careful planning, good time management, and smooth transitions?

   1   2   3   4   5   6   7   8   9   10

8. **Questions**: Did the speaker demonstrate knowledge, confidence, courtesy, and interest?

   1   2   3   4   5   6   7   8   9   10

Additional Comments/Suggestions

The Project Proposal

Chapter 7

The Assignment

The project proposal is the final draft of the project you have worked on all term. Like the oral presentation, it should be a leadership statement that puts information into action by proposing a research-justified solution to a well-defined problem. Unlike the presentation, though, it must adhere to a specific format, which is presented below and illustrated in the sample papers that follow. The guidelines for preparing this final paper may not conform to those of your workplace or those requested for specific grant applications you might be considering. These guidelines, though, should be readily adaptable to any real-world submission. We encourage you to revise your final project for submission in your workplace or in your future graduate work, but for the time being focus on fulfilling the requirements of our class. Please consult with your instructor if there are any discrepancies between the parameters presented here and the instructions included in a published Request for Proposals.

Remember that the heart of the proposal is a problem, paradigm, and plan that work together to create a unified concept. The paradigm should grow organically out of the way you define the problem, and the plan you present should be clearly rationalized by the paradigm. If you unify and focus your argument, you will be able to present a well-organized and logical paper.

The final draft of the project proposal must be from 15 to 20 pages inclusive, single-spaced (though your Works Cited should be double-spaced in keeping with MLA guidelines). You should also be sure to do the following:

- Strive for a consistent professional tone throughout.
- Number your pages clearly.
- Provide coherence to your paper using rhetorical, design, and signposting strategies.
- Use clearly distinguished headings and subheads to help guide your reader through the parts of each section.
- When appropriate, use bullets or numbers to list items for easy comprehension.
- Label and number all graphs and figures for easy reference.
- Unify your paper with a consistent typography and style.

- Polish your writing for style and emphasis.
- Proofread for errors in spelling, grammar, and syntax.

The Parts of the Proposal

[handwritten: no resume in proposal]

The formal aspects of the final proposal help you to present your overall argument in a way that is useful for your reader. There are fourteen parts of the project proposal, most of which should be labeled and presented in order (with the exception of visual graphic aids, which should ideally be incorporated into the body of the paper with individual titles):

1. Cover Letter—generally one full page (not numbered or titled) *[handwritten: To pation   not counted toward]*
2. Title Page—one page (not numbered or titled)
3. Abstract—one page (Roman numeral i) *[handwritten: Summary A-Z of plan not part of 8-10]*
4. Table of Contents—one page (Roman numeral ii)
5. Table of Figures—one page (Roman numeral iii)
6. Executive Summary—one to two pages (Roman numerals iv–v)
7. Introduction—generally more than two pages (Arabic numeral 1+)
8. Literature Review (or Research) *[handwritten: How you will achieve paradigm shift]*
9. Plan (or Procedures)
10. Budget
11. Discussion (~~perhaps~~ including an Evaluation Plan)
12. Works Cited *[handwritten: MLA format]*
13. Visual Aids (or Figures)—incorporated into the text when possible
14. Appendix (if necessary)

[handwritten left margin: 8-10 pages]

[handwritten right: 8-10]

[handwritten: 4 models of success   6 referee'd articles]

[handwritten: 1 foundational theory]

1. Cover Letter

Like the cover letter that accompanied your résumé, this letter of transmittal is intended to explain and interpret the attached document. It should explain why the reader has received your proposal, and it should try to persuade the reader to examine it closely, offering details about the content intended to interest or intrigue him or her. The letter of transmittal should respond to the situation of reading and answer the reader's likely questions: "Why is this on my desk?" and "Why should I read it when I have a dozen other things to do?"

The transmittal letter can take the form of a letter (for a reader outside of your organization) or memo (for a reader within your organization). While an increasing number of transmittals are written in e-mail form, where the proposal is usually an attached file, we ask that you adhere to the traditional paper forms for the purposes of this course.

If it is a letter, it should follow the full block style, in which all of the elements are flush with the left margin in this order:

1. Return address (your name and address)
2. Date (for the purposes of the class, use the due date of the final proposal)
3. Recipient's address (including name, title, organization, and business address)
4. Salutation ("Dear" plus formal address and name)

5. Body (see discussion below)

6. Closing ("Sincerely") and signature

If you are using the letterhead of a specific organization, you will not need to include your address. If the cover letter is prepared as a memo, then it should be written on company stationery (or facsimile) and prepared in memo form:

1. To: (addressee's full name)

2. From: (your full name and handwritten initials)

3. Date: (today's date)

4. Subject: (a line indicating your proposal topic)

5. Body: (see discussion below)

Many of the rules for writing the cover letter to accompany your résumé obtain here. Since your imagined reader probably attended your presentation (or at least you created a context where he or she was imagined in the room), you may want to begin by reminding the reader of that event, explaining that this is the full version of that proposal. Whether or not you have met your reader before, begin by explaining why you sent him or her your proposal and why it should be of interest. Emphasize what you know about the reader's interests and highlight the principal way in which this proposal matches those interests.

The central paragraph (or central two paragraphs) should offer an overview of the project, highlighting salient details about the problem, paradigm, and plan. Again, point to those aspects of your project most likely to interest your reader.

The final paragraph should invite further contact, offering the most convenient way for the reader to get in touch with you (perhaps by phone or e-mail).

2. Title Page

The page should include the following information:

- Project title

- Submitted by: Your full name and title (or position)

- Submitted to: Your addressee's full name, title, and business address

- Date

You should also indicate somewhere near the bottom of the page the course for which this paper was prepared, your instructor's name, and any class information requested by your instructor. (This way if your paper gets lost it won't end up on the desk of the imagined audience but will have a chance of getting returned.)

The title of your project should be carefully chosen and crafted for maximum communication in the shortest space. It is one of the first things the reader sees of your report, and it will become the means of referencing it to others. The more communicative power it has, the more effective it will be. Strive to be both clear and memorable. Remember that you can use a two-part title, especially if you want to give your project a catchy title followed by a more technically specific one.

There are many ways to design the title page, and you should do what looks and works best for your specific project. Use white space, color, and other page elements to design an attractive image that is consistent with the document design as a whole. You might want to use graphics or pictorial lettering to highlight your topic.

3. Abstract

[handwritten: What your proposal contains "plan to, hope to"]

The abstract should be clearly labeled as an "abstract" at the top of the page and should be no more than one or two paragraphs in length. The purpose of the abstract is to tell busy people (or their secretaries) how to file your report. It should be written from a disinterested perspective, providing a balanced view of the project idea as though written by an outside party. Usually it is written in the third person or uses passive voice to avoid naming the agent. For the purposes of this class, you should write a relatively long, informative abstract that includes details about your overall argument and covers elements of the problem, paradigm, and plan (in that order). Be sure to indicate your rationale and what specific action you want to take. Aim to be maximally communicative within minimal space—generally between 150 and 300 words.

4. Table of Contents

Clearly label and design your table of contents for easy use. Recognize that the table of contents has two main uses: it helps readers locate the information that interests them most (this is especially true of long reports) and it gives your reader an overview of the project and its parts. You should list all parts of the project listed above (excluding the cover letter, title page, and visual aids), along with any important subheads. Number the opening parts (abstract, table of contents, table of figures, and executive summary) with small Roman numerals (i, ii, iii) and then use Arabic numbers (1, 2, 3) beginning with the introduction section. Use whatever design elements you can to help make the information clear and usable—indenting subheads, using ellipses to link section names and page numbers, and aligning all related parts. The style and font should be consistent with the design throughout your document.

You can work up a table by carefully laying out the items in it, but many word processing programs, such as Microsoft Word, will generate a table for you.

5. Table of Figures

If your table of contents is short, you might include your table of figures (clearly labeled) on the same page. Otherwise, it should occupy its own page. Ideally, each figure and illustration you use should have a number for easy reference. List the number and title of each figure along with the page on which it appears.

6. Executive Summary   *[handwritten: # 1 very important, top American plus]*

The executive summary should be clearly labeled. This is usually the last thing you write, but it is often the first (and sometimes only) thing that your audience will read closely. It is a "miniature" or condensed version of the paper itself written for busy executives (hence the name). Basically, the executive summary presents your whole argument, *in the order of the paper itself,* with key details and evidence, all in only 10 percent of the space of the whole paper (generally no more than two pages for a twenty-page proposal). A reader should be able to understand your entire project (including problem, paradigm, and plan) after having only read these two pages. Generally, you should cite critical evidence and sources here, but you should not include illustrations. Unlike the abstract, which is intended for description only, the executive summary can contain persuasive language.

In writing some parts of the paper, you may feel like you are repeating yourself. To an objective reader of the entire document, there may seem to be an element of redundancy. However, you should recognize that while you may present the same information several times in different parts of the report, each part is intended, in a sense, for a different reader. This part is written for the busy executive. The body of the report is written for the (perhaps same) executive who has time for a closer examination of your ideas.

[handwritten: page and 1/2]

[handwritten: Actual Research and implementation Cite your research]

7. Introduction

State your case — *persuasive*

There are two purposes for the introduction: <u>to present information about the problem you will address and to forecast your overall argument.</u> Here is where you will want to offer all the information you have on the problem you seek to address. You should try to quantify or define the problem and offer images that help clarify and emphasize the key aspects of it. <u>Focus on those aspects of the problem that will most interest your reader,</u> and suggest by the way you examine or define the problem a direction for approaching it. Close the introduction with a forecasting statement giving your reader a sense of your argument to follow and providing a transition to the next part.

8. Literature Review (or Research)

This is the section in which you present, analyze, and integrate your paradigm research into your proposal. The literature review section should open with some reference to the problem (especially by way of transition from the introduction), but it should focus mostly on the justification for your project. The research you present should explain why you will approach the problem in a particular way; it should also provide a unified rationale for the specific plan of action you describe in your plan. Thus the paradigm is essential for unifying your paper because it shows how the plan of action you will propose is a logical approach to the problem you have defined. Remember, there are two sides to paradigms—they are represented by **theory** and by **models of success**. These elements work together to provide justification for your specific course of action.

While each of you will have to explore research in a way unique to your topic, all of you should strive to show that you are not merely asserting your approach to the problem based on opinion, politics, or personal view, but that there is a consensus of opinion or a well-documented trend or development that supports your idea. You will want to discuss theories that form the basis for your assumption that the plan you have in mind will be effective—offering evidence and authority to show that your plan is responding to a body of knowledge in a particular field. If you are planning experimental work that grows out of a well-established scientific paradigm, you should review the tradition of work in the field that you are building on in your research. You will also discuss examples of similar or related projects you are using as models, focusing on the procedures and plans that worked in those instances and emphasizing the positive results achieved. Remember that the main purpose of the research is to justify your plan of action. Thus, if you plan to educate people about a specific environmental issue, you will likely want to focus more on an effective way (or paradigm) of educating people than you will on that environmental issue (though you will need research on that as well).

One of the purposes of the literature review is to establish your authority, which will stand or fall based on the quality of the research you cite. By demonstrating your command over recognized or paradigmatic research, you show that you have the knowledge and expertise to make valid recommendations. You should strive to find the most useful and authoritative research whenever possible, and you should discuss published research (ideally, research that has been subjected to peer review). Many projects will, however, call for a wide range of research sources, including articles, books, Internet sources, published government statistics, interviews, surveys, field studies, calculations, and experimental results. You should do your best to evaluate sources and use only the most solid in building your literature review. To use low-quality materials in constructing your paper is equivalent to using low-quality materials in building a house, and your product will be evaluated and graded accordingly.

9. Plan (or Procedures)

models of success — needs relevance to plan
what aspects will you adopt?

The plan should be as specific as possible and should follow logically from your research. How it is presented will depend upon the specific project you have in mind. If you are proposing a workplace project, you might focus on how your idea will be implemented (perhaps providing a flowchart or time line). If you are proposing to do an experiment, you should lay out the specific procedures you

logistical and logical action to impress the patron and event papers. also attract population

will use. If you are building something, you will want to describe how it will be built and provide diagrams. You might wish to reference research to support the specific choices you are making, though the research section should provide the bulk of your rationale.

10. Budget

The budget should list everything you will need for your project, from salaries to supplies. Some items may require explanation, which you should supply here as well. You should arrange the cost of your budget items in aligned accountant's columns to make your addition clear.

11. Discussion (or Evaluation Plan) *1 full page*

Generally your paper should conclude by summing up your project and making a final pitch for its value. If you are proposing a project whose results can be tested in some way, then you should also offer an evaluation plan.

12. Works Cited *MLA format*

This section should list all sources of information cited in your paper in alphabetical order. The list of Works Cited should be prepared according to MLA Style, covered in the *MLA Style Guide* in Chapter Four. For those who want extra guidance, you might consult *The MLA Handbook*, which is available in the reference section of any campus library.

13. Visual Aids (or Figures)

You should have at least three graphic aids that are visual representations of numerical information. These might include graphs, tables, charts, or maps. In addition to these three, you may include drawings, photographs, flowcharts, maps, organization charts, Gantt charts, time lines, diagrams, or floor plans. Each visual graphic aid should be numbered (e.g., Figure 1, Figure 2, etc.) and should have a title. If the graphic is based on information from a source, then you should have a citation line at the bottom (i.e., Source: Alvarez 26). If you can incorporate your graphics into the body of the paper, do so. If you cannot incorporate your graphics, then include them at the end in an appendix or inter-paginate them directly following the first reference to them.

14. Appendix (optional)

If you have other information that doesn't exactly fit into your text, you could include it as an appendix (which is literally appended to the end of your document). For example, if you cite a map or chart which is too big to be incorporated into the body of your text, you could label it as Appendix A. Be sure to list it under Appendices in your table of contents, and refer to it in the text (i.e., See Appendix A, p. 20).

Sample Final Proposals

What follows are typical samples of student work, as with the previous assignments, presented for illustrative purposes. This section is included to generate discussion, provide the opportunity for objective critique, and facilitate practicing of contentious peer review. These final proposals are not provided to represent a particular grade or to distinguish between passing and failing work. As with all representative examples, these papers have a variety of strong and weak moments. We encourage you to utilize the course grading criteria to attempt to situate these papers, with the guidance of your instructor. Hopefully, while you are revising your work, this experience will help you to identify the usual moments of achievement, as well as areas that would benefit from improvement.

Margaret Simms
52 Xavier Drive
New Brunswick, New Jersey 08901

December 12, 2011

C. Travis Webb
Chairperson
Young Americans Center
3550 E. 1st Avenue
Denver, Colorado 80206

Re: Achieving Personal Financial Success for Rutgers Students

Dear Mr. Webb,

Young Americans Center (YAC) is a leader in providing financial education to America's Youth. Recently, the project known as Young Ameritowne is impacting the lives of children as young as fifth grade. CEO Richard Martinez says that "every transaction is an educational opportunity," exemplifying the YAC's commitment to improving children's financial futures ("Teaching Kids About Money"). The children are learning, in real "town" scenarios, how to budget and manage money. This is something even adults today can benefit from, says Fox anchor Joana Corals ("Teaching Kids About Money"). In fact, a group in-between children and adults can also *greatly* benefit from financial education; and they are college students.

College students are an important group, as they are America's youth on the verge of entering "our free enterprise system" (yacenter.org). For the college students of today, economic climates and job markets are more challenging to deal with, as "the recession drags painfully on," which places these students on high priority for financial knowledge (mybudget360.com). Personal financial knowledge is the ability to make well-informed financial decisions like budgeting, investing, and managing risk. It is critical to financial success, and thus, it is imperative that college students are provided a personal finance education.

To address this problem, college students must have the opportunity to learn critical financial concepts, just as the fifth-graders in Denver have done. It is likely this process will begin with workshops, and eventually lead to formal classes. I hope you will agree that the YAC is an ideal institution to begin helping college students achieve personal financial success. This, in conjunction with YAC's mission statement, in "developing the financial literacy of young people," is the goal of this proposal (yacenter.org). If you have any questions or comments please feel free to call 732-632-8876 or e-mail me at msimms@rutgers.edu. Thank you for taking the time to review my proposal.

Sincerely,

Margaret Simms

Margaret Simms

Achieving Personal Financial Success for Rutgers Students

A proposal to provide personal financial education

Submitted by:
Margaret Simms

Submitted to:
C. Travis Webb
Chairperson
Young Americans Center
3550 E. 1st Avenue
Denver, Colorado 80206

December 12, 2011

Prepared for:
Writing for Business and Professions
Professor James Martin

Abstract

In this paper, it is proposed that Rutgers University Students in New Brunswick, New Jersey, be provided with a personal financial education. The education component that is proposed is grounded in three main concepts: budgeting, investing, and managing risk. Additionally, this paper discusses the financial literacy of college students, and argues for a lack thereof. College students, particularly at Rutgers, may be called "financially illiterate." Presented here is evidence illustrating that students do not understand critical financial concepts and are not wholly prepared for their financial future. Using Amartya Sen's capability theory, this proposal follows his claim that a "capability" is a function that allows a person to participate in the world, and prosper. Sen adds that it is part of society's job to improve every individual's "capability." This paper uses financial literacy as a "capability" and thus argues it is essential to one's well-being. Further, other programs have been used, with similar goals to this proposal, as a basis for a plan called "RU Learning Personal Finances?" and they are discussed. These programs are referred to as "Models of success" and are as follows: Junior Achievement program in Texas, Banking at School program in Illinois, and CashCourse in Texas. Each model of success contains an educational component, although treated differently in terms of scale.

This proposal seeks to implement workshops for Rutgers students to attend, where they will learn the basics of personal finance. Two Business School staff members, along with two members of the Young American Center, will present each workshop. Workshops, as discussed in step two, will consist of an educational component covering budgeting, investing, and managing risk, followed by an interactive group activity. Step three proposes to encourage a "Budget Wizard" Web site for Rutgers students to utilize free of charge.

Table of Contents

Table of Figures

Executive Summary

Personal financial knowledge is critical to achieve personal financial success. It dictates one's financial behavior, as "people with low financial literacy are more likely to have problems with debt, and less likely to accumulate wealth," which are also factors that affect one's overall well-being (Lusardi 360). Sufficient financial knowledge may be called "financial literacy," which is "the ability to make informed judgments and effective decisions regarding the use and management of money" (Gavigan 24). Financial literacy would not only allow an individual to accumulate wealth, but also to then budget and manage it effectively, invest it to preserve for the future, and to understand financial resources such as loans and credit cards. Unfortunately, today's American college students lack such knowledge, and are thus, "financially illiterate." Financial illiteracy among United States college students is of particular concern, as they are the incoming generation of the country; they will replace their parents and grandparents out in the "real world." Further, they face a peculiar challenge in today's market as the economy slows, causing some economists to call it "the worst financial crisis since the Great Depression" (Gavigan 24). Further, American students are "characterized increasingly by high levels of debt," student loans are now averaged at $22,900.00, atop of an average $4,138 in credit card debt (Chatzy 23). Even after graduation students still seem to lack financial knowledge as "the number of bankruptcies among young people under age 25 has grown by 50% since 1991" exemplifying the lack of personal finance knowledge (njaes.rutgers.edu). When it comes to credit cards, research shows that students are not using them properly, and in fact, most do not understand them. In a Sallie Mae survey, "64 percent would have liked to receive information [about credit cards] in high school and 40 percent as college freshmen" which also indicates the lack of financial education that circulates in the United States. The same survey found that "many college students [are using them] to live beyond their means—not just for convenience" and "sixty percent [were surprised] at how high their balance had reached" (salliemae.com).

Currently, the students at Rutgers University in New Brunswick, New Jersey, are facing these same issues. According to the most recent Rutgers Financial Aid report, students graduating in four years accumulate $17,411 in loan debts, alone. In a survey of current Rutgers students 39% of students indicated they owe more than $10,000 in student loans. When asked about investments, 75% indicated they do not know how to invest their money; rather, they do not have preserved funds for the future. The data indicates that Rutgers students are falling into the same overall patterns as other American college students. They accumulate debt, and are then not prepared to deal with it post-graduation, as indicated by the rise of bankruptcies. In the same survey, 87% of Rutgers students said they use one to two credit cards, while 82% also said that they do not know the APR rate on their cards, which is already a warning sign of ignorance when it comes to credit cards. A report from the Rutgers University Student Affairs Committee also stated, "Student financial management and credit-card debt are important issues facing students at Rutgers," and they were appalled by how easy it was for students, with blank credit history, to obtain one or more credit cards (senate.rutgers.edu/credcard.html). "Such early entanglements can [actually] hinder their ability to accumulate wealth" while on the other hand, if students receive a sound personal finance education, they can be better equipped for a successful financial future (Lusardi 358).

Many researches blame higher education institutions for a lack of emphasis on personal finance. Even going back to high school, "very little of the student's studies focus on dealing with financial matters such as bank accounts, investments, credit cards, [and] loans" (Avard 321). It seems financial education, even for basic concepts, have been scarce in the lives of students. It is vital that we implement opportunities for financial education to students, especially before they graduate and enter the "real world." The consequences for failing to implement such an education are massive. Scholars agree that "when individuals cannot manage their finances, it becomes a problem for society," expanding the scope of this problem to nationwide (Avard 332). Mark Kantrowitz of finaid.org recently spoke to this concern stating, "Student loan debt has become a macroeconomic factor; it affects the economy." Given our current economic climate, which includes a "dismal job market," students' financial literacy is at a heighted concern (qtd. in Rosen "Student Debt: America's Next Bubble?"). As individuals, research finds that students with heavy debt loads are anxious about it, causing stress and confusion when it comes to finances. Further, it has been found to "[influence] major labor decisions" and may leave students in jobs where they are unhappy, and even unsuccessful (Lusardi 359).

For this financial literacy problem, we may look to Amartya Sen's "capability theory." To Sen, a "capability" is a freedom that a person has to lead one kind of life or another. Based on one's capabilities, we may "judge how well someone's life is going," as we often call one's "well-being" (Robeyns 60–61). Within his theory, Sen believes it is part of society's job to improve citizens' "capabilities," and help them be "full social persons," and be active in the world (Johnson 123). Financial literacy is an example of a capability that students will use to secure their financial well-being, which includes basic functions like food and shelter to more luxurious possessions. Further, financial literacy will allow them to be social persons by participating in the world economy, via investments or simply being able to afford products available. Further, Sen finds formal education as a means of improving one's capability. By providing financial education, students can begin to improve that capability and work toward a successful financial future. Further, students' lives after graduation will be made much easier with the understanding of money and how to easily manage it, rather than "have it be a stressful (and foggy) task" (Johnson 124). Some programs have been implemented around the country, in the effort to improve this capability.

The Junior Achievement Program (JA) in Dallas, Texas, known as "JA Personal Finance," is taught at the high school level over several weeks. The JA program has students work in groups and simulate running a bank, where students had to assume real world positions. The program was successful in increasing students' financial knowledge, particularly in tracking expenses, saving money, and feeling confident making their own financial decisions. After the program, 46.5% of the students said that saving their money in a savings account was the most important thing they had done. However, the criticism of this program is lack of access to financial institutions, as many of the students are low-income. Perhaps more than 46.5% of the students would have opened a savings account if they had access to one (Johnson 128). Other programs have also worked on financial literacy capabilities, but in different ways.

Take for instance the Banking at School program, which "has regained popularity as concern about financial literacy has grown" (Johnson 129). The program was initiated by the State of Illinois Treasurer's Office for students in the fourth to the eight grades. The program sets schools up with participating banks and credit unions, who then sends a representative to the school once a month to collect deposits from the students. The banks and credit unions open these accounts for free, and students can access them once they reach eighteen years of age. Sen's theory also applies here, as he believes that people should have the "real opportunity to accomplish what we value" as a society, which includes wealth. The Banking at School program gave students a "real opportunity" simply by granting them access to a financial account. In addition, teachers taught the following chapters in their classes: "What is money?, Why do people save?, What are banks for and how do they work?, Where does money come from?, and The World of Work," none of which include a money management lesson (lba.org). As a result of the program, "over 200,000 students [are] participating in the state's bank-at-school program," which indicates all of those students will have money saved. However, a drawback to this program may be the lack of emphasis on money management. Once the students withdraw their saved money, they will need the "capability" to manage it.

To tap specifically into money management skills, a college Web site known as CashCourse, offers a free program called "Budget Wizard." The Budget Wizard allows students to enter personalized information such as their income and expenses, and Budget Wizard will print out a budget, along with tips for the students to stay within it. It will produce charts and graphs tracking student's spending habits. Texas Tech University administration has taken initiative to actively encourage students to use Budget Wizard. For instance, they share it with parents and students at orientations, they encourage mentors to spread the word to help peers manage money and debt, they place it on popular Web sites, such as the financial aid site, and they have created an attractive pocket-sized 20 dollar bill flyer to "catch students' eyes and point them to CashCourse throughout the year" (cashcourse.org). The results of their effort at Texas Tech has landed them in the top 20 schools for CashCourse Web site traffic for 2011, after only signing up for CashCourse in 2008. Texas Tech tactics can also be used at Rutgers, only after implementing a "first step."

The first step to address this problem at Rutgers is to implement workshops on the Rutgers campus, and thereby inform students that personal financial knowledge is attainable. We will conduct three 80-minute workshops where students will learn *budgeting, savings, and managing risk*. Geri Anderson and Phyllis Gage of YAC will team up with Rutgers Business School Professors Guarino and Kedia to plan and present the workshops. The Professors are an ideal choice, as they are knowledgeable in basic financial concepts that will be covered and they are accustomed to teaching these topics to undergraduates.

At the workshop, Professors Guarino and Kedia will present a PowerPoint, teaching basic lessons on budgeting, investing, and managing risk. Specific content will include: Budget Wizard in budgeting, stocks in investing, and credit cards in managing risk. After the presentation, students, who are already seated in groups, will engage in a group activity that involves role-play. Role-play activities will give students the opportunity to act as if they were in a "real world" financial situation. The groups will have to make real-world decisions in terms of investments and loans. Hereafter, the professors will take over and explain each answer while presenting some "answer" slides for about fifteen minutes. Then, Geri Anderson and Phyllis Gage will join Professors Guarino and Kedia onstage for this section, and encourage students to ask questions about anything they learned, about YAC, or what else they can do. The last thing the four members will leave the students with is a reminder to register on CashCourse.org to use the Budget Wizard. This last step is to encourage YAC's mission at Rutgers to continue beyond the workshops.

Introduction

Personal finance is an everyday function, and a key skill for life. However, American college students are ill-equipped to deal with personal finances, and therefore lack 'financial literacy.' "Financial literacy is the ability to make informed judgments and effective decisions regarding the use and management of money" (Gavigan 24). A person with sufficient financial literacy will make judgments based on the understanding of financial risk, such as taking out a certain loan or credit card. Financial literacy also enables a person to make healthy financial decisions such as saving, budgeting, and investing for the future.

Unfortunately, college students, usually 18–24 years old, in the United States are "financially illiterate" (Gavigan 24). A study at Texas A&M University indicated that college freshman "are unable to balance a checkbook, and most have no insight into the basic survival principles involved with earning, spending, saving and investing" (Avard 334). Another study indicated that a majority of freshmen do not have a "financial plan," which is critical during this transitional period from financial dependence to independence. This also indicates that students may be thinking about what major to choose, but not how they will manage their expenses during school. During their time at school, students are "constantly accumulating debt, through student loans and credit cards," and "may not realize how their current debt can negatively affect their future credit rating," and even hinder their financial goals (Henry 245). It is reported that "this year's freshmen will likely emerge with average debt well above 2011 grads: $4,138 in credit-card debt atop their $22,900 in student loans" which is a heavy burden to walk away from college with (Chatzy 23).

A survey of college seniors in the nation's four-year public colleges reported a 5% increase in overall debt since 2009. The same report found that at least 22% of this debt was from private loans, which "are one of the riskiest ways to pay for college [as] they typically have higher costs and provide minimal relief if you are struggling to meet your monthly repayment obligations" (mybudget360). The aforementioned means of debt, credit cards, also impedes students' personal financial success. Credit cards can be useful tools, like to build a solid credit history, however students seem to misuse them. A recent Sallie Mae study found that "many college students use credit cards to live beyond their means—not just for convenience" and "sixty percent [were surprised] at how high their balance had reached" (salliemae.com). "Lack of personal financial knowledge place students at a greater financial risk for having large and perhaps unmanageable, debt burdens," and will make life post-graduation more difficult (Lawrence 5).

By the time students graduate, they will likely be dealing with other major financial decisions, such as buying a house, starting a family, or thinking about retirement. Students today are also facing a complex and volatile financial market, that some economists are calling "the worst financial crisis since the Great Depression" (Gavigan 24). Today's college students are "characterized by high levels of debt," making their financial literacy a particular concern (Lusardi 359). Their debt load consists of both loan and credit card debt, which is shown in the chart below, collectively. Shown here is the student loan debt for 2011, which for the first time, has surpassed credit card debt. According to "My Budget 360, investing ideas for preserving wealth," this kind of situation is cryptic, as student loans cannot be discharged with bankruptcy. Instead, the lenders " will garnish your wages, tax refunds, and even Social Security payments" until they are paid in full (mybudget360.com).

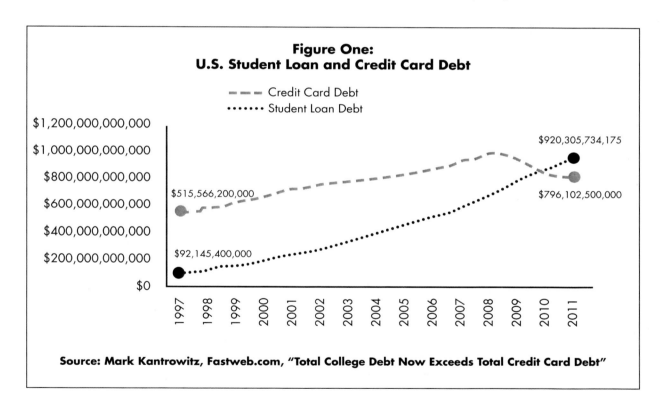

Figure One:
U.S. Student Loan and Credit Card Debt

Source: Mark Kantrowitz, Fastweb.com, "Total College Debt Now Exceeds Total Credit Card Debt"

The questions here are then: Are students aware of the implications of taking out loans, and do they understand credit card interest rates, or how to use them? Further, can they efficiently manage and invest their money to avoid such hazardous debt, and a stressful financial future? The evidence indicates that their knowledge in these areas is dangerously low, and in need of improvement. Neal Godfrey, of *ABA Banking Journal* states, "Our kids simply don't learn the financial facts of life . . . We live in the largest capitalist nation in the world, and our children graduate from high school without a clue about finance," and as shown here, they then graduate college without significant improvement (qtd. in Manton, et al. 44). In a 2009 consumer report, 84% of American college students admitted that they needed more education on financial management. Further, 64% would have liked to receive financial education in high school, and 40% would have liked to receive financial education during their freshman year of college ("Study finds rising number"). Adding to this concern, the Rutgers Cooperative Extension found that, "Many of New Jersey's young adults are leaving school without the knowledge and skills necessary to make critical life decisions (e.g., wise use of credit, developing a spending plan, purchasing auto insurance)." This raises an alarming concern for current Rutgers University students, as 86% of them are from the state of New Jersey (njaes.rutgers.edu).

The Problem Hits Home at Rutgers

College students at Rutgers are a direct reflection of the university, and as they enter in the world, the students will represent America. A report from the Rutgers University Student Affairs Committee stated, "Student financial management and credit-card debt are important issues facing students at Rutgers," and they were appalled by how easy it was for students, with blank credit history, to obtain one or more credit cards (senate.rutgers.edu/credcard.html). In a survey of current Rutgers students, shown below in Figure 2, 87% said they use one to two credit cards, while 82% also said that they do not know the APR rate on their cards. This becomes a concern, as this may be a trap for students to get caught in high debt.

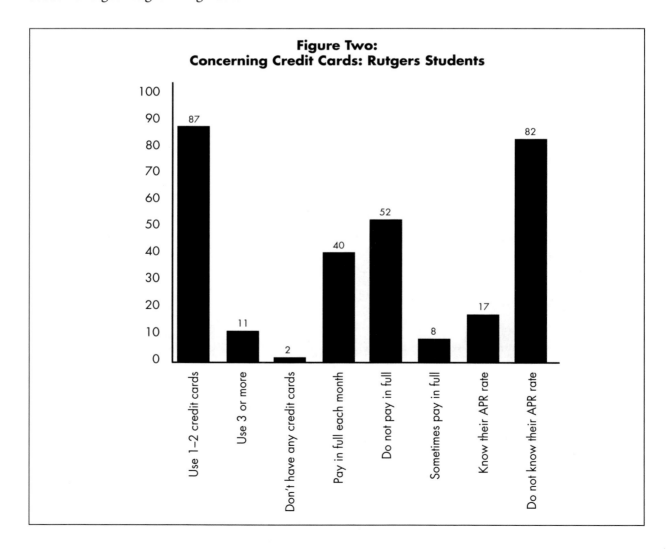

**Figure Two:
Concerning Credit Cards: Rutgers Students**

In addition to credit card debt, evidence shows students are inevitably prone to student loan debt. As of now, the most recent Rutgers Financial Aid report shows that students graduating in four years accumulate $17,411 in loan debts, alone. This amount also increases when a student takes longer than expected to graduate. Moreover, Rutgers has increased tuition by 4.0% for the coming year, which will obligate students to take out even bigger loans (news.rutgers.edu). A student member of the Rutgers Board of Governors spoke for her peers during the tuition debate, explaining that students are "working multiple jobs, accruing debt and, in one case, relying on a grandfather's second mortgage to afford school" (Mulvihill 1). Such cases exemplify the great lengths to which students go to pursue an education. In the same aforementioned survey, shown in Figure 3, 39% of students indicated they owe more than $10,000 in student loans. What is more alarming is that 68% of students indicated that they do not have any investments, such as stocks or bonds, and worse, 75% said they do not know *how* to invest. This indicates a lack of readiness for their future. Lastly, 84% of Rutgers students do not have a written budget because they do not know *how*, which indicates their lack of knowledge in managing money. Again, we may question students' financial knowledge, and their preparedness for a successful financial future; it is a lack thereof that presents the problem.

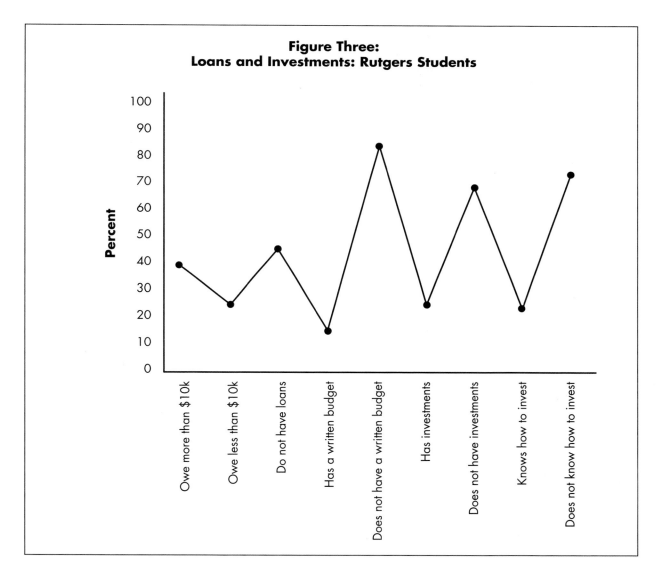

**Figure Three:
Loans and Investments: Rutgers Students**

The problem begins, or rather is not addressed, beginning at the high school level, where curriculum "does not focus on dealing with financial matters such as bank accounts, investments, mutual funds, mortgages, credit cards, loans, and taxes," and students are immediately put at risk (Manton 43). Although educators do find financial education to be of high importance, they "are reluctant to add one more thing to the curriculum given this era of high-stakes testing" (Gavigan 24). Another root to the problem is actually students' parents, who have a strong influence on their financial knowledge. A 2010 collection of personal finance statistics reveals that 56% of young adults attribute their knowledge of money management to their parents. Unfortunately, many "adults [today] have not mastered basic economic skills," and may not do justice to their children in this area (Gavigan 25). In fact, American consumer bankruptcy has increased to 1.4 million per year from 1.1 million in 2008 ("Making the case for financial literacy" 8). Further, and more importantly here, many researchers account the problem to *higher education institutions*, where there is a lack of emphasis on students' personal finance education (Avard 332). Specifically at Rutgers, there is no personal finance course required in the general education curriculum.

Repercussions of low financial literacy in college students are immense. For the students, research finds that heavy debt loads "are causing anxiety and influencing major labor decisions" and may leave students in jobs where they are unhappy, or even unsuccessful. In addition, "students with high credit card debt are having trouble getting good jobs because employers are reviewing credit reports," which is an aspect of job hunting many students are unaware of (Lusardi 359). Further, lack of knowledge on how to deal with debt, or manage current income can leave students in a financial blur, or not knowing what to do. In fact, "the number of bankruptcies among young people under age 25 has grown by 50% since 1991" exemplifying the lack of personal finance knowledge even after graduation (njaes.rutgers.edu). Additionally, scholars agree that "When individuals cannot manage their finances, it becomes a problem for society," expanding the scope of this problem from students to nationwide (Avard 332). Mark Kantrowitz of finaid.org recently spoke to this concern stating, "Student loan debt has become a macroeconomic factor; it affects the economy." Given our current economic climate, which includes a "dismal job market," students' financial literacy is at a heighted concern (qtd. in Rosen "Student Debt: America's Next Bubble?"). It would be detrimental to our country, and to these individual students, if they were deprived of an opportunity to be financially educated.

Literature Review

Capability Theory, by Amartya Sen = *foundational theory*

"Increasing consumer financial literacy is [also] a public policy objective to improve welfare" especially as the gap between rich and poor increases (Huston 296). The work of Amartya Sen has long impacted public policy and social sciences, specifically, with his theory known as "capability theory." To Sen, a "capability" is a freedom that a person has to lead one kind of life or another. Based on one's capabilities, we may "judge how well someone's life is going," as we often call one's "well-being" (Robeyns 60–61). The theory has also helped many scholars in "comparing how well two persons (or societies) are doing," which brings us back to college students reflecting Rutgers and America. If we improve a student's "capability" to manage and understand money, we have done our job, as according to Sen, it is part of society's job to develop these capabilities in citizens, one way being through a formal education (Johnson 123). "This relates to the need to educate students on personal finance," as they need to develop this capability in order to secure their well being in the world (Johnson 124). A student's life will be made much easier with the understanding of money and how to easily manage it, rather than "have it be a stressful (and foggy) task" as it often can be (Johnson 124). In the most extreme case, the capability theory refers to "the real opportunity to avoid poverty," and as data above shows, student debt is growing, and potentially can become a "serious deprivation" for them (Robeyns 69). The problem of "financial illiteracy" is one to solve and prevent, thus we can implement programs that catch the problem sooner rather than later.

Junior Achievement Program, Dallas, Texas *model*

Some programs have already been set in motion to improve this "capability" of financial literacy in students specifically through "a formal education," such as the Junior Achievement Program (JA) in Dallas, Texas (Johnson 123). The JA program, known as "JA Personal Finance," is taught at the high school level over several weeks, and involves real-world stimulations and role-play. All the simulations and role-plays set out to show students how they might manage wealth effectively. They focus mainly on concepts in the banking industry and get the students to simulate running a bank. The program was successful in increasing students' financial knowledge, particularly in tracking expenses, saving money, and feeling confident making their own financial decisions. After the program, 46% of the students said that saving their money in a savings account was the most important thing they had done. However, the criticism of this program is lack of access to financial institutions, as many of the students are from low-income families. It is possible, especially as the aforementioned rich and poor gap grows, that more students will be from low-income or struggling families. We must be prepared to also give students access to apply what we teach them. Perhaps even more than 46.5% of the students would have opened a savings account if they had access to one (Johnson 128).

Banking at School, Illinois *model*

Another program is the Banking at School program, which "has regained popularity as concern about financial literacy has grown" and the program continues to grow and develop (Johnson 129). One such example took place in Illinois, initiated by the State of Illinois Treasurer's Office, for students in the fourth to the eight grades. Sen's theory also explains part of improving a "capability" is the ability or "real opportunity to accomplish what we value" and "money" or "financial success" is certainly a value in society, as its power allows one to participate in the world, as well as obtain basic survival functions, like food and shelter. Sen refers to this as the opportunity to be a full social person (Robeyns 62). Turning back to financial education, students must have the "real opportunity" to begin managing money, which is part of what Banking at School does. The program matches a school with a participating bank or credit union, and a representative visits the school once a month to collect deposits, which provides the students with real access to improve their "capability." Hereafter the program began, "Illinois reports over 200,000 students participating in the state's bank-at-school program," and the students can access the money as they please once they turn eighteen. In addition, teachers added a financial education component to the curriculum. Their chapters were as follows: "What is money?, Why do people save?, What are banks for and how do they work?, Where does money come from?, and The World of Work" (lba.org). However, none of these focus specifically on management, which is an important component of personal finance. Once they reach eighteen years of age and are able to withdraw the money, they must be able to manage it properly, and even start to think in futurity. For instance, some students at that point may be headed off to college where evidence shows students still don't have the "capability" to manage money. Thus, it is important to address the issue of management.

CashCourse.org, Texas Tech University ~~Model~~

Moreover, some programs have been dedicated to teaching students money management. For instance, the CashCourse program at Texas Tech University. The capability theory calls for "the means or resources necessary for [a] capability" to be achieved and realized, and CashCourse is an exemplar Web site of this concept. Cashcourse.org is a college Web site that teaches students money management, specifically budgeting, using their program known as "Budget Wizard" (cashcourse.org). The Budget Wizard is always readily available and customized for each individual student, as they can enter their current income and expenses. They may change the information at any time, for example, they may make less money during finals, or they may have more expenses during a particular month. The Budget Wizard will then produce charts and graphs displaying how a student spends their money, and from there it will print out a budget for the student to follow. The budget wizard makes creating a budget simple and provides tips for students to stay within their budget. On Cashcourse.org, they say, "Sticking to a budget while in college can help you meet personal goals such as studying abroad, staying out of or reducing your debt, and allowing you to be better prepared for unexpected expenses and emergencies. It also helps you think about long-term financial goals and helps establish positive behaviors before you're out in the "real" world."

At Texas Tech University, administration strives to promote the Web site at every opportunity. They share it with parents and students at orientations, they encourage mentors to spread the word to help peers manage money and debt, they place it on popular Web sites, such as the financial aid site, and they have created an attractive pocket-sized 20 dollar bill flyer to "catch students' eyes and point them to CashCourse throughout the year" (cashcourse.org). The results of their effort at Texas Tech has landed them in the top 20 schools for CashCourse Web site traffic for 2011, after only signing up for CashCourse in 2008. Best of all, signing up is free for all colleges and universities, which makes CashCourse a great resource for any school budget. A drawback to this program, as with the aforementioned, is the lack of education on actually accumulating wealth, or rather, investing for the future. It is vital that we merge all the concepts mentioned in each of these programs, and emphasized in research, which would include budgeting, investing, and managing risk. Further, "while financial education is very important for adults, it can have the greatest overall life impact on young people," as they have not established too many financial habits yet, thus "education can mold their habits more effectively" (gpo.gov).

Plan: RU Learning Personal Finances?

Step One: Gaining Recognition

"RU Learning Personal Finances" is a plan to kick off financial education at Rutgers, and will be grounded in the aforementioned concepts: budgeting, investing, and managing risk. Bankruptcies and irresponsible credit card use among students, as discussed earlier, calls for budgeting. Further, students admitted their lack of knowledge on investments, which is defined as "saving present resources for future use through the use of saving accounts, stocks, bonds or mutual funds" that can all be crucial during retirement, or buying a house (Huston 303). Finally, managing risk will be to teach students important components of credit cards, such as APR rates, and how to use them, and also include loan provisions, and risks of different types of loans. These concepts will be embedded in "RU Learning Personal Finances" to proceed in our goal of promoting financial literacy, and therefore promote personal financial success for Rutgers students.

The first step is to establish recognition for the (YAC) on the Rutgers campus. Geri Anderson, a board member of YAC, may be elected as the head of this project. One way to reach the students is through social networking. "A Facebook Page gives a voice to any . . . organization to join the conversation with their audience on Facebook" and many of Rutgers' students are on Facebook already (facebook.com). We will create a Facebook page, titled RU Young Americans Center. This is a free account, and students may add this page to their personal Facebook account and have access to any content we put on the page. The page will be a place for mission statements and information about past projects, such as Ameritowne for students' viewing. More importantly, it will contain a schedule of YAC's workshops being held on campus, which will be discussed later in more detail. Facebook will also allow us to post news feeds, which will reach the students immediately, giving them any necessary updates. It would also allow the students to post comments or questions, for instance, if they would like to see another workshop at a certain time, or if they have a question about something they learned about in a workshop. Geri Anderson may update the page, and respond to any feedback we receive on it.

Next, we will create a free e-mail account on Gmail so that we may establish a mailing list. The address will be as follows: RUYAC@gmail.com. This is an optimal choice of communication, especially for students who may not use Facebook, because students are often checking e-mail for their classes. An associate from the YAC bank in Denver may assist Geri with this part of the project. The associate will be paid at an hourly rate, so that in addition to assisting in the workshops, they will spend about fifteen minutes checking this e-mail daily. This will also require sending e-mail announcements for upcoming workshops.

Once these two accounts are established, we will reach out to Career Services on College Avenue, who may send an e-mail out to their mass e-mail list, which consists of all current Rutgers New Brunswick students. Career services will send out messages about the YAC workshops in a timely fashion, free of charge. In fact, many events and workshops are advertised at Rutgers this way. The e-mail includes the date, time, location, and a brief explanation of the workshop. Further, the e-mail provides a link for students to register for the event via "CareerKnight," which is also a courtesy of career services. Up to forty-five students will be able to register for each of the three workshops.

Step Two: Innovative Workshops

Step two is an integral part of "RU Learning Personal Finances?" We will hold three 80-minute long workshops where students will learn budgeting, investing, and managing risk. A group of four qualified individuals will be in charge of the workshops, and their responsibilities will include planning as well as conducting the workshops. The group will require two members from the YAC, Geri Anderson who is head of the project, and her fellow YAC board member, Phyllis Gage. They will oversee the workshops to ensure the security of YAC's mission. The two remaining members of the group will be professors from the Rutgers Business School faculty. The first is Arthur Guarino, who teaches finance, including introductory and management courses, and also has experience working as a securities arbitrator in the financial industry. The second professor is Simi Kedia who teaches finance and economics, and was an assistant manager for Citibank before coming to Rutgers (rutgers.edu).

The Business School professors will be asked to volunteer in creating the workshop. However, if they do not wish to volunteer their services, we will compensate them a flat rate, which is reflected in the budget below. The Business School professors are an ideal choice, as they are knowledgeable in many topics that will be covered (budgeting, investing, credit cards, and loans) and they are accustomed to teaching these topics to undergraduates. The team (the professors, YAC board members, and YAC associates) will plan and write out a PowerPoint presentation in three "planning meetings" estimated at two hours each. The goal is to have not only an attractive PowerPoint, but to have meaningful content that is easy to understand. We want students to learn the basic concepts of budgeting, investing, and managing risk.

The workshops will take place at Rutgers Student Center, in room 410, which provides a comfortable space for up to forty-five people. As part of the cost for the room, the Rutgers Student Center will arrange the room in tables, so that students may sit in groups. This will be important for the final part of the workshop, which will be discussed later. There will be snacks, catered by Au Bon Pain who will also set it up, and beverages purchased by the team. In the front of the room, there will be two chairs for the Rutgers Business School members, who will present the PowerPoint slideshow on a projector behind them. Professors Guarino and Kedia will also be provided with a microphone, which is also included in the price of the room. The two YAC members will be able to circulate the room after they introduce themselves and YAC's mission at the start of the workshop. The associate will also be there to assist in handing out any paperwork, setting up beverages, and generally assist in keeping things running smoothly.

In the first forty-five minutes, we will present the PowerPoint. The PowerPoint presentation is ideal because the room package was available with a projector and large screen for viewing. In room 410, all students will be able to face the screen and see the PowerPoint, while also taking notes, if they so please, on their personal note pads that we will ask them to bring. Professors Guarino and Kedia will alternate verbally explaining the slides, and they will work out these logistics in the three "planning meetings." The presentation will cover each of the three topics for fifteen minutes each. Some highlights of each section include: "Budget Wizard" in budgeting, stock market tips in investing, and building healthy credit in managing risk. Unlike the programs in the Literature Review section, we have merged three aspects of personal finance, instead of one or two.

Next, we will have students engage in a group activity, similar to what the JA program in Texas did, and role-play. Whereas the JA program had students simulate running a bank, we will have students simulate making decisions about purchasing investments and applying for loans. This is because 75% of Rutgers students admitted not knowing how to invest, and further, the overall loan debt has now surpassed credit card debt. As per the lesson preceding this activity, students should be able to point out what investments would be more "financially sound" than another, for instance a mutual fund is better to invest in than a car. Further, they should practice understanding loans, as in percentages, and terms like "borrower" and "lender," as well as repayment options. We will hand out a worksheet for them to write out their answers on, as they first discuss what they think as a group, for about fifteen minutes. Then, the professors will take over and explain each answer while presenting some "answer" slides, for about fifteen minutes.

Hereafter, there will be about fifteen minutes for questions and answers. Geri Anderson and Phyllis Gage will join Professors Guarino and Kedia on-stage for this section, and encourage students to ask questions about anything they learned, about YAC, or what else they can do. The last thing the four members will leave the students with is a reminder to register on CashCourse.org to use the Budget Wizard.

Step Three: CashCourse

The use of CashCourse will be an ongoing effort as well for Rutgers administration to continue. Like Texas Tech University, Rutgers may continue to advertise the free use of Cashcourse.org. This can be a message YAC leaves to Rutgers administration, but will be out of this project budget. Nonetheless, Rutgers may consider the actual Web site is free, and the only cost would be paper advertisements. Texas Tech also used links on popular Web sites, which is also something free of cost for Rutgers to utilize. Step three is to ensure that YAC's mission on campus continues to spread beyond the "RU Learning Personal Finances?" workshops.

Budget

Section 1: Salaries

EHW x HR = FR (FR)

This times the hourly rate = Flat rate

Name	Flat rate (bls.gov) (FR)	Estimated hours of work (EHW)
Geri Anderson > different skills?	$1344.00	20 hours
Phyllis Gage	$1344.00	20 hours
Professor Arthur Guarino	$1060.00	15 hours
Professor Simi Kedia	$1060.00	15 hours
Associate	$324.00	9 hours

Salaries have been extracted from bls.gov occupational handbook. They are calculated based on median salary, broken down by months and into days. Each member will vary in salary and in number of days work compensated. Although their work is broken down by hours, they will be paid based on "days" work, because we want to encourage enthusiasm in the project. Further, the members are taking time out of their normal jobs, which we want to be courteous and grateful of.

The YAC members, Geri Anderson and Phyllis Gage, will be paid as education administrators, with six days of work compensated. The professors will be paid their normal salary as associate professors for five days. The associate, based on administrative assistant salary, will be compensated three days, which includes checking RUYAC gmail account. These amounts are reflected in the "Section 1" chart above.

The "estimated hours" above includes planning meetings, estimated at two hours each. This time will be used to decide content, how they will conduct the session, and other logistics. All persons involved have a dedicated four hours for the actual workshops and three hours each of personal preparation time. Planning and preparation is important, as we want to ensure that what we present at the workshops is the most sophisticated, and up-to-date, while also maintaining a clear and understandable lesson for the students.

Total for Salaries: $5,132.00

Section 2: Advertisement

Item	Cost	Manufacturer
Poster	$60.00 (scc.rutgers.edu)	SCC at Alexander Library
Group Worksheets	$118.00 (staples.com)	135 copies from Staples

The poster will be outside of the student center during the three days of the actual workshop. The group worksheets are for the group activity during the workshops, where students can write their answers.

Total for Advertisement: $178.00

Section 3: Workshop

Component	Cost	
Room 411 Rutgers Student Center	$3,775.00 (getinvolved.rutgers.edu/ reservespace)	For all sessions: Includes table set up, projector, screen, and 2 microphones
Food: Au Boin Pan	$700.00 (aubonpain.com/catering)	For all sessions: Includes mini cookies, brownies, and fresh berries
Beverages: Shop Rite	$60.00 (shoprite.com)	For all sessions: 24 packs of Poland spring water
Iced Tea	$30.00	For all sessions: 32 packs of Ssips Iced Tea boxes

The Rutgers Student Center price package includes set up in our room, room 411. There will be tables set up where a group of five students can be seated at each table. This will not only make it comfortable for snacking, but also make group work easily accessible. With a maximum of forty-five students, there would be nine groups during this time. This package also includes a projector and screen to display a PowerPoint presentation of key concepts: budgeting, investing, and managing risk. Microphones for Professors Guarino and Kedia are also included here.

Total for Workshop: $4565.00

Section 4: YAC members travel

Airfare (Denver to Newark)	$495.00/ticket/non-stop/ round trip (delta.com)	3 tickets economy seats
Car ride (Newark to New Brunswick)	$89.00 (giantslimo.com)	1 car for 3 people

We would like to compensate the YAC members travel expenses, as they will be coming to New Brunswick from Denver, Colorado. The total for three airplane tickets (for Geri Anderson, Phyllis Gage, and the associate) from Delta airlines is $1480.00. The car to pick the YAC members up from the airport will be $89.00. Total travel expenses are: $1569.00.

Total for travel: $1569.00

TOTAL FOR ALL: "Achieving Personal Financial Success for Rutgers Students" : $11,444.00

Discussion and Evaluation Plan

The degree of financial literacy one has will inevitably affect their financial behavior, and ultimately, their well-being in the world. College students, of all backgrounds and majors, will face financial challenges and decisions. College students today, in particular, face a financial world that is becoming more complex and challenging (Avard 321). As they graduate, they may be buried in debt, confused about buying a house, or budgeting their current income and more importantly will be the new faces of the United States workforce. Therefore, it is vital that they have the knowledge and tools to deal with those challenges. If we fail to do so, consequences for the students can be stressful and almost unmanageable. *Newsweek* satires the issue by stating "by the time they graduate, they'll be well versed in Faulkner, microbiology, or Mandarin—but chances are, they won't have even a basic command of financial tasks like living on a budget," thus, they must be prepared (Chatzy 23).

"We have a financial-literacy crisis in America" and we must cope by providing such education (Chatzy 24). As earlier mentioned, low financial literacy among citizens can easily become a problem for society. Factors such as high bankruptcy rates, less spending or consumerism, decreased business, or unpaid loans, can drive the economy downward, as we currently see in 2011. If we begin to educate and fuel students' financial literacy, we can help their, and our nation's, future. If we induce this proposal, we can begin to combat the financial literacy crisis among the next generation of America.

As an evaluation plan, we may follow up with students the semester before they graduate with a second survey on financial literacy. Students should ideally feel more confident answering the questions. In addition, more of them should answer "yes" to questions such as: Do you have any investments? Do you have a written budget? Do you know the APR rate on your credit card? Further, we may evaluate Internet traffic on the "Budget Wizard" to examine students' use of this budgeting tool. To track traffic is made simple by the free assistance of cashcourse.com administration. These evaluation tools will assist us in examining the outcomes of this proposal to help students at Rutgers achieve financial success. In the furthest outlook, we may evaluate how Rutgers' curriculum board responds to our workshops. "Since this subject matter is so important to a college graduate, perhaps universities should regard financial knowledge as being a component of their general education program," and with success of "RU Learning Personal Finances?" perhaps Rutgers will adopt this notion (Avard 333). If so, we may use this as a long-term evaluation.

Appendix A

RU Learning Personal Finance?

The Young Americans Center
at RU!

Our Mission: As experts in financial education, we are committed to developing the financial literacy of young people through real-life experiences and hands-on programs purposefully designed to enable them to <u>prosper</u> in our free enterprise system.

Do you know how to budget, invest for the future, or effectively manage money? Do you understand your loans or credit cards, and how to properly use them?

How can you achieve
<u>Personal Financial Success?</u>....

Come join us and **<u>learn how</u>** at one of our valuable and interactive workshops:
Monday, February 2nd at 8 p.m.
Tuesday, February 3rd at 7 p.m.
Wednesday, February 4th at 7 p.m.

Room 411 in the Rutgers Student Center on College Avenue.
Refreshments will be served.

Please register with career services on CareerKnight
(HURRY! Max is 45 students)

Works Cited

Avard, Stephen, et al. "The Financial Knowledge of College Freshmen." *College Student Journal* 39.2 (2005): 321–39. Print.

cashcourse.org. Web. 2011.

Chatzky, Jean. "The Student Financial Crisis." *Newsweek* 158.10 (2011): 23. Print.

Gavigan, Karen. "Show Me the Money Resources: Financial Literacy for 21st-Century Learners." *Library Media Connection* 28.5 (2010): 24–7. Print.

"Financial Literacy Education: What do Students Need to Know to Plan for the Future? Hearing before the committee on education reform." *Gpo.gov.* Web. 28 Oct. 2003.

Henry, Reasie A., Janice G. Weber, and David Yarbrough. "Money Management Practices of College Students." *College Student Journal* 35.2 (2001): 244. Print.

Hite, Nancy Groneman, et al. "Personal Finance Education in Recessionary Times." *Journal of Education for Business* 86.5 (2011): 253–7. Print.

Hoffman, Michael J. R., Karen S. McKenzie, and Susan Paris. "Paper Or Plastic?" *CPA Journal* 78.9 (2008): 16–20. Print.

Huston, Sandra. "Measuring Financial Literacy." *The Journal of Consumer Affairs.* 44.2 (2010): 296–315. Print.

Johnson, Elizabeth, and Margaret S. Sherraden. "From Financial Literacy to Financial Capability among Youth." *Journal of Sociology & Social Welfare* 34.3 (2007): 119–46. Print.

Joo, So-hyun, John E. Grable, and Dorothy C. Bagwell. "Credit Card Attitudes and Behaviors of College Students." *College Student Journal* 37.3 (2003): 405. Print.

Kantrowitz, Mark. *finaid.org.* Web. 2011.

Lawrence, Frances C., et al. *Credit Card Usage of College Students: Evidence from Louisiana State University* (Research Information Sheet #107). Baton Rouge, LA: Louisiana Agricultural Center (2003): 1–27. Print.

lba.org. Web. 2011.

Lusardi, Annamaria. "Financial Literacy among the Young." *Journal of Consumer Affairs* 44.2 (2010): 358–80. Print.

"Making the Case for Financial Literacy—2010." *Jumpstart.org.* Updated April 2010, *Jumpstart.org.* Web. 26 Nov. 2011.

Manton, Edgar J., et al. "What College Freshmen Admit To Not Knowing About Personal Finance." *Journal of College Teaching & Learning* 3.1 (2006): 43–54.

Moore, Marguerite, and Jason M. Carpenter. "The Impact of College Student Money Attitudes on Credit Responsibility." *College Student Journal* 43.4 (2009): 1116–24. Print.

Mulvihill, Geoff. "Rutgers Raises In-state Tuition by 1.8% after Board Cuts Planned Hike in Half." *The Associated Press* 14 July 2011. Print.

"Mybudget360.com". Web. 2011.

njaes.rutgers.edu. Web. 2011.

Office of Media Relations. *Rutgers, The State University of New Jersey, Media Relations.* Web. 20 Oct. 2011.

"Report of the Rutgers University Senate Student Affairs Committee and Executive Committee: Student financial management and credit card debt." Web. 5 November 2011.

Robeyns, Ingrid. "Sen's Capability Approach and Gender Inequality: Selecting Relevant Capabilities." *Feminist Economics* 9.2–3 (2003): 61-92. Print.

Rosen, James. "Student Debt: America's Next Bubble?" *foxnews.com.* 19 Apr. 2011. Web. 2 December 2011.

Scott, Matthew S. "Avoid the Credit Card Trap." *Black Collegian* 37.3 (2007): 62–4. Print.

Seyedian, Mojtaba. "Improving Financial Literacy of College Students: A Cross-Sectional Analysis." *College Student Journal* 45.1 (2011): 177–89. Print.

"Study finds rising number of college students using credit cards for tuition." *salliemae.com.* Sallie Mae, April 2009. Web. 2 December 2011.

Supiano, Beckie. "For Students, the New Kind of Literacy is Financial College Offer Programs in Managing Money. (Cover Story)." *Chronicle of Higher Education* 55.2 (2008): A1–A38. Print.

"Teaching Kids about Money." Fox News. Denver, Colorado. 6 Oct. 2011. Television.

"YAcenter.org". Web. 2011.

Christine Redmond
466 Oak Street
Metuchen, New Jersey 08840

July 19, 2012

Brian Colvin
Associate Athletic Director of Finance and Administration
Louis Brown Athletic Center
83 Rockafeller Road
Piscataway, New Jersey 08854

Dear Mr. Colvin,

It is in the nature of Rutgers University to always strive for excellence, and its athletic department follows suit by giving student-athletes like me the opportunity to succeed. Sports teams at Rutgers have consistently faced and met challenges both on and off the field, especially the softball program. While it continues to make accomplishments, the team faces financial struggles that have undoubtedly hindered the program's success.

The Rutgers softball team does not generate revenue, and it has sub-par facilities that fail to compete with its Big East counterparts. The athletic department will be alleviating some of its own financial stresses by fixing a problem like this for the program. Impending budget cuts have recently shed a light on spending issues, and the future of a non-revenue sports program like the softball team depends on a plan of action. I am calling this issue to your attention because a project of this scale would need funding from the department. I also understand that you coordinated a $6-million renovation project of Fordham's athletic facilities where you were last employed before joining the Rutgers community.

Enclosed is a copy of a business proposal to expand the softball facilities at Rutgers. The proposal outlines the steps needed to turn the Rutgers' softball team into a revenue-generating sport. By making aesthetic upgrades to the field along with adding stadium seating, the team will have the benefits of charging admission to games, renting out the stadium for outside use, and holding camps and clinics to generate profit. This plan includes several models from successful Big East programs such as the University of South Florida, the University of Notre Dame, and the University of Louisville. The proposal also includes a budget for the plan. Overall, the complex will be transformed into a facility that the softball organization, the athletic department, and the university can be proud of.

Thank you for taking the time to read my proposal. If you have any questions, please do not hesitate to contact me by phone at (732) 890-4326 or by e-mail at credmond@rutgers.edu.

Sincerely,

Christine Redmond

Christine Redmond

Avoiding a Budget Crisis:

A Proposal to Update the Rutgers Softball Facilities

Submitted by:
Christine Redmond

Submitted to:
Brian Colvin
Associate Athletic Director of Finance and Administration
Louis Brown Athletic Center
83 Rockafeller Road
Piscataway, New Jersey 08854

Prepared for:
Writing for Business and Professions
19 July 2012

Abstract

Impending budget cuts draw attention to spending issues within the Rutgers athletic department, namely the allocation of its resources to non-revenue sports. Without generating profit, these sports are limited in terms of spending which puts them at a disadvantage as compared to other Big East programs. The softball team has suffered the consequences of a tight budget and inadequate resources. Research has shown the positive effects of team loyalty and certain stadium factors on spectator attendance, as well as the relationship between psychological commitment and customer retention in sports. Other Big East softball programs including the University of South Florida, the University of Notre Dame, and the University of Louisville have implemented this research into a plan of action and updated their facilities in order to generate profit and have consequently seen increases in revenue, fan attendance, and overall satisfaction.

This proposal discusses the implementation of a facilities update to turn the softball team into a revenue-generating sport at Rutgers University. The update will include aesthetic changes to the infield and outfield, the reconstruction of both dugouts, and the creation of stadium seating to accommodate more fans and provide the opportunity to charge admission to the games. The stadium will also feature a concession stand and will be available for outside use including camps, clinics, and tournaments. This proposal includes a detailed, step-by-step plan along with a budget for the project.

Table of Contents

Table of Figures

Executive Summary

The profits that have been generated within the athletic department at Rutgers are insufficient to offset its spending habits, and this discrepancy poses a risk to the financial health of the athletic department, the university, and its students. The current revenue that is being generated from the university's sports teams isn't enough to reduce funding from the school, which places the athletic department in the face of yet another budget cut. The softball team is one of several at-risk, non-revenue sports at Rutgers.

In order for a non-revenue sport to generate profit, it must engage in profit-maximizing behavior. However, this cannot occur when a program like the softball team fails to bring in revenue yet spends over $900,000 on an annual basis. Nonetheless, there is hope to turn things around for the organization. Charging admission is a start, but it's not enough. Research has shown that by offering a comfortable venue that fulfills fans' needs, fans will act like customers and repeat their purchasing habits in favor of the softball program. They will continue to purchase tickets and merchandise and become loyal spectators. Fans experience psychological motivations that stadium features can deliver in order to financially benefit the softball team.

Marketing this stadium experience is also important. Fans will have a more positive experience if they get a lot of "bang for their buck," so to speak. By offering special events and promotions, spectators are drawn to attend games. According to research, building a fan base is the key to an organization's success. Sport marketing has the opportunity to appeal to an entirely new audience, which will boost attendance and profit for the program.

This proposal includes several models of success from the University of South Florida, the University of Louisville, and the University of Notre Dame. Each school has adapted these theories to fit their program's needs and has seen drastic increases in revenue. We can use these schools as models of success for a similar plan to be implemented at Rutgers.

The proposal outlines the steps needed to turn the softball team into a revenue-generating sport. First, by adding stadium seating along with making aesthetic upgrades to the field, the team will have the benefits of building a fan base, charging admission to games, and holding camps and clinics to generate profit. These upgrades include replacing the infield dirt and outfield grass, reconstructing both dugouts, and adding a press box and concession area.

This plan calls for an architectural company to design updated facilities. Thus, the athletic department will allocate a budget, and based on this budget the company will proceed with construction. This plan is flexible and can be easily adapted for any financial plan, but a feasible cost for this entire project would be two million dollars.

Introduction

The profits that have been generated within the athletic department at Rutgers have been deemed insufficient and pose a risk to the financial health of the university and its students. According to *Bloomberg News*, it is costing the average student nearly $1,000 in student fees to support Rutgers' sports teams (Bloomberg). In other words, when a student pays his or her tuition bill for the year, $1,000 goes solely to the athletic department. If that wasn't enough, out of fifty-four surveyed schools, Rutgers' athletics took the most money ($28.5 million) from its university budget last year. According to financial reports filed with the National Collegiate Athletic Association (NCAA), Rutgers was one of thirty-three schools that lost money and subsequently increased its university financial support budget from the previous year (Bloomberg).

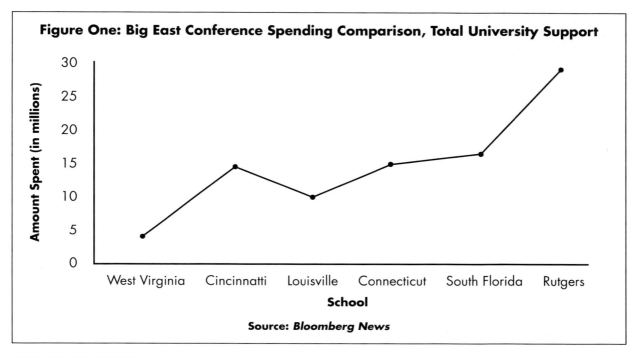

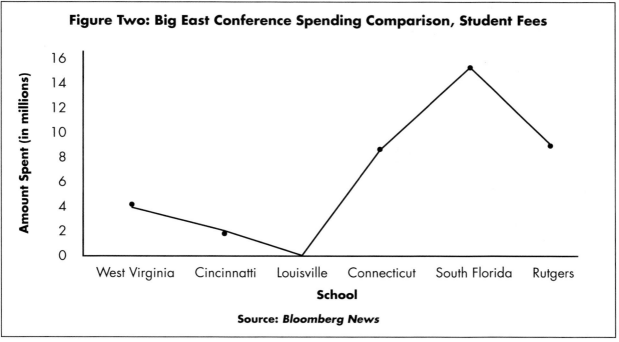

The current revenue that is being generated from our sports teams isn't enough to reduce funding from the school. If funding isn't reduced, budget cuts will begin to affect non-revenue sports at Rutgers, leaving the softball program at a clear disadvantage. With less money flowing into the organization, the program faces the inability to effectively recruit quality players and the inability to travel in order to compete at a high level. Additionally, because the budget supports coaches' salaries and benefits, as well as scholarships and summer school funding, these areas will face losses that are difficult to recover. A more severe repercussion is the threat of cutting yet another Olympic sport at Rutgers, which has become a very prominent and tangible fear. In 2006, six sports were cut from the athletic department including heavyweight crew, lightweight crew, men's and women's fencing, men's swimming and diving, and men's tennis. Without a way to generate revenue, cuts could affect the softball team as well.

The Rutgers faculty council has recently weighed in on the issue at hand, and rightfully so. The council believes that academics are losing out because of the massive amount of money flowing into the athletic department. Subsequently, on March 30 they voted in demand of "$5 million of cuts in university funding of athletics by fiscal 2016 and a referendum on sports fees required of students" (Bloomberg). This has been a continuing debate among faculty and administration, and it certainly promises to give the athletic department a tough time avoiding yet another budget cut. However, a stable revenue-generating plan of action would certainly point the university in the right direction to at least put a dent in the debt caused by Rutgers' sports teams.

As previously mentioned, *Bloomberg News* surveyed fifty-four public institutions including Rutgers University. Schools that were successful in reducing university funding had a major similarity attributing to their success. The athletic budget funds nineteen non-revenue sports here at Rutgers (taking out football, men's basketball, and women's basketball), something that no other school does. The Olympic sports at Rutgers rely heavily on funding from the university in order to keep their respective programs afloat. Currently, the softball program brings in zero dollars in revenue. It does not charge admission to games, and it does not offer a concession stand. Bleachers holding a capacity of only about 150–200 people are the only form of seating. On an average weekend game, fans include mostly family members of the players plus the occasional recruit, never amounting to more than one hundred people. What this program does, on the other hand, is use hundreds of thousands of dollars of department resources to fund scholarships, trips, post-season funds, salaries, and benefits. In the 2010–2011 year, the team spent over $900,000.

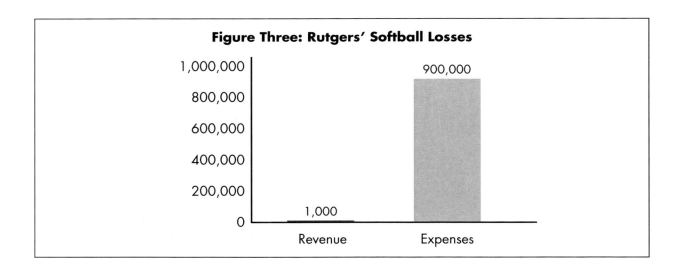

This is not to take credit away from the team. For its third consecutive season, the softball program made it to the Big East championship in 2012. It had quite a few individual record-setting performances along with several notable victories this past season including wins over Texas State (43), Notre Dame (29), and Syracuse (22). The team finished its 2012 campaign ranked 70th overall out of 289 Division 1 teams ("NCAA Division 1 Softball Rankings").

While the softball team at Rutgers continues to make remarkable accomplishments, it still does not have the facilities to show for all its success. The university is in the midst of a multi-million dollar addition to the Livingston campus that includes state-of-the-art facilities. The softball field is an eyesore in the middle of a beautiful renovation, so it seems only natural that the athletic fields are included in this project. By updating these facilities, the program will have the ability to generate revenue and not rely so heavily on the athletic budget for support. Thus, budget cuts will not affect the team's scholarships, salaries, benefits, summer school funding, or post-season funding. Cutting the sport will not be realistic, and the organization along with the athletic department will be able to breathe again. This plan is crucial for the financial health of the athletic department and ultimately, the university.

Literature Review

The Rutgers softball team does not generate revenue, subjecting it to department-wide budget cuts and, more seriously, the termination of the program as a whole. In order to stay afloat, the organization must find a way to create profits in order to be more self-sufficient and not rely so heavily on the athletic department's budget.

Research to Support Updating Facilities

Profit maximizing behavior is essential for any serious sports team or organization to stay afloat. It is reasonable to assume that a private firm, or in this case the athletic department, "is interested in its profits and that higher profits are better than lower profits" (Bradley). If the Rutgers athletic department has any hope in preserving its nineteen non-revenue Olympic sports teams, it must make its primary interest to generate profit. Aju Fenn proposes in his article entitled "Sports Economics" that, like any other business, there are two sides to the profit equation when it comes to sports economics: revenues and costs. Currently in the softball program this equation is incredibly lopsided, where costs peak near one million dollars, and revenues stay at zero.

One of the most basic forms of revenue (and consequently the simplest to calculate) is from admission. It is calculated by multiplying the average cost of admission by the number of attendees present at a competition (Fenn). Last year the Rutgers football team made 9.3 million dollars in revenue from ticket sales alone (Bloomberg). In order to alleviate the lopsided revenue to cost ratio, the softball team will have to charge admission to the games. However, as noted by Hoye et al. in *Unique Aspects of Managing Sport Organizations*, simply charging admission is not enough. Fans are encouraged to attend competition based on what the experience offers. While external factors such as the weather might be important in determining attendance at a game (Fenn), these circumstances are not controllable. On the other hand, the athletic department does have control over creating an atmosphere that is enjoyable for teams, the officiating crew, and fans alike. Attending a sports competition can be related to a consumer purchasing a product. These consumers, or in this case the fans, develop emotional attachments to the product, or team, they support. Ultimately, they experience psychological motivations that drive them to attend games (Hoye et al.). If fans are able to experience this psychology, it will influence their motivations and ultimately boost attendance for Rutgers softball.

It is important to market the stadium experience for fans, and to do so the softball field must be upgraded. According to Michael Silk in his article *Sports Stadiums*, building these facilities "has become a central component of revitalization . . . and stadiums have become among the most effective vehicles for advancement within an organization" (Silk). In other words, the softball team will experience a positive outcome by making updates to the field. The program will make strides toward generating revenue since stadiums are so beneficial to an organization's financial health.

It is clear that every detail counts when it comes to sport marketing and fan retention. In a 2012 study on customer retention in sports organization marketing, Gordon Gray and Stacia Wert-Gray found that the likelihood of customer retention increases with successful relationship marketing. Essentially by strengthening the fan-team relationship, they found fans were likely to return to the stadium for future events (Gray). Furthermore, they found that a high degree of fan loyalty resulted in increased consumption related to that team (Gray). In fact, loyal spectators are the key to an organization's success because, "they exhibit behavior such as the repeat purchasing of tickets and continual attendance, which benefit the sports organization" (Bee). Though fan loyalty to a team on account of its performance and history is instrumental in explaining why spectators attend games, the stadium's surroundings play just as important of a role in determining spectator's attendance inclinations (Wakefield). In other words, regardless of a team's track record, fans are almost guaranteed to return when the stadium experience provides them with more bang-for-their-buck, so to speak.

This "bang" has a lot to do with what the venue offers for fans. A stadium will only be as good as the perks it offers to spectators. Fundamentally, the stadium experience must be marketed "as more than just a game" (Wakefield). By doing so, fans will experience positive associations and return for future events. In addition to the money spent by fans to attend sporting events, "there are also millions of dollars spent each year on sports memorabilia—clothing, hats, collectibles, and so forth" (McDonald). While this trend is most prevalent at a professional level, creating a facility that sells merchandise still has the opportunity to bring in money for the softball program. A sports venue will draw more fans if it offers "attractive and comfortable facilities, good views of play, easy accessibility, and a large scoreboard. Other external factors that may influence fans' decisions are the price; special promotions; and even what other leisure alternatives are offered" (Hoye et al.). Many organizations also run camps or clinics that attract prospective youth players. According to Colleen Bee and Mark Havitz in their article assessing the relationship between involvement and fan attraction, "an individual's attraction to the sport and his/her involvement with the sport has a direct influence on the development of a psychological commitment to a related sports event" (Bee). Thus, by using these facilities to run clinics, the softball program has the opportunity to turn these young players into prospective fans who have a positive psychological attachment to the program and will become loyal customers.

It is not surprising, then, that notable Big East programs, specifically the University of South Florida, the University of Louisville, and the University of Notre Dame offer most, if not all, of the above-mentioned amenities.

The University of South Florida

After speaking in a telephone interview with Chris Paras, the Assistant Athletics Director of Facilities at the University of South Florida, it became evident as to why USF made it to the Women's College World Series in the 2012 season. As Mr. Paras pointed out, the formula is simple. His state-of-the-art facilities attract the top recruits in the nation. These recruits produce wins for the program. And as this organization has shown, fans will support a winning program.

It was clear to the athletic department at USF that the time had come for change. So, as part of a revitalization plan to update a number of athletic facilities on-site, the softball program received a brand new, state-of-the-art stadium. Previously, what they had was in need of maintenance. The life expectancy of certain facilities was up, and some teams didn't even have buildings to use. As Mr. Paras put it, when it came to the department's facilities the athletic program was "really limited with potential as far as being a Big East contender." Though the NCAA puts a limit on how much a program can charge to enter a game, increasing numbers in attendance have certainly made an impact. With the new updates the stadium can accommodate more fans, expanding from only a couple hundred seats to about 750. The program is able to sell more tickets as a result of having larger facilities, which increases its potential revenue.

The USF softball field is not only used for practice and competition within the organization. The program runs camps, as well as doing some internal sharing within the university. In fact, the stadium has been turned into a movie theatre where people are able to pay a small admission fee to sit in the stands and enjoy a movie on the big-screen scoreboard. The program has been able to enjoy a steady profit by renting out the stadium for outside activities.

The University of Louisville

At the University of Louisville, a similar scheme is used to produce profit within the organization. Ulmer Stadium "can accommodate up to 2,200 fans, features field lighting, home and visiting bullpens, and a climate-controlled press box and a video board" ("Ulmer Stadium"). While Rutgers would not need such an expansive renovation, these accommodations have attributed to much of Louisville's success.

The ten-year-old venue offers state-of-the-art upgrades that attracted a large crowd for the 2011 Big East Championship. More recently, the stadium was selected as a host site for the 2012 NCAA Softball Regional as it was three years earlier in 2009. Similarly to USF's field, Ulmer Stadium is used not only for practice and competition, but also for high school softball games, tournaments, and team camps ("Ulmer Stadium"), all of which are revenue-generating events for the university's athletic department. The facility also has a stand set up along the bottom level of the stadium that sells Louisville softball merchandise. Fans have yet another way to buy into Louisville softball because of this amenity.

The University of Notre Dame

Melissa Cook Stadium at the University of Notre Dame is yet another example of an update that has given back to the organization in more ways than one. According to my correspondence with Assistant Athletics Director of Event Management Monica Cundiff, there was a laundry list of reasons for creating the new stadium such as, "allowing more fans to attend games and being able to host post-season, conference, and NCAA tournaments." The list goes on and the stadium serves other purposes including, "giving the student-athletes a better experience by playing in a nicer stadium and having a locker room and team room on-site so the student-athletes have somewhere else to go for down time as well as studying."

According to Ms. Cundiff, since the stadium was built in 2008, there has been a tremendous growth in fan attendance and revenue. The program has also made a more extensive marketing effort toward the promotion of the Notre Dame softball team in order to "build a fan base and promote the games." Most of the program's profit comes from ticket revenue and group sales.

Similar to Rutgers, Notre Dame's previous facility, Ivy Field, did not charge admission to games. Ms. Cundiff indicated that on a typical Saturday or Sunday when the weather was nice in South Bend, the crowd at Ivy Field ranged from about 150 to 200 fans, which is about the maximum capacity of Rutgers' current softball field. Now, on the other hand under those same conditions, between 500 and 750 people will buy tickets and attend a game. "You can say the stadium has something to do with it for sure," Ms. Cundiff confirmed, "and the increase in marketing efforts is instrumental." These marketing efforts are manifested in advertising and extensive media coverage.

Notre Dame hosted the 2012 Big East Championship tournament just four years after the stadium's unveiling in 2008, attesting to its success as a leading Division I facility. While the stadium has several features benefitting players and coaches for both the home and visiting teams, it also boasts "Wi-Fi capabilities, a family picnic lawn, chair back and bleacher seating, a concessions area, interior restrooms, and a common area which make the new Cook Stadium a very fan friendly place to enjoy a softball game" ("Melissa Cook Stadium"). The stadium can accommodate 850 fans and its primary use is practice and competition ("Melissa Cook Stadium").

Plan

Populous© architectural company was responsible for the expansion of the softball facilities at the University of South Florida as well as the expansion of the football stadium at Rutgers. They are familiar with what it will take to update our facilities and they are familiar with Rutgers University itself, making them an excellent candidate for this proposal. Typically the university will pitch a budget to the architectural company, and based on this number the company will draw up a plan. While this project is flexible in terms of the products and equipment used in construction, research has shown that there are some "must-haves" in order for a stadium to be successful in generating revenue.

Stadium Seating

Stadium seating will replace the bleachers that are currently the only form of seating, allowing for a greater maximum capacity to hold more fans during competition. All three models offer stadium seating in their facilities, as it has the opportunity to build a fan base and retain fans that will return for future events. It also increases the potential revenue an organization can make. This upgraded seating will provide good views of play, easy accessibility, and comfort, which according to research, are essential in attracting and retaining spectators. There will be a main entrance that includes a ticket area so admission can be charged upon entrance into the facilities, an essential aspect of generating profit. Although the NCAA caps admission costs, Rutgers can use a pricing scheme similar to those seen around the league. The team can also sell season tickets.

The stadium will also incorporate a press box and a new sound system for in-game entertainment to keep fans and players satisfied while meeting the needs of the athletic communications department, who must use the press box for game coverage.

Concessions

A concession stand will be built within the stadium, which will offer some staple food and drink items for fans to purchase. These items include those found at Rutgers football, basketball, and baseball games such as fountain drinks, water, candy, and other snacks. This provides yet another way to generate profit while keeping fans satisfied during game days that frequently last upward of four hours. All three models offer concession stands at their respective venues.

Aesthetic Upgrades

The infield dirt and outfield grass will be replaced along with both the home and visiting dugouts. Using products such as Hilltopper Infield Mix© and bluegrass sod will ensure minimal maintenance in the future while providing a top-of-the-line playing surface now. The dugouts will be reconstructed for more accessibility, aesthetic appeal, and better views of play. As research and models have shown, these aesthetic upgrades go a long way in appealing to fans and prospective recruits. According to this research, fans will enjoy a sports venue if it offers attractive facilities, which can be achieved by replacing the infield dirt, outfield grass, and dugouts. Each model has received some sort of aesthetic upgrade on its playing field within the last ten years.

Stadium Marketing

The athletic department could build a beautiful new stadium for the softball team, but have their efforts go unnoticed. As Notre Dame softball illustrates, marketing is key. By marketing the stadium, the general public will become aware of the program's facilities and events. This is an essential step in building a fan base. Just as other Rutgers sports events, camps, and clinics are advertised via the Web, radio, or at other athletic competitions, the softball program will have to follow suit. These advertisements will inform the public and turn them into potential consumers buying into Rutgers softball.

Budget

There are several directions that the stadium could go in based on input from the architectural company and a budget from the athletic department. Typically construction management or architectural companies create a plan in keeping with the budget allocated by the athletic department. Several things will need to be taken into account when calculating the budget for this proposal. These include: the cost of labor, equipment costs, and facility maintenance for the updated field. Additionally, the budget will take into account the cost of employing staff for ticket sales and a concession area during events.

This proposal provides flexibility in its design and price, which will be beneficial for the athletic department. For instance, construction costs will vary based on the materials chosen for the updates. Certain materials have their advantages, while others come at a hefty price. With that said, it is impossible to accurately predict the exact cost of this project. However, outlined below are some figures, which can be calculated to get a ballpark number that will be suitable for the Rutgers softball team's needs.

Cost of Labor

According to the Occupational Outlook Handbook, architects earned $34.88/hour on average in 2010. The athletic department will allocate a budget to the architectural company who will in-turn draw up a plan for the project.

Construction equipment operators made $18.97/hour while construction laborers earned $13.66/hour.

Cashiers made $8.89/hour, which will account for the approximate cost to hire people for ticket sales and the concession stand. In the 2012 season, the Rutgers softball team played 15 home games. Each game lasted for approximately two hours, making the total cost for both a concession worker and someone to work ticket sales $533.40.

Equipment Costs

Depending on the materials used for this project, stadium seats could range in price. The cost of a press box and sound system will also depend on the architectural company and the department's budget. Both the home and visiting dugouts will be completely renovated in this project.

Infield dirt is typically made up of a combination of sand, silt, and clay. However, ready-made products such as Hilltopper Infield Mix made by Stabilizer® Solutions are available. According to their Web site, 440 pounds of soil should be applied to newly constructed infields. (Stabilizer® calls for one pound of dirt per 25 square feet, and the infield is approximately 11,000 square feet.) It will cost approximately $20 per fifty-pound bag, which totals $176. The 29,000-square foot outfield will be covered with bluegrass sod, which costs approximately $0.34 per square foot totaling $9,860. Sustainability is crucial in the financial aspect of this project. By using top-of-the-line supplies now, little to no maintenance will be needed later on.

Cost to Maintain Facilities

Grounds maintenance workers earned $11.41/hour in 2010 according to the Occupational Outlook Handbook. Supplies needed to maintain the facilities include extra bases, chalk, and infield dirt. Equipment needed to maintain the facilities includes an irrigation system to account for the new infield and outfield updates.

Final Cost

Again, while it is impossible to predict the exact cost of a facilities update, the athletic department can pitch a number to an architectural company who will draw up a plan based on this budget. Based on comparables, this project will not be inexpensive and can reach costs of two million dollars. This is a feasible number that incorporates the needs of the program. The athletic department will have to fund the bulk of this project, but there is always an option to fundraise. Below is an itemized breakdown of approximate costs for this project. These numbers are based off of the three models in this proposal, as well as price quotes by construction companies and equipment companies. It is important to know that this is a list used for the purposes of itemizing costs, and takes into account the minimum and maximum budget for this project.

Figure Four: Itemized Cost Breakdown

Category	Cost
Cost of Labor:	
Construction and Architect	$218,120
Cashier	$540
	$218,660
Cost of Equipment:	
Infield	$176
Outfield	$9,860
Stadium Seating	$280,000
Dugouts	$10,000
Press Box and Sound System	$50,000
Concessions	$20,000
	$370,036
Maintenance Cost:	
Labor	$41,000
Supplies	$486
Equipment	$7,000
	$48,486
Total	**$637,182–$2,000,000**

Giving Back to RU

Rutgers softball will generate revenue by offering the amenities outlined in this plan. Simply charging admission alone will create profit even if the program fails to increase its fan base. Realistically, if the program maintained its usual crowd of about 150, this plan puts about $575 in the softball team's pocket in one day.

Figure Five: Admission Prices and Potential Revenue

Ticket	Number of Fans	Ticket Cost	Total
Adult	100	$5.00	$500
Child	25	$0.00	$0
Senior	25	$3.00	$75
			$575

The time it would take to make the money back from construction would be based on the aggressiveness of advertising and marketing. As the research and models have shown, marketing is the key to building a fan base, and it also accounts for fan retention. Consequently these fans will be responsible for the profits generated within the Rutgers softball program.

Discussion

The softball fields at Rutgers are in need of maintenance and upgrades. These proposed changes have the opportunity to turn the program into a revenue-generating sport, which will alleviate some of the financial issues within the athletic department. Research shows that fan retention and successful sport marketing can be achieved by creating a certain stadium atmosphere. Collegiate programs such as the University of South Florida, the University of Louisville, and the University of Notre Dame are reaping the benefits of state-of-the-art stadiums that help promote their respective program and the university as a whole.

Upgraded facilities are no longer a luxury for collegiate programs—they have become a necessity. In order for the Rutgers softball team to avoid a budget cut or, more severely, the termination of the program as a whole, it must take action. A plan to start generating revenue is essential for the financial health of the organization. Not only will a stadium alleviate some of the financial issues in the athletic department, but it will also be a facility that Rutgers athletics can rely on to produce profit. Most importantly, it will be something the university and its affiliates can be proud of.

Works Cited

Bee, Colleen, and Mark Havitz. "Exploring the relationship between involvement, fan attraction, psychological commitment and behavioural loyalty in a sports spectator context." *INTERNATIONAL JOURNAL OF SPORTS MARKETING & SPONSORSHIP.* 11.2 (2010): 140–57. Print.

Bradley, Michaele. "Profit Maximization." *21st Century Economics: A Reference Handbook.* Ed. Rhona C. Free. Thousand Oaks, CA: SAGE, 2010. 110–25. *SAGE Reference Online.* Web. 20 Jun. 2012.

Eichelberger, Curtis, and Elise Young. "Rutgers Football Fails Profit Test As Students Pay $1,000." *Bloomberg News.* Bloomberg, 06 May 2012. Web. 13 Jun. 2012.

Fenn, Aju. "Sports Economics." *21st Century Economics: A Reference Handbook.* Ed. Rhona C. Free. Thousand Oaks, CA: SAGE, 2010. 533–42. *SAGE Reference Online.* Web. 13 Jun. 2012.

Gray, Gordon, and Stacia Wert-Gray. "Customer retention in sports organization marketing: examining the impact of team identification and satisfaction with team performance." *INTERNATIONAL JOURNAL OF CONSUMER STUDIES.* 36.3 (2012): 275–81. Print.

Hoye, Russell, Matthew Nicholson, and Aaron Smith. "Unique Aspects of Managing Sport Organizations." *21st Century Management: A Reference Handbook.* Thousand Oaks, CA: SAGE, 2007. 502–10. *SAGE Reference Online.* Web. 13 Jun. 2012.

McDonald, Becky. "Sports Promotion." *Encyclopedia of Public Relations.* Thousand Oaks, CA: SAGE, 2004. 807–09. *SAGE Reference Online.* Web. 20 Jun. 2012.

"Melissa Cook Stadium." *The Official Site of Notre Dame Athletics.* University of Notre Dame. Web. 13 Jun. 2012.

"NCAA.com." *NCAA Division 1 Softball Rankings.* NCAA. Web. 20 Jun. 2012.

Occupational Outlook Handbook. U.S. Bureau of Labor Statistics. Web. 9 Jul. 2012.

Silk, Michael. "Sports Stadiums." *Encyclopedia of Urban Studies.* Ed. Ray Hutchison. Thousand Oaks, CA: SAGE, 2009. 763–67. *SAGE Reference Online.* Web. 20 Jun. 2012.

"Ulmer Stadium." *University of Louisville Official Athletic Site–Facilities.* Louisville Athletics. Web. 13 Jun. 2012.

"USF Softball Stadium." *Official Athletics Website of the University of South Florida.* USF Athletics. Web. 13 Jun. 2012.

Wakefield, Kirk. "The effects of team loyalty and selected stadium factors on spectator attendance." *Journal of Sport Management.* 9.2 (1995): 153–72. Print.

Chapter 7 ■ Final Proposal Workshop I

Please fill out the following form for your partner. Feel free to write comments on the drafts as well.

Cover Letter and Title Page

Does the cover letter . . .

1. directly address the funding source? _____yes _____no

2. explain why the reader has received this proposal? _____yes _____no

3. persuade the reader to examine this plan closely? _____yes _____no

4. offer details about the content of the plan? _____yes _____no

5. appear in full block form and include all six elements
   (return address, date, recipient's address, salutation, body, closing)? _____yes _____no

Is the cover letter . . .

1. signed? _____yes _____no

2. free of all grammatical and typographical errors? _____yes _____no

Does the title page . . .

1. include all five elements (project title, name of sender
   name of recipient, date, return information)? _____yes _____no

2. catch the attention of the reader? _____yes _____no

3. have a title appropriate to the plan? _____yes _____no

Is the title page . . .

1. visually appealing? _____yes _____no

2. free of all grammatical and typographical errors? _____yes _____no

What parts of the drafts did you like the most?

What parts of the drafts need the most improvement?

Abstract

1. Is the document clearly labeled as an "Abstract" at the top of the page? _____ yes _____ no
2. Is the document written from a third-person perspective? _____ yes _____ no
3. Does the document provide a balanced view of the project idea? _____ yes _____ no
4. Does the document cover elements of the problem, paradigm, and plan (in that order)? _____ yes _____ no
5. Does the document indicate a specific course of action? _____ yes _____ no
6. Is the document between 150 and 300 words and no longer than two paragraphs in length? _____ yes _____ no
7. Is the document single-spaced, in 12 point Times New Roman type? _____ yes _____ no
8. Is the document free of errors in grammar, usage, and/or sentence structure? _____ yes _____ no
9. Is the document presented in a clear, readable form? _____ yes _____ no
10. Would this document encourage me to read this plan? _____ yes _____ no

What is the one part of the draft you liked the most?

What is the one part of the draft that needs the most improvement?

Table of Contents and Table of Figures

1. Are these documents clearly labeled and presented in a logical and readable form? _____ yes _____ no
2. Are these documents free of errors in grammar, spacing, and punctuation? _____ yes _____ no

Additional Comments/Suggestions:

Chapter 7 ■ Final Proposal Workshop I

Please fill out the following form for your partner. Feel free to write comments on the drafts as well.

Cover Letter and Title Page

Does the cover letter . . .

1. directly address the funding source?   _____yes _____no

2. explain why the reader has received this proposal?   _____yes _____no

3. persuade the reader to examine this plan closely?   _____yes _____no

4. offer details about the content of the plan?   _____yes _____no

5. appear in full block form and include all six elements
   (return address, date, recipient's address, salutation, body, closing)?   _____yes _____no

Is the cover letter . . .

1. signed?   _____yes _____no

2. free of all grammatical and typographical errors?   _____yes _____no

Does the title page . . .

1. include all five elements (project title, name of sender
   name of recipient, date, return information)?   _____yes _____no

2. catch the attention of the reader?   _____yes _____no

3. have a title appropriate to the plan?   _____yes _____no

Is the title page . . .

1. visually appealing?   _____yes _____no

2. free of all grammatical and typographical errors?   _____yes _____no

What parts of the drafts did you like the most?

What parts of the drafts need the most improvement?

Abstract

1. Is the document clearly labeled as an "Abstract" at the top of the page?   _____ yes _____ no

2. Is the document written from a third-person perspective?   _____ yes _____ no

3. Does the document provide a balanced view of the project idea?   _____ yes _____ no

4. Does the document cover elements of the problem, paradigm, and plan (in that order)?   _____ yes _____ no

5. Does the document indicate a specific course of action?   _____ yes _____ no

6. Is the document between 150 and 300 words and no longer than two paragraphs in length?   _____ yes _____ no

7. Is the document single-spaced, in 12 point Times New Roman type?   _____ yes _____ no

8. Is the document free of errors in grammar, usage, and/or sentence structure?   _____ yes _____ no

9. Is the document presented in a clear, readable form?   _____ yes _____ no

10. Would this document encourage me to read this plan?   _____ yes _____ no

What is the one part of the draft you liked the most?

What is the one part of the draft that needs the most improvement?

Table of Contents and Table of Figures

1. Are these documents clearly labeled and presented in a logical and readable form?   _____ yes _____ no

2. Are these documents free of errors in grammar, spacing, and punctuation?   _____ yes _____ no

Additional Comments/Suggestions:

Chapter 7 ■ Final Proposal Workshop I

Please fill out the following form for your partner. Feel free to write comments on the drafts as well.

Cover Letter and Title Page

Does the cover letter . . .

1. directly address the funding source?   _____yes _____no

2. explain why the reader has received this proposal?   _____yes _____no

3. persuade the reader to examine this plan closely?   _____yes _____no

4. offer details about the content of the plan?   _____yes _____no

5. appear in full block form and include all six elements
   (return address, date, recipient's address, salutation, body, closing)?   _____yes _____no

Is the cover letter . . .

1. signed?   _____yes _____no

2. free of all grammatical and typographical errors?   _____yes _____no

Does the title page . . .

1. include all five elements (project title, name of sender
   name of recipient, date, return information)?   _____yes _____no

2. catch the attention of the reader?   _____yes _____no

3. have a title appropriate to the plan?   _____yes _____no

Is the title page . . .

1. visually appealing?   _____yes _____no

2. free of all grammatical and typographical errors?   _____yes _____no

What parts of the drafts did you like the most?

What parts of the drafts need the most improvement?

Abstract

1. Is the document clearly labeled as an "Abstract" at the top of the page? _____ yes _____ no

2. Is the document written from a third-person perspective? _____ yes _____ no

3. Does the document provide a balanced view of the project idea? _____ yes _____ no

4. Does the document cover elements of the problem, paradigm, and plan (in that order)? _____ yes _____ no

5. Does the document indicate a specific course of action? _____ yes _____ no

6. Is the document between 150 and 300 words and no longer than two paragraphs in length? _____ yes _____ no

7. Is the document single-spaced, in 12 point Times New Roman type? _____ yes _____ no

8. Is the document free of errors in grammar, usage, and/or sentence structure? _____ yes _____ no

9. Is the document presented in a clear, readable form? _____ yes _____ no

10. Would this document encourage me to read this plan? _____ yes _____ no

What is the one part of the draft you liked the most?

What is the one part of the draft that needs the most improvement?

Table of Contents and Table of Figures

1. Are these documents clearly labeled and presented in a logical and readable form? _____ yes _____ no

2. Are these documents free of errors in grammar, spacing, and punctuation? _____ yes _____ no

Additional Comments/Suggestions:

Chapter 7 ■ Final Proposal Workshop II

Please fill out the following form for your partner. Feel free to write comments on the drafts as well.

Executive Summary

1. Is the document clearly labeled as an Executive Summary at the top of the page? _____ yes _____ no

2. Is the document within the two-page guideline? _____ yes _____ no

3. Does the document follow the order of the full proposal? _____ yes _____ no

4. Does the document provide key details and evidence? _____ yes _____ no

5. Does the document use persuasive language? _____ yes _____ no

6. Is all source material cited appropriately in MLA format? _____ yes _____ no

7. Is the document single-spaced, in 12 point Times New Roman type? _____ yes _____ no

8. Is the document free of errors in grammar, usage and/or sentence structure? _____ yes _____ no

9. Is the document presented in a clear, readable form? _____ yes _____ no

10. Would this document encourage someone to read the full plan? _____ yes _____ no

Which part of the draft did you like the most?

Which part of the draft needs the most improvement?

Additional Comments/Suggestions:

Chapter 7 ■ Final Proposal Workshop II

Please fill out the following form for your partner. Feel free to write comments on the drafts as well.

Executive Summary

1. Is the document clearly labeled as an Executive Summary at the top of the page?   _____ yes _____ no

2. Is the document within the two-page guideline?   _____ yes _____ no

3. Does the document follow the order of the full proposal?   _____ yes _____ no

4. Does the document provide key details and evidence?   _____ yes _____ no

5. Does the document use persuasive language?   _____ yes _____ no

6. Is all source material cited appropriately in MLA format?   _____ yes _____ no

7. Is the document single-spaced, in 12 point Times New Roman type?   _____ yes _____ no

8. Is the document free of errors in grammar, usage and/or sentence structure?   _____ yes _____ no

9. Is the document presented in a clear, readable form?   _____ yes _____ no

10. Would this document encourage someone to read the full plan?   _____ yes _____ no

Which part of the draft did you like the most?

Which part of the draft needs the most improvement?

Additional Comments/Suggestions:

Chapter 7 ■ Final Proposal Workshop II

Please fill out the following form for your partner. Feel free to write comments on the drafts as well.

Executive Summary

1. Is the document clearly labeled as an Executive Summary at the top of the page? _____ yes _____ no

2. Is the document within the two-page guideline? _____ yes _____ no

3. Does the document follow the order of the full proposal? _____ yes _____ no

4. Does the document provide key details and evidence? _____ yes _____ no

5. Does the document use persuasive language? _____ yes _____ no

6. Is all source material cited appropriately in MLA format? _____ yes _____ no

7. Is the document single-spaced, in 12 point Times New Roman type? _____ yes _____ no

8. Is the document free of errors in grammar, usage and/or sentence structure? _____ yes _____ no

9. Is the document presented in a clear, readable form? _____ yes _____ no

10. Would this document encourage someone to read the full plan? _____ yes _____ no

Which part of the draft did you like the most?

Which part of the draft needs the most improvement?

Additional Comments/Suggestions:

Chapter 7 ■ Final Proposal Workshop III

Please fill out the following form for your partner. Feel free to write comments on the drafts as well.

Introduction and Literature Review

Does the introduction . . .

1. attempt to quantify or define the problem?   _____ yes _____ no

2. include visuals that help clarify and emphasize the key aspects
   of the problem?   _____ yes _____ no

3. focus on the aspects of the problem that would most interest
   the reader?   _____ yes _____ no

4. suggest a direction for approaching the problem?   _____ yes _____ no

5. close with a forecasting statement giving the reader a sense of the
   argument to follow and providing a transition to the next section?   _____ yes _____ no

Is the introduction . . .

1. single-spaced, in 12 point Times New Roman font?   _____ yes _____ no

2. free of all grammatical and typographical errors?   _____ yes _____ no

Does the literature review . . .

1. open with a reference to the problem?   _____ yes _____ no

2. focus on the paradigm of the project?   _____ yes _____ no

3. explain why the problem will be approached in a particular way?   _____ yes _____ no

4. provide a unified rationale for the specific plan of action?   _____ yes _____ no

5. show how the plan of action proposed is a logical approach
   to the problem defined?   _____ yes _____ no

6. include the most useful and authoritative sources (especially those
   subject to peer review)?   _____ yes _____ no

Is the literature review . . .

1. single-spaced, in 12 point Times New Roman font?   _____ yes _____ no

2. free of all grammatical and typographical errors?   _____ yes _____ no

What parts of the drafts did you like the most?

What parts of the drafts need the most improvement?

Additional Comments/Suggestions:

Chapter 7 ■ Final Proposal Workshop III

Please fill out the following form for your partner. Feel free to write comments on the drafts as well.

Introduction and Literature Review

Does the introduction . . .

1. attempt to quantify or define the problem?   _____ yes _____ no

2. include visuals that help clarify and emphasize the key aspects
   of the problem?   _____ yes _____ no

3. focus on the aspects of the problem that would most interest
   the reader?   _____ yes _____ no

4. suggest a direction for approaching the problem?   _____ yes _____ no

5. close with a forecasting statement giving the reader a sense of the
   argument to follow and providing a transition to the next section?   _____ yes _____ no

Is the introduction . . .

1. single-spaced, in 12 point Times New Roman font?   _____ yes _____ no

2. free of all grammatical and typographical errors?   _____ yes _____ no

Does the literature review . . .

1. open with a reference to the problem?   _____ yes _____ no

2. focus on the paradigm of the project?   _____ yes _____ no

3. explain why the problem will be approached in a particular way?   _____ yes _____ no

4. provide a unified rationale for the specific plan of action?   _____ yes _____ no

5. show how the plan of action proposed is a logical approach
   to the problem defined?   _____ yes _____ no

6. include the most useful and authoritative sources (especially those
   subject to peer review)?   _____ yes _____ no

Is the literature review . . .

1. single-spaced, in 12 point Times New Roman font?   _____ yes _____ no

2. free of all grammatical and typographical errors?   _____ yes _____ no

What parts of the drafts did you like the most?

What parts of the drafts need the most improvement?

Additional Comments/Suggestions:

Chapter 7 ■ Final Proposal Workshop III

Please fill out the following form for your partner. Feel free to write comments on the drafts as well.

Introduction and Literature Review

Does the introduction . . .

1. attempt to quantify or define the problem? _____ yes _____ no

2. include visuals that help clarify and emphasize the key aspects of the problem? _____ yes _____ no

3. focus on the aspects of the problem that would most interest the reader? _____ yes _____ no

4. suggest a direction for approaching the problem? _____ yes _____ no

5. close with a forecasting statement giving the reader a sense of the argument to follow and providing a transition to the next section? _____ yes _____ no

Is the introduction . . .

1. single-spaced, in 12 point Times New Roman font? _____ yes _____ no

2. free of all grammatical and typographical errors? _____ yes _____ no

Does the literature review . . .

1. open with a reference to the problem? _____ yes _____ no

2. focus on the paradigm of the project? _____ yes _____ no

3. explain why the problem will be approached in a particular way? _____ yes _____ no

4. provide a unified rationale for the specific plan of action? _____ yes _____ no

5. show how the plan of action proposed is a logical approach to the problem defined? _____ yes _____ no

6. include the most useful and authoritative sources (especially those subject to peer review)? _____ yes _____ no

Is the literature review . . .

1. single-spaced, in 12 point Times New Roman font? _____ yes _____ no

2. free of all grammatical and typographical errors? _____ yes _____ no

What parts of the drafts did you like the most?

What parts of the drafts need the most improvement?

Additional Comments/Suggestions:

Chapter 7 ■ Final Proposal Workshop IV

Please fill out the following form for your partner. Feel free to write comments on the drafts as well.

Plan, Budget, and Discussion

Does the plan . . .

    1. transition logically from the research?   _____ yes _____ no

    2. focus on how the idea will be implemented?   _____ yes _____ no

    3. reference research to support the writer's choices?   _____ yes _____ no

    4. present information clearly?   _____ yes _____ no

    5. consider all possibilities in justifying its recommendations?   _____ yes _____ no

Is the plan . . .

    1. organized logically?   _____ yes _____ no

    2. free of unanswered questions or areas of confusion?   _____ yes _____ no

    3. single-spaced, in 12 point Times New Roman font?   _____ yes _____ no

    4. free of all grammatical and typographical errors?   _____ yes _____ no

Does the budget . . .

    1. list everything needed for the project?   _____ yes _____ no

    2. explain items that may be unfamiliar to the reader?   _____ yes _____ no

Is the budget . . .

    1. arranged in aligned accountant's columns?   _____ yes _____ no

    2. single-spaced, in 12 point Times New Roman font?   _____ yes _____ no

    3. free of all mathematical, grammatical, and typographical errors?   _____ yes _____ no

Does the discussion . . .

    1. conclude by summing up the project?   _____ yes _____ no

    2. make a final pitch for the value of the project?   _____ yes _____ no

    3. offer an evaluation plan for testing the results?   _____ yes _____ no

Is the discussion . . .

1. single-spaced, in 12 point Times New Roman font? _____ yes _____ no

2. free of all grammatical and typographical errors? _____ yes _____ no

Which parts of the drafts did you like the most?

Which parts of the drafts need the most improvement?

Additional Comments/Suggestions:

Works Cited

1. Is the document clearly labeled as a list of Works Cited at the top of the page? _____ yes _____ no

2. Does the document contain a minimum of ten published sources? _____ yes _____ no

3. Are there various types of sources represented (books to develop a theoretical framework, scholarly journals for detailed models, etc.)? _____ yes _____ no

4. Are at least 50% of the references cited from scholarly sources? _____ yes _____ no

5. Is the document formatted in proper MLA citation style (alphabetized, indented after first line, publication elements ordered correctly, etc.)? _____ yes _____ no

6. Is the document correctly spaced, in 12 point Times New Roman type, with one-inch margins? _____ yes _____ no

7. Is the document free of errors in grammar, punctuation, and capitalization? _____ yes _____ no

Additional Comments/Suggestions:

Chapter 7 ■ Final Proposal Workshop IV

Please fill out the following form for your partner. Feel free to write comments on the drafts as well.

Plan, Budget, and Discussion

Does the plan . . .

1. transition logically from the research?   _____ yes _____ no

2. focus on how the idea will be implemented?   _____ yes _____ no

3. reference research to support the writer's choices?   _____ yes _____ no

4. present information clearly?   _____ yes _____ no

5. consider all possibilities in justifying its recommendations? _____ yes _____ no

Is the plan . . .

1. organized logically?   _____ yes _____ no

2. free of unanswered questions or areas of confusion?   _____ yes _____ no

3. single-spaced, in 12 point Times New Roman font?   _____ yes _____ no

4. free of all grammatical and typographical errors?   _____ yes _____ no

Does the budget . . .

1. list everything needed for the project?   _____ yes _____ no

2. explain items that may be unfamiliar to the reader?   _____ yes _____ no

Is the budget . . .

1. arranged in aligned accountant's columns?   _____ yes _____ no

2. single-spaced, in 12 point Times New Roman font?   _____ yes _____ no

3. free of all mathematical, grammatical, and typographical errors? _____ yes _____ no

Does the discussion . . .

1. conclude by summing up the project?   _____ yes _____ no

2. make a final pitch for the value of the project?   _____ yes _____ no

3. offer an evaluation plan for testing the results?   _____ yes _____ no

Is the discussion . . .

1. single-spaced, in 12 point Times New Roman font? _____ yes _____ no
2. free of all grammatical and typographical errors? _____ yes _____ no

Which parts of the drafts did you like the most?

Which parts of the drafts need the most improvement?

Additional Comments/Suggestions:

Works Cited

1. Is the document clearly labeled as a list of Works Cited at the top of the page? _____ yes _____ no

2. Does the document contain a minimum of ten published sources? _____ yes _____ no

3. Are there various types of sources represented (books to develop a theoretical framework, scholarly journals for detailed models, etc.)? _____ yes _____ no

4. Are at least 50% of the references cited from scholarly sources? _____ yes _____ no

5. Is the document formatted in proper MLA citation style (alphabetized, indented after first line, publication elements ordered correctly, etc.)? _____ yes _____ no

6. Is the document correctly spaced, in 12 point Times New Roman type, with one-inch margins? _____ yes _____ no

7. Is the document free of errors in grammar, punctuation, and capitalization? _____ yes _____ no

Additional Comments/Suggestions:

Chapter 7 ▪ Final Proposal Workshop IV

Please fill out the following form for your partner. Feel free to write comments on the drafts as well.

Plan, Budget, and Discussion

Does the plan . . .

1. transition logically from the research? _____ yes _____ no

2. focus on how the idea will be implemented? _____ yes _____ no

3. reference research to support the writer's choices? _____ yes _____ no

4. present information clearly? _____ yes _____ no

5. consider all possibilities in justifying its recommendations? _____ yes _____ no

Is the plan . . .

1. organized logically? _____ yes _____ no

2. free of unanswered questions or areas of confusion? _____ yes _____ no

3. single-spaced, in 12 point Times New Roman font? _____ yes _____ no

4. free of all grammatical and typographical errors? _____ yes _____ no

Does the budget . . .

1. list everything needed for the project? _____ yes _____ no

2. explain items that may be unfamiliar to the reader? _____ yes _____ no

Is the budget . . .

1. arranged in aligned accountant's columns? _____ yes _____ no

2. single-spaced, in 12 point Times New Roman font? _____ yes _____ no

3. free of all mathematical, grammatical, and typographical errors? _____ yes _____ no

Does the discussion . . .

1. conclude by summing up the project? _____ yes _____ no

2. make a final pitch for the value of the project? _____ yes _____ no

3. offer an evaluation plan for testing the results? _____ yes _____ no

Is the discussion . . .

1. single-spaced, in 12 point Times New Roman font? _____ yes _____ no

2. free of all grammatical and typographical errors? _____ yes _____ no

Which parts of the drafts did you like the most?

Which parts of the drafts need the most improvement?

Additional Comments/Suggestions:

Works Cited

1. Is the document clearly labeled as a list of Works Cited at the top of the page? _____ yes _____ no

2. Does the document contain a minimum of ten published sources? _____ yes _____ no

3. Are there various types of sources represented (books to develop a theoretical framework, scholarly journals for detailed models, etc.)? _____ yes _____ no

4. Are at least 50% of the references cited from scholarly sources? _____ yes _____ no

5. Is the document formatted in proper MLA citation style (alphabetized, indented after first line, publication elements ordered correctly, etc.)? _____ yes _____ no

6. Is the document correctly spaced, in 12 point Times New Roman type, with one-inch margins? _____ yes _____ no

7. Is the document free of errors in grammar, punctuation, and capitalization? _____ yes _____ no

Additional Comments/Suggestions:

Chapter 7 ■ Final Proposal Evaluation

1. The proposal includes all necessary sections and is within the page-length requirement.

    1   2   3   4   5   6   7   8   9   10

2. The proposal strives to persuade (and address the needs of) its audience.

    1   2   3   4   5   6   7   8   9   10

3. The proposal clearly describes and/or quantifies a viable problem, using published research and fieldwork.

    1   2   3   4   5   6   7   8   9   10

4. The proposal attempts a challenging and/or original task.

    1   2   3   4   5   6   7   8   9   10

5. The proposal is based upon relevant and/or innovative scholarly research.

    1   2   3   4   5   6   7   8   9   10

6. The Works Cited page includes the required number of sources and is presented in MLA format.

    1   2   3   4   5   6   7   8   9   10

7. The research is organized into a clearly and carefully delineated paradigm.

    1   2   3   4   5   6   7   8   9   10

8. The plan of action follows logically from the research and is specifically described to the audience.

    1   2   3   4   5   6   7   8   9   10

9. The proposal places sources in logical relation to each other and to the project as a whole.

    1   2   3   4   5   6   7   8   9   10

10. The proposal is fully justified by the published research.

    1   2   3   4   5   6   7   8   9   10

11. The proposal engages possible complications suggested by the research or the plan.

    1   2   3   4   5   6   7   8   9   10

12. The transitions and headings help guide the reader through the project.

    1   2   3   4   5   6   7   8   9   10

13. The visuals are appropriate and effective at conveying information to the reader.

    1   2   3   4   5   6   7   8   9   10

14. The writing is fluent and virtually error-free.

    1   2   3   4   5   6   7   8   9   10

15. The proposal exhibits an overall attractive appearance and visually appealing design.

    1   2   3   4   5   6   7   8   9   10